I0803093

IMAGES
of America

BEAVER COUNTY

On the Cover: This photograph was taken in 1902 in Beaver County, Oklahoma Territory. Many of the men here helped trail cattle, build ranches, file on homesteads according to the Homestead Act, and settle the area. Pictured here, from left to right, are (first row) Charles Beebe, Frank Long, Frank Maple, Frank Laughrin, Judge Neese, Frank Brown, Billy Quinn, and E. C. Savoy with son Ernie Savoy; (second row) Ed Hibbs, Dr. Munsell, Frank Madison, Fred C. Tracy, Judge Tannehill, Shorty Jones, Bill White, Tom Judy, and Horace Potname; (third row) Billy Palmer, Carter Tracy, George Perry, George Heath, George Winters, Mr. Groves, Mr. Rizley, Brent Lewis, James Lane, and Lon Haskell. (Jones and Plummer Trail Museum.)

IMAGES
of America

BEAVER COUNTY

V. Pauline Hodges, Harold Kachel,
and Joe Lansden

ARCADIA
PUBLISHING

ISBN 978-0-7385-8350-1

Published by Arcadia Publishing
Charleston, South Carolina

Printed in the United States of America

Library of Congress Control Number: 2010932263

For all general information, please contact Arcadia Publishing:
Telephone 843-853-2070
Fax 843-853-0044
E-mail sales@arcadiapublishing.com
For customer service and orders:
Toll-Free 1-888-313-2665

Visit us on the Internet at www.arcadiapublishing.com

This book is dedicated to those courageous and hearty pioneer ranchers and farmers who dared to come to a new land; build towns, schools, and churches; and make a new life for themselves and their families. It is also dedicated to the descendants of the folks who were kind enough to provide the pictures herein, as well as to the memory of Pearl Sharp and her daughter Louise who preserved most of the pictures that, upon their deaths, were donated by Alice Spohn Newton to the Jones and Plummer Trail Museum. Many of those photographs are used in this book. Dedication is also in memory of Fannie Judy who provided financial support and years of her time as a volunteer worker at the Jones and Plummer Trail Museum to preserve artifacts and information about the history of our area.

Contents

Acknowledgments		6
Introduction		7
1.	Prehistory Beginnings	9
2.	Business in No Man's Land Grows	21
3.	Attempts at Establishing Law and Order	45
4.	Beaver County Becomes Part of Oklahoma	57
5.	Homesteaders and Punkin' Rollers	63
6.	The Coming of the Railroads	105
7.	The Dust Bowl Destroys Farms	111
8.	Oil and Gas Discovery Changes the Area	119
9.	Present-day Beaver County	123

ACKNOWLEDGMENTS

Special thanks to Kathal Bales who scanned the historical pictures for this book. Without her excellent assistance, the book never would have been completed. Kathal is a member of the Lansden publishing family of Beaver County and only recently returned to Beaver in time to help with the publication of this history.

Other appreciation goes to the publication committee of the Beaver County Historical Society and to the board of directors who made access to historical pictures possible. Those on the committee are Julie O'Reilly (JO'R), Jerry Venable, Robbie Hancock, Brenda Maness, Cheley McAlister, and Leora Bridgewater. These dedicated citizens gave hours of their time to access and sort old pictures to be used. Special thanks to the *Herald Democrat* for allowing use of its archives. Thanks, too, to June Whisenant Kissock (RJK), Iris Harrington Lochner (IHL), Betty Janzen (BJ), Shirley Dirks Kroeker (SDK), Amy-Beth Epp (ABE), Bill Leonard (WLL), Jean Peckham (JP), Harold Kachel (HSK), Joy Savage (JS), Frank Healy IV (FDHIV), Brent Lansden (BL), and Joe Lansden (JWL) who made special efforts to locate specific pictures upon our request. Unless otherwise noted, all images appear courtesy of the Jones and Plummer Trail Museum. These, in turn, were "rescued" from the Beaver Museum when the owners died and the building was sold, so their true origins are unknown.

Other citizens who contributed their family photographs and who found pictures for use in the book are also appreciated. It took time and effort to locate these, as well as some trepidation to loan them out because they are irreplaceable. We were disappointed not to be able to use all the donated pictures because of limited space in the book, but we are grateful for your efforts.

Introduction

The history of the area known as Beaver County is unique. Over time, the area existed under five flags—Spain, France, Mexico, the Republic of Texas, and the Oklahoma Territory—before it became a part of the State of Oklahoma in 1907. For 70 years, it belonged to no state or nation and had no official law and order; hence it was sometimes referred to as "No Man's Land." Until statehood, the area included all of the territory today known as the Oklahoma Panhandle, from the 100th to the 103rd meridians, and between 36'30" and 37" parallels. These two parallels were set by extension of the Mason-Dixon Line when Texas became a slave state and by the terms of the Missouri Compromise when Kansas became a free state. Even during the time that the area belonged to the Oklahoma Territory, the area known as Beaver County included all of that land just described, with Beaver City as the capital of the territory.

However, millions of years before modern history, the area experienced interesting eras with dinosaurs, mastodons, mammoths, and prehistoric people who left behind writings and the remains of their buildings. There were seas, land upheavals, prehistoric drainage ditches, primitive Native American tribes, and buffalo and other native animals—all of which left their marks on the land.

The authors, through pictures, have tried to capture the essence of the prehistoric period as well as the times in which Spanish explorers, modern Native Americans, cattle trails, ranchers, homesteaders, religious immigrants and recent Hispanic immigrants, feed yards, hog farms, railroads, and gas and oil wells changed the landscape and the population to make the unique location what it is today. The authors especially included the pioneers of the late 1800s and early 1900s who were the ancestors of the people that now occupy Beaver County. Fortunately these more recent residents have preserved pictures that capture their ancestors' times and preserve their history. However, the authors did not have as many pictures donated as they wished, especially of the early towns, and they had limited access to the records in the Jones and Plummer Trail Museum; many of the museum's pictures were used.

Readers should note that Beaver City was the original name of the town, but in the 1920s, as more newcomers came to the area to live, folks began using just the word "Beaver" to refer to the county seat. Since most of the beaver dams from which the name was derived had disappeared, it was perhaps appropriate to shorten the name.

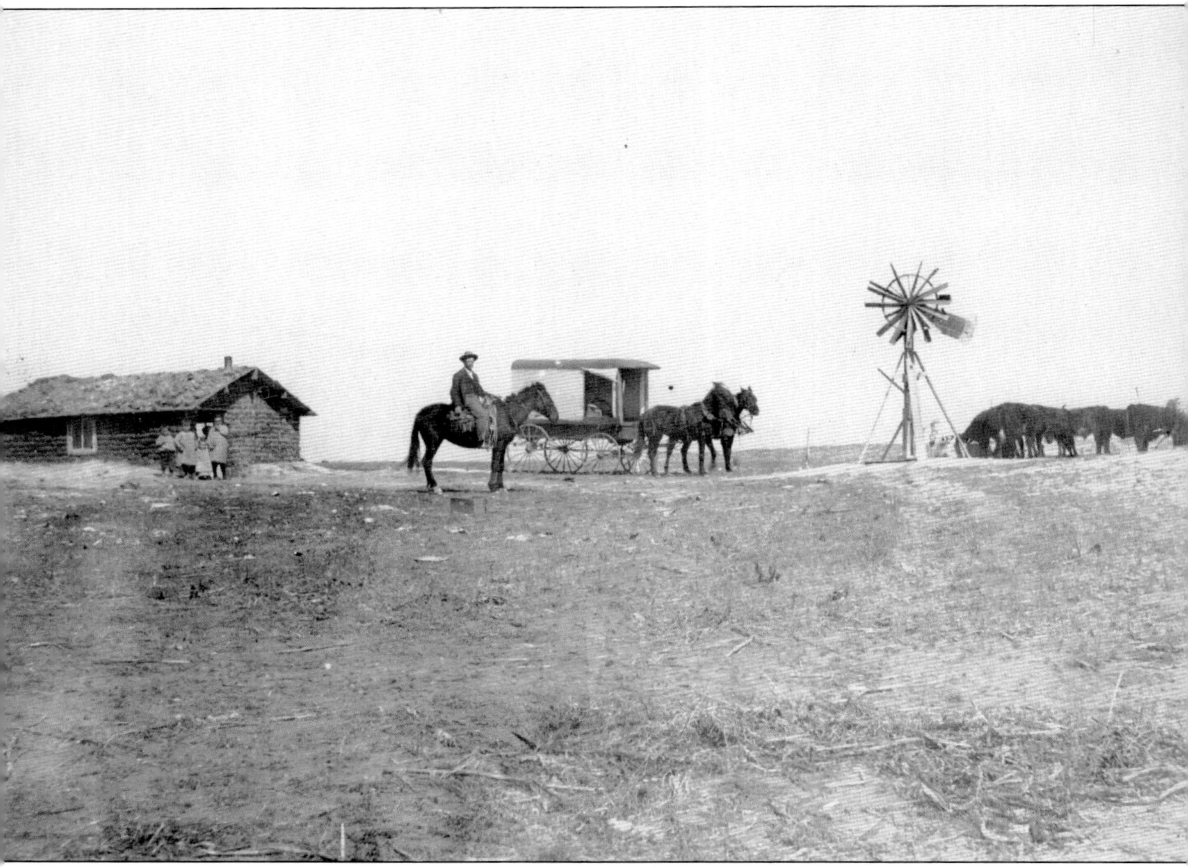

Pictured is an early pioneer with his horses and buggy in front of a typical sod house in a settlement of the county in the late 1800s.

One

Prehistory Beginnings

At first, Beaver County was one county that encompassed all of what was then known as "No Man's Land." Some of the first and larger ranches in Beaver County were Rafter H, the Rafter Cross, the OK, and the Anchor D. The Ox Ranch was the first cattle ranch established with headquarters in No Man's Land. Other cattle ranch outfits were the 101, the LV, the CCC, the NF, the LUK, the KK, and many smaller operations.

There were many large ranches in Texas, and it is believed that some men, such as Jim Neighbors, thought cattle could be driven north to the railhead in Dodge City, Kansas. Then the cattle could be shipped to markets in the East, making for large profits. One of the first trails north was the Tascosa Trail, which did lots of business in the 1870s and 1880s.

The Ed Jones and Joe Plummer Trail was one of the later trails, and it probably was first used to haul buffalo hides. With the buffalo gone, cattlemen started to use it to trail thousands of head of cattle to market. James Lane had been over the freight trail several times, and in 1880 he built a sod house and corral on the south side of Beaver River. This is where most of the cattle herds stopped for a rest period on the Jones and Plummer Trail, and it became the first business in what would later become Beaver City, Oklahoma. Lane then built a second sod house, both with two rooms each. The Lane family lived in one and kept a stock of guns in the other and used it as a public sleeping room. The bed for the travelers was no more than a couple of blankets and some buffalo robes on the floor.

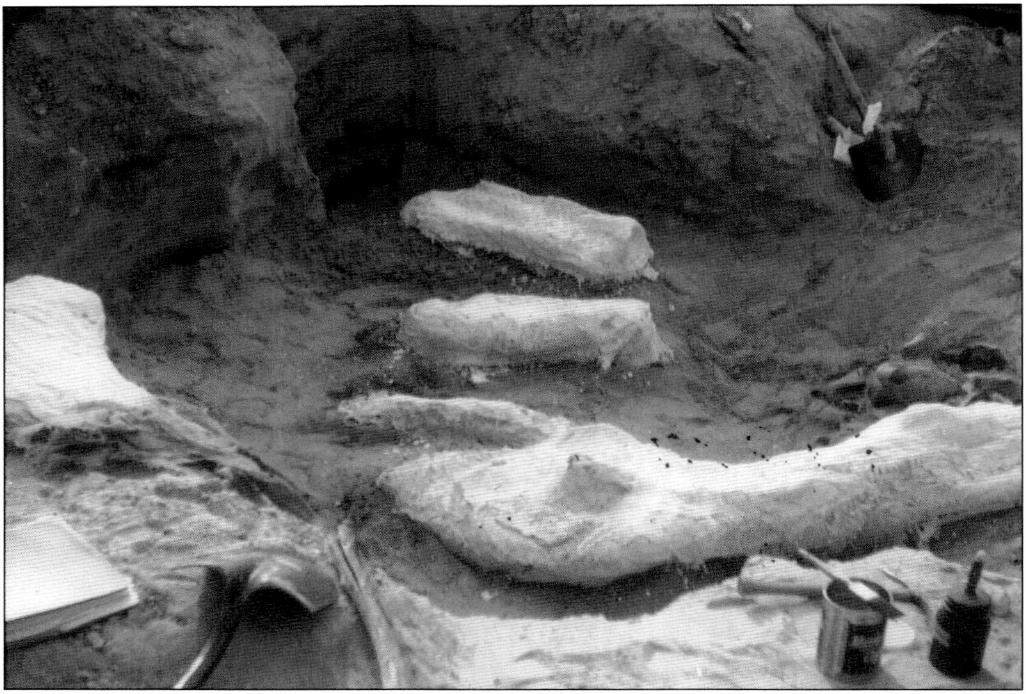

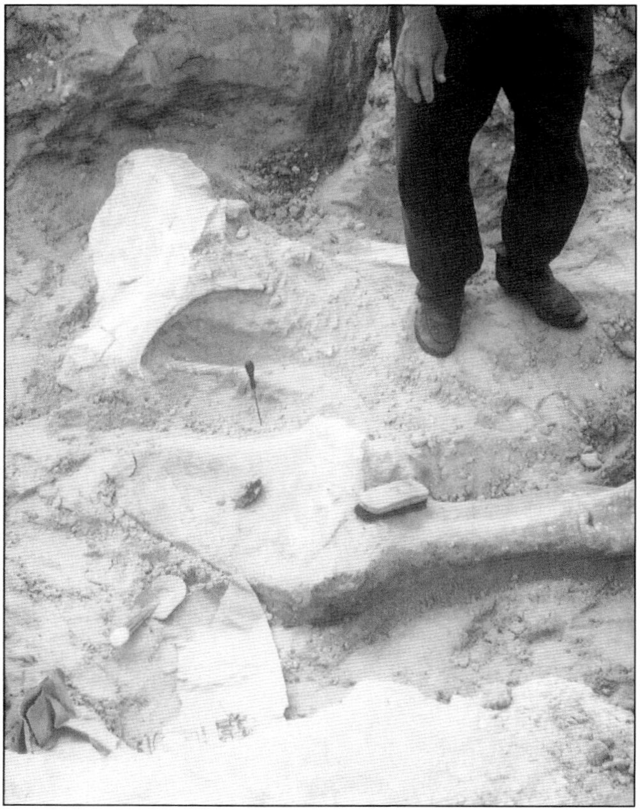

This mastodon excavation took place on the Billy Wilson ranch. The animal is estimated to be 50 million years old. (HSK.)

This mastodon was exhumed by the No Man's Land Museum in Goodwell, Oklahoma, with Dr. Nolan McWhirter and Dr. Harold Kachel in charge. (HSK.)

A buffalo wallow, located west of the present town of Forgan, is in this photograph. Wallows were common when buffalo were plentiful and hunting buffalo was all the rage. (HSK.)

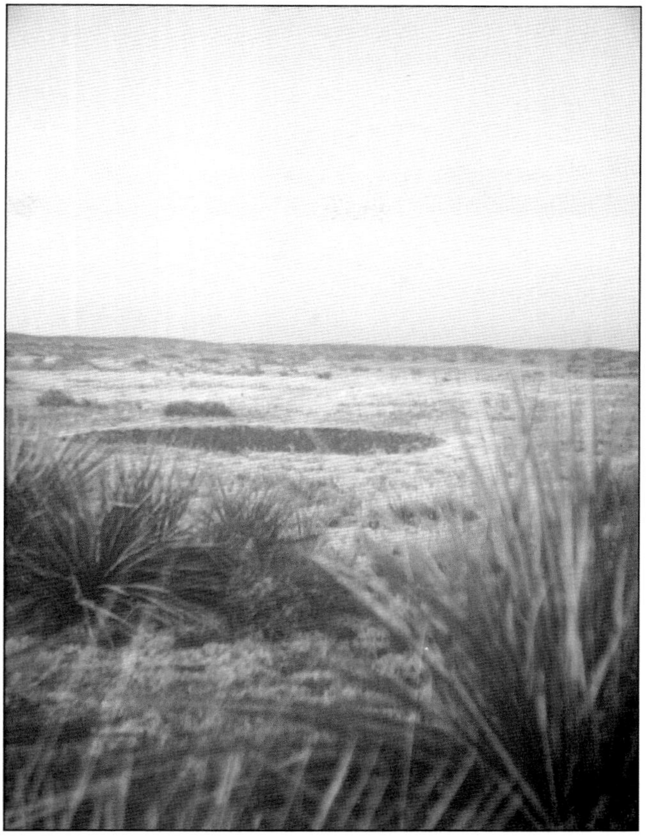

Sand hills, or dunes, are part of the chain of formation on the north side of the river for nearly 200 miles. The area just north of Beaver is today the Dunes State Park and has picnic areas, camping areas, and an ATV area. (BL.)

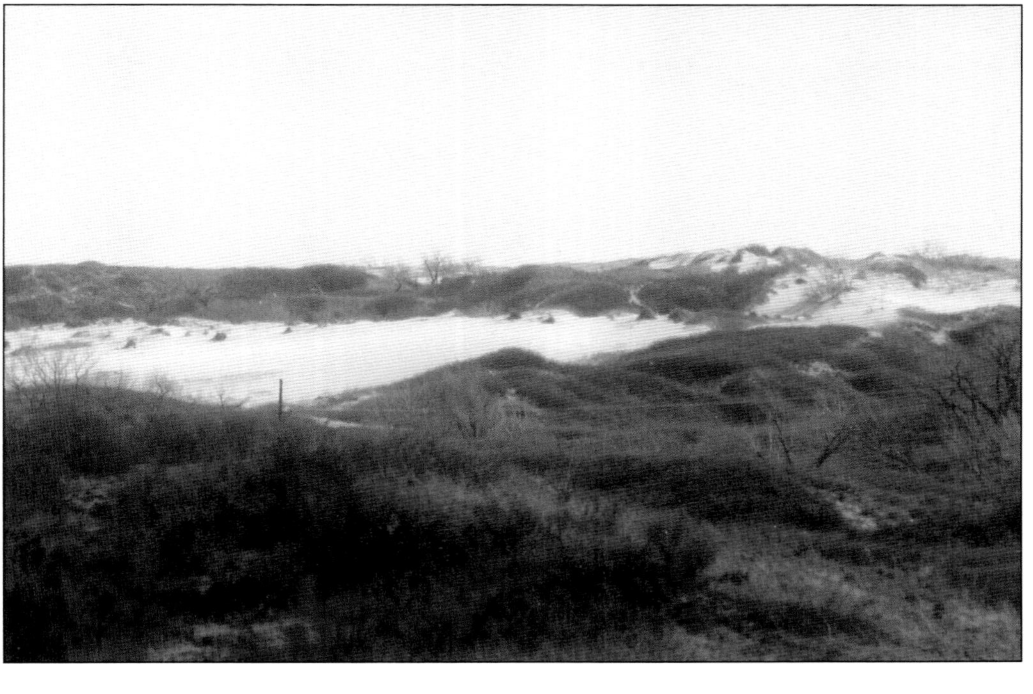

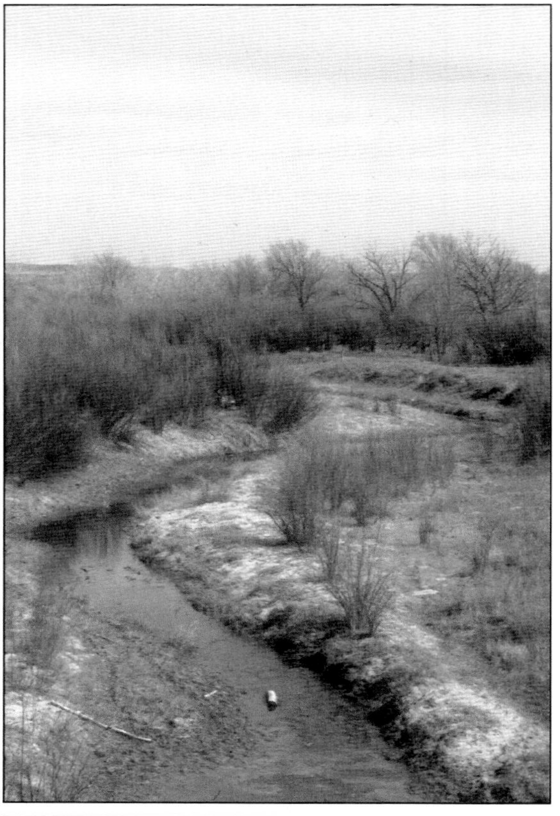

The Beaver River, after which the county is named, provided water and was a reason that early settlements were located here. (BL.)

This view shows the plains before homesteaders plowed it up, making it easily blown away during the Dust Bowl of the 1930s. (BL.)

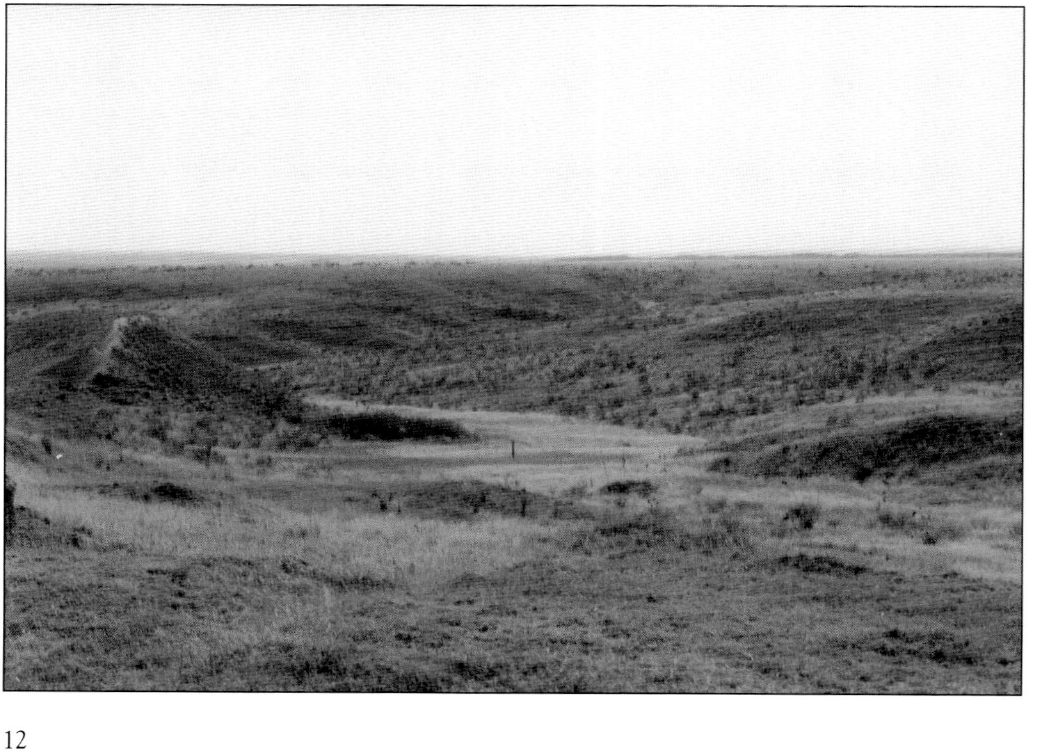

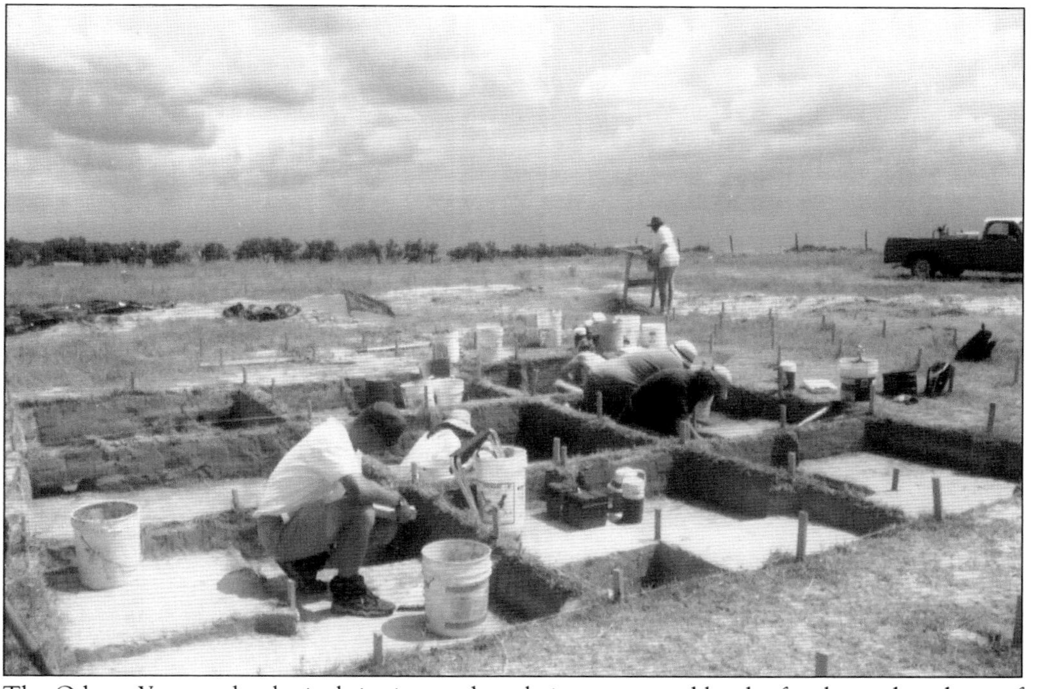

The Odessa Yates archeological site is seen here being excavated by the faculty and students of the University of Oklahoma. This site is carbon dated to the year 1346 A. D. (HSK.)

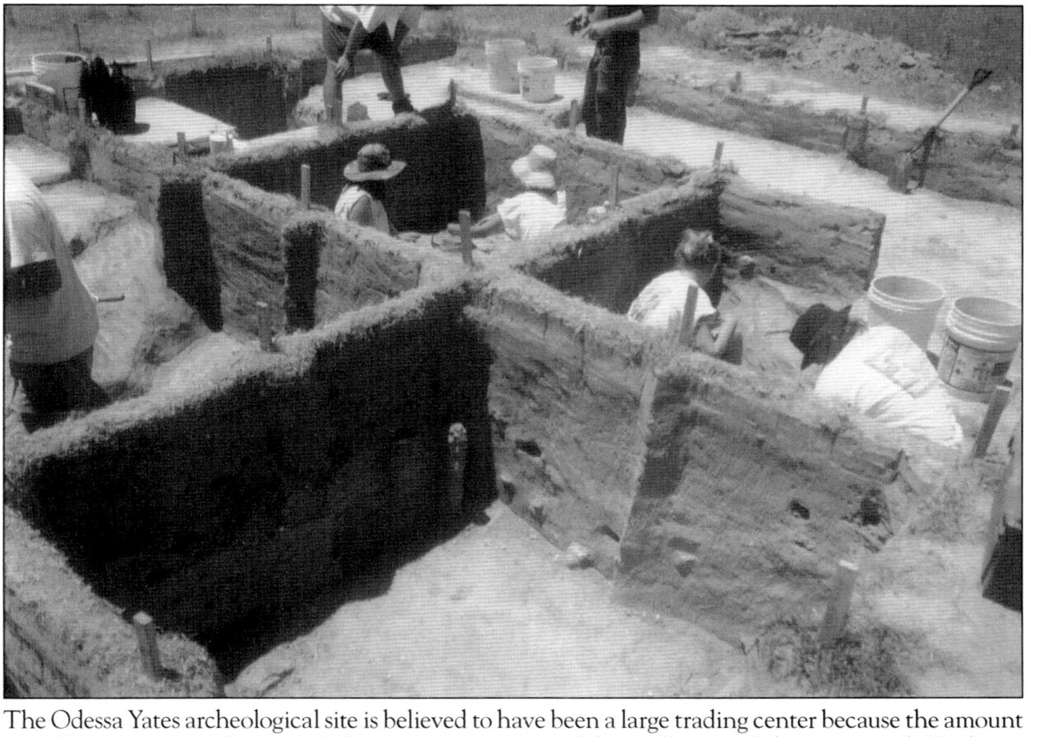

The Odessa Yates archeological site is believed to have been a large trading center because the amount of different items and materials found there originated from all around the country. (HSK.)

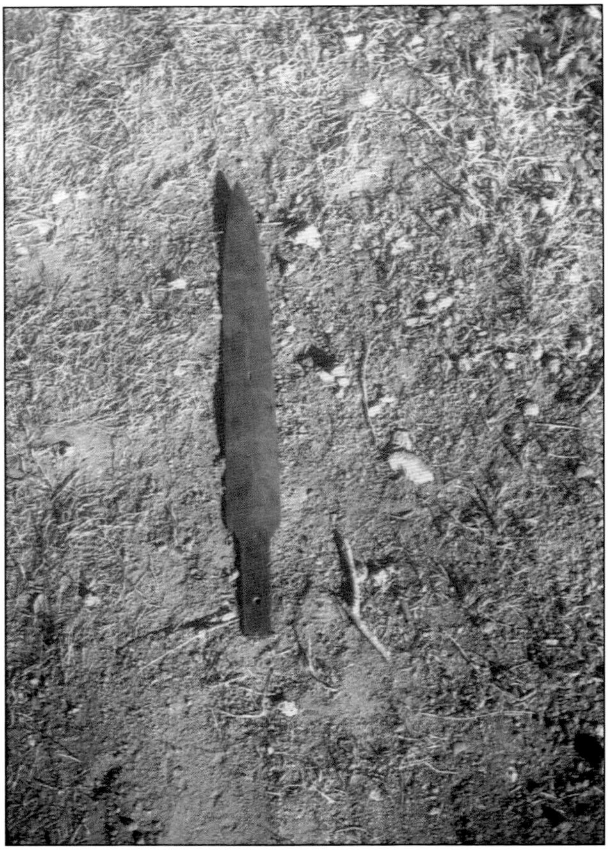

In 1541, Francisco Vasquez de Coronado, an early Spanish explorer who came through the southwestern United States searching for the Seven Cities of Cibola, left armor and other artifacts in the New Mexico, Oklahoma Panhandle, and Kansas areas. This Mexican-style lance point was used by Mexican buffalo hunters in 1300–1600 A.D., around the time of Coronado. (HSK.)

This Coronado marker is located at the junction just east of the present town of Forgan. The early exploration and settlement of people from Spain, Mexico, and New Mexico Territory is often ignored, but Coronado and the sheep ranchers near Carrizo (now Kenton) were the first known non–Native Americans to cross or occupy the area of Beaver County in modern history. The markings in caves near Kenton indicate that there might have been others in prehistoric times. (JWL.)

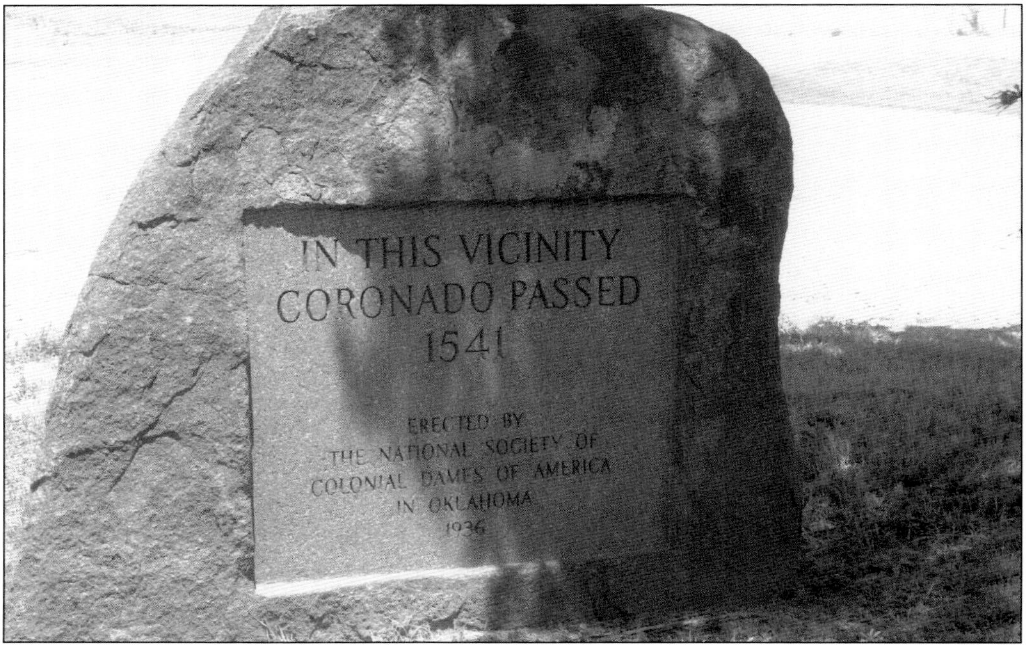

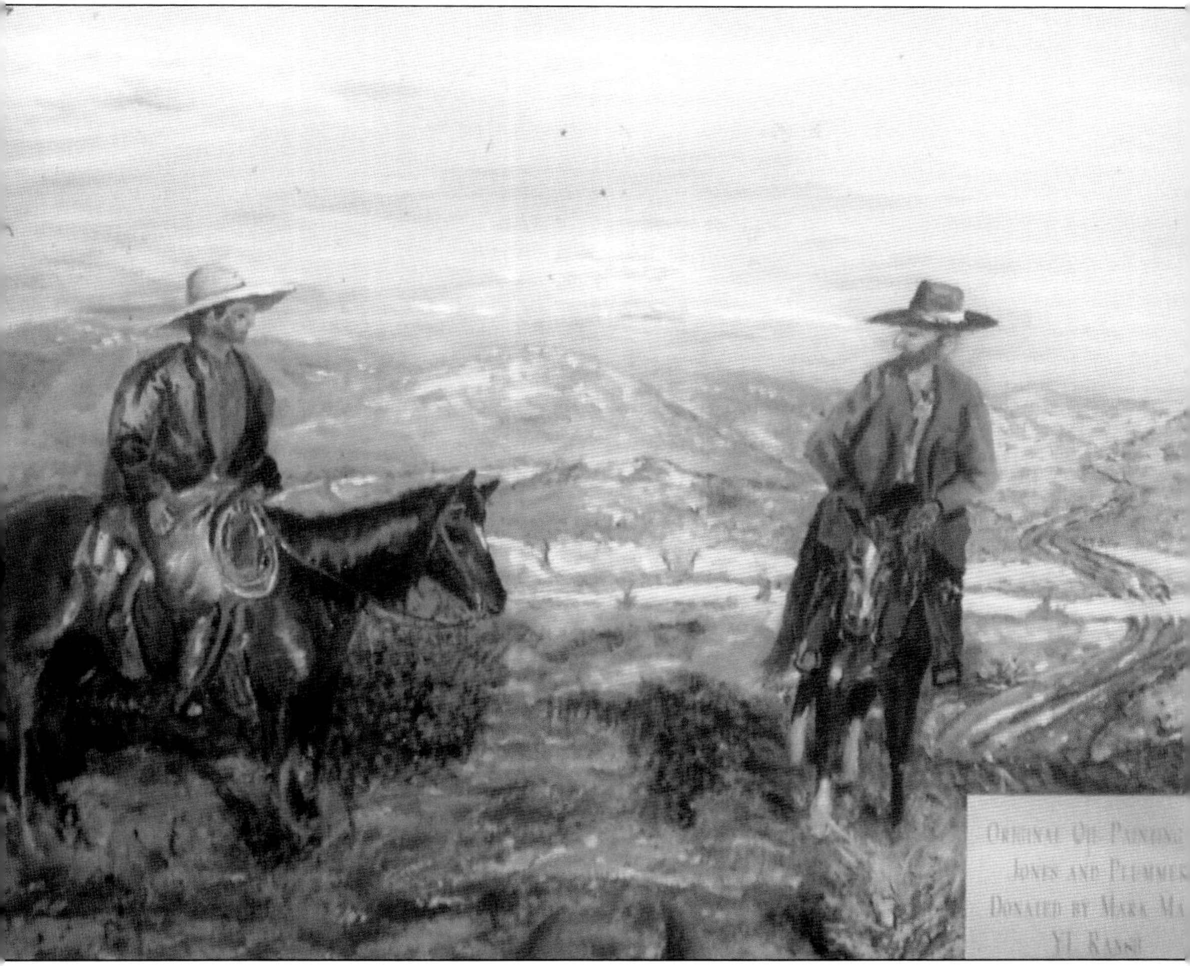

This painting of Ed Jones (left) and Joe Plummer, freight haulers for whom the Jones and Plummer Trail is named, was done by the late Mark Mayo, a prominent rancher and owner of the historic YL Ranch. (JWL.)

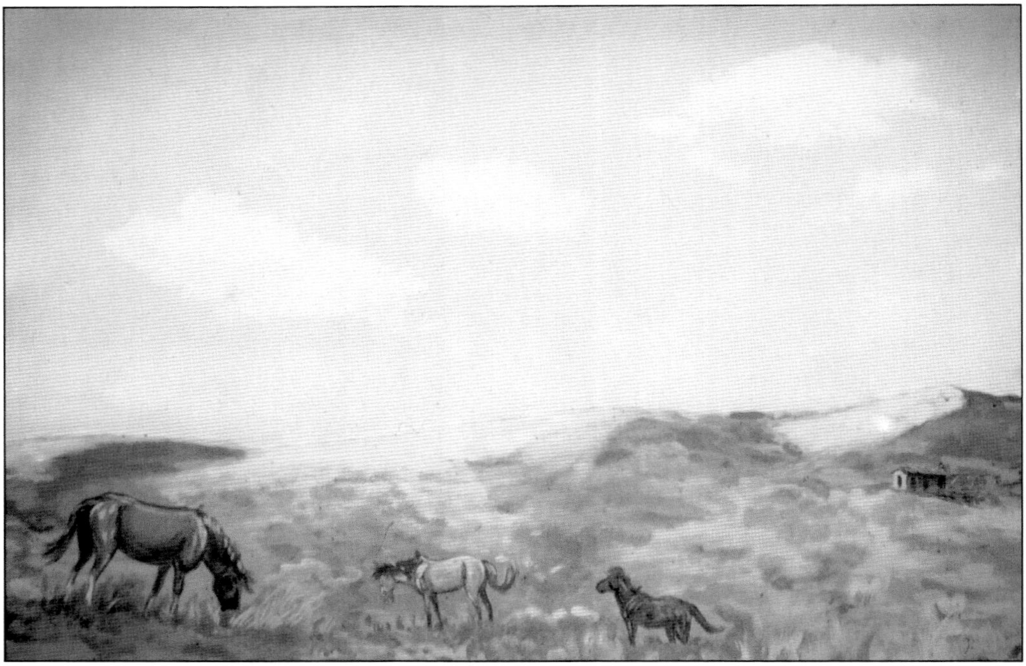

The painting of the first post office north of Beaver City in the sand hills is a mural by the late Jim Calhoon. It is displayed on the wall of Ned and Darlene's Restaurant in Beaver. This post office only lasted a short time before it was moved to the Jim Lane trading post, which was the first building in what would become Beaver City in 1879 because of its site on the Jones and Plummer Trail. (HSK.)

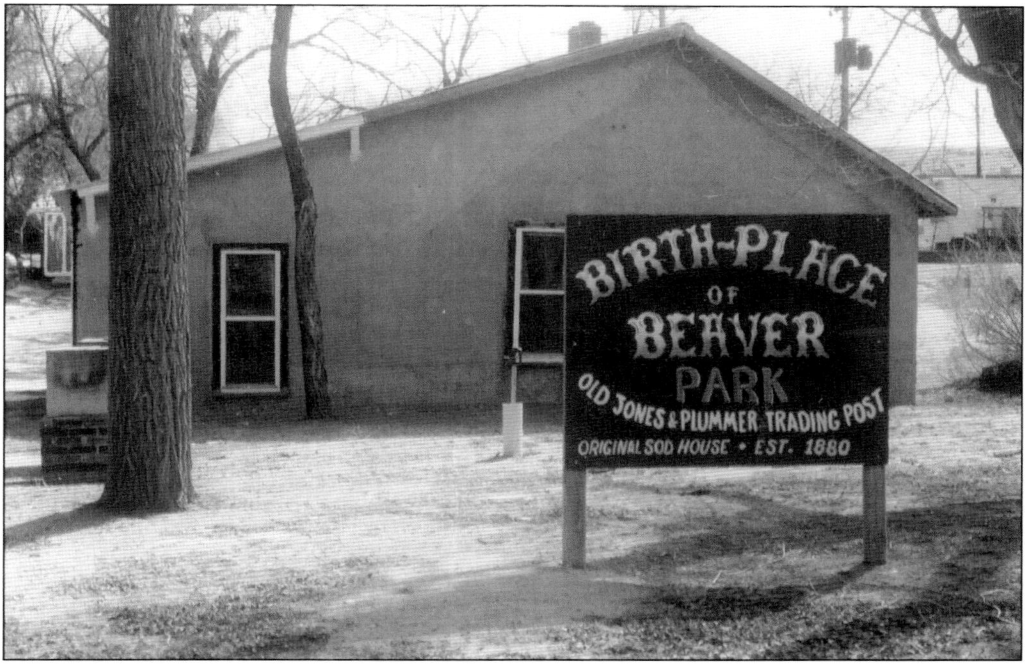

The Jim Lane trading post was the site of the second Beaver Post Office. It provided accommodations for the freighters and their horses in the corral behind the store. (HSK.)

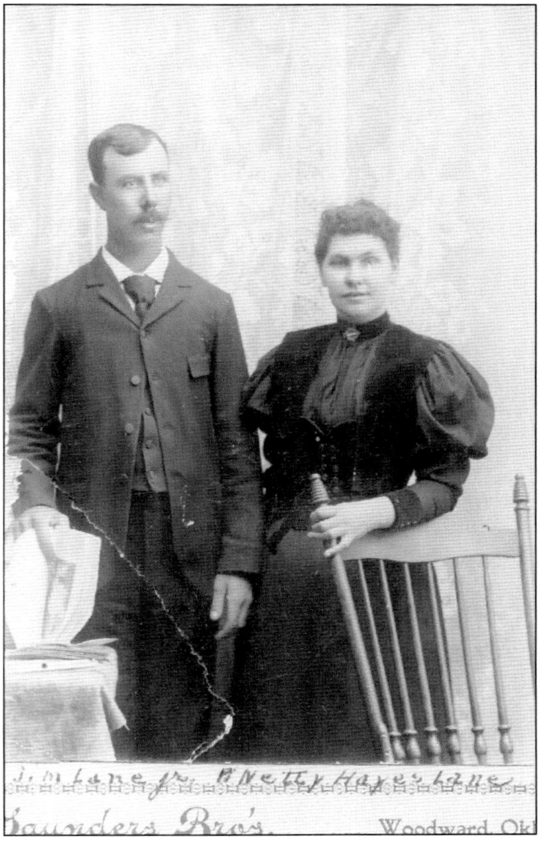

Jim Lane and Netty Hayes Lane were the first residents of what would become Beaver City. Their original business was in Woodward.

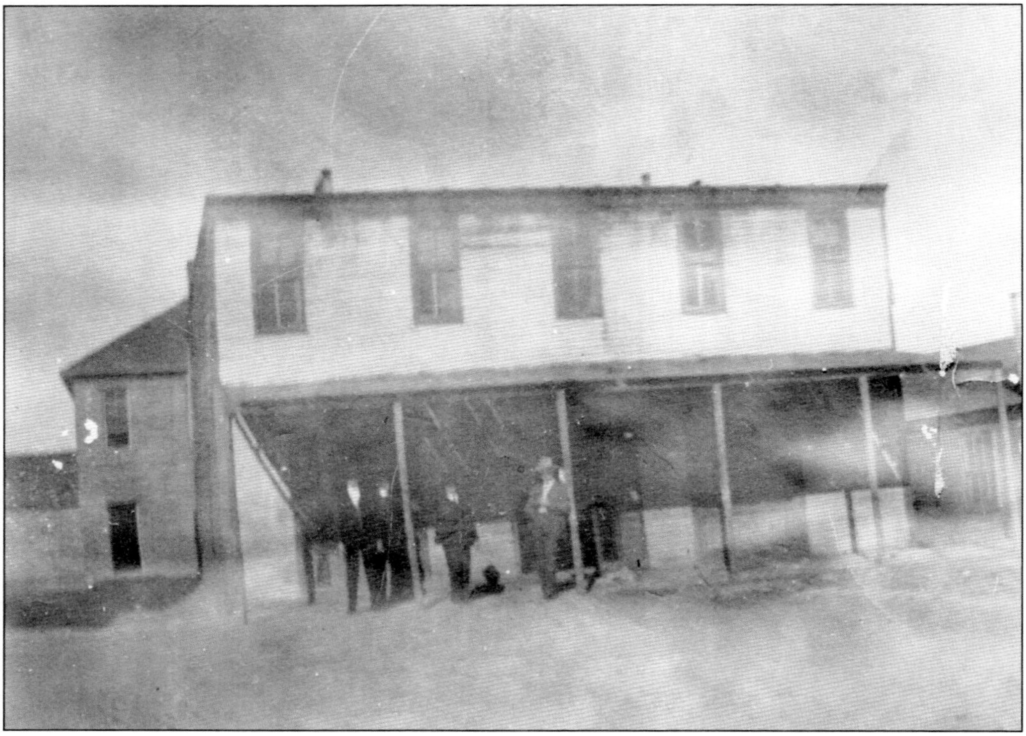

This is the original Beaver County Courthouse. It was located on what is now Douglas Avenue, on the site of the present Duckwall Variety Store. The courthouse burned in 1910, and its stone replacement was located on Second Avenue.

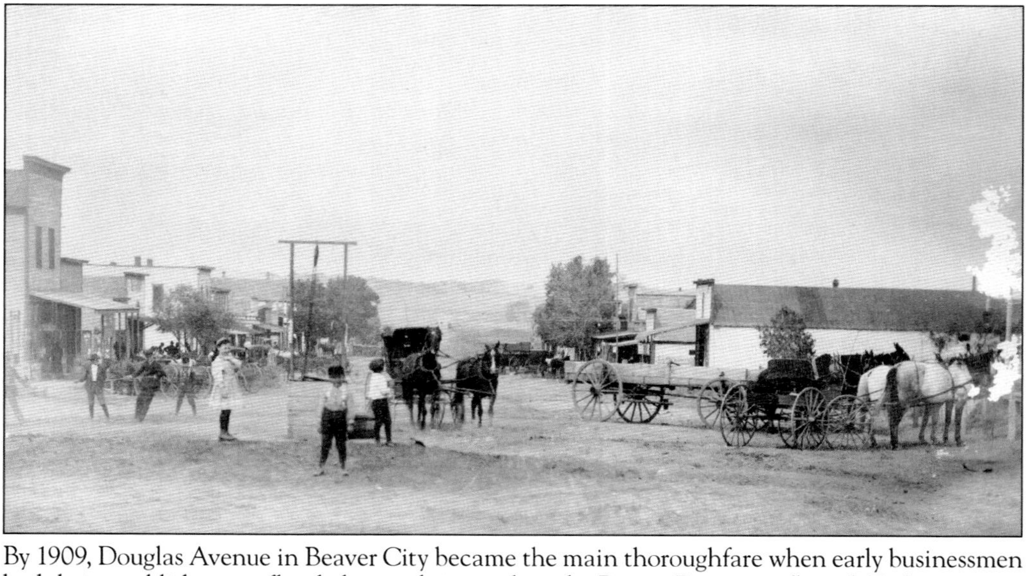

By 1909, Douglas Avenue in Beaver City became the main thoroughfare when early businessmen had their establishments flooded several times when the Beaver River overflowed. Today it serves as the main street while the original Main Street that ran east and west is now home to elevators and construction businesses, as well as a few residences. The former Main Street's street sign today reads "Old Main Street."

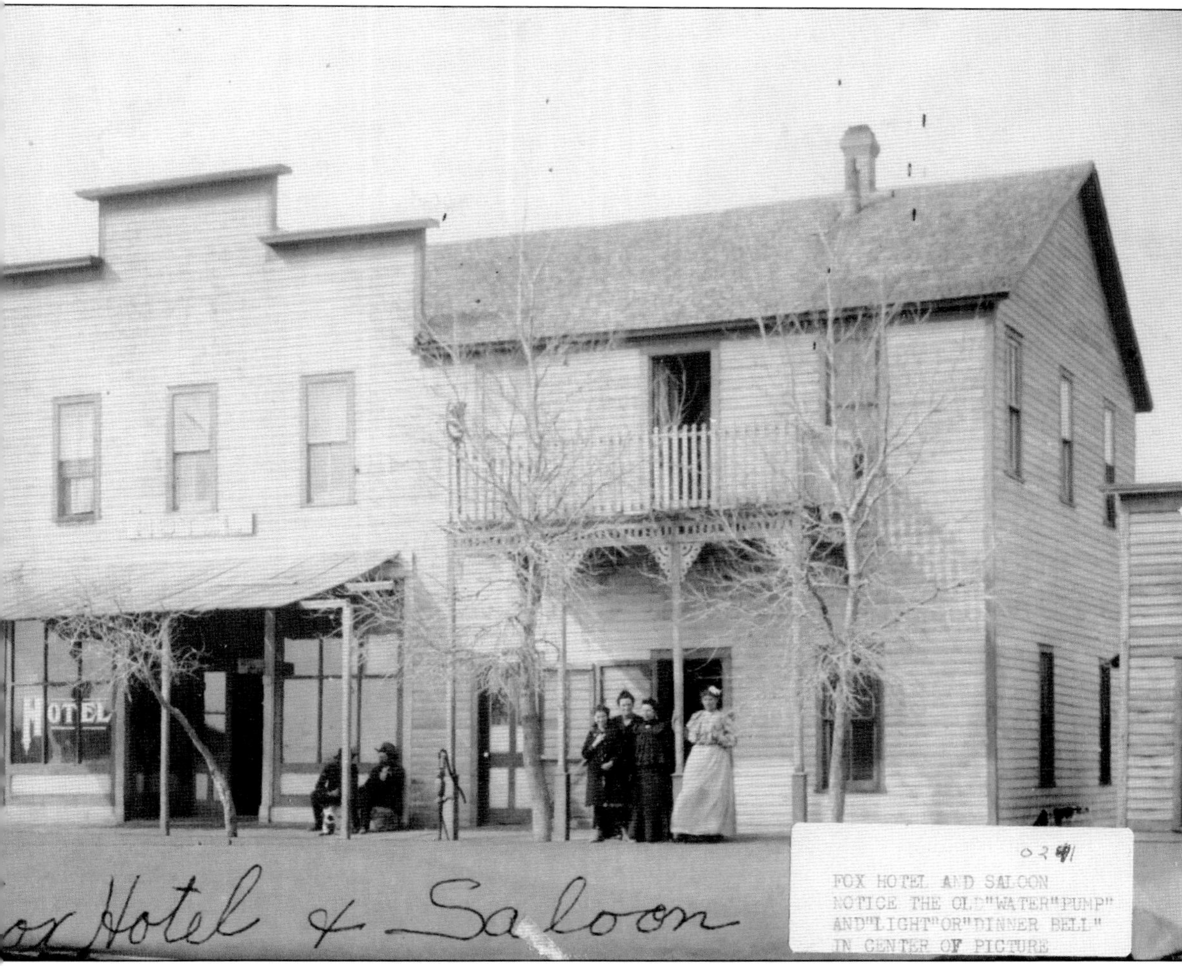

The Fox Hotel and Saloon was a very popular watering hole in the 1880s and 1890s, as well as into the 20th century. Notice the old water pump and the light or dinner bell in the center of the picture.

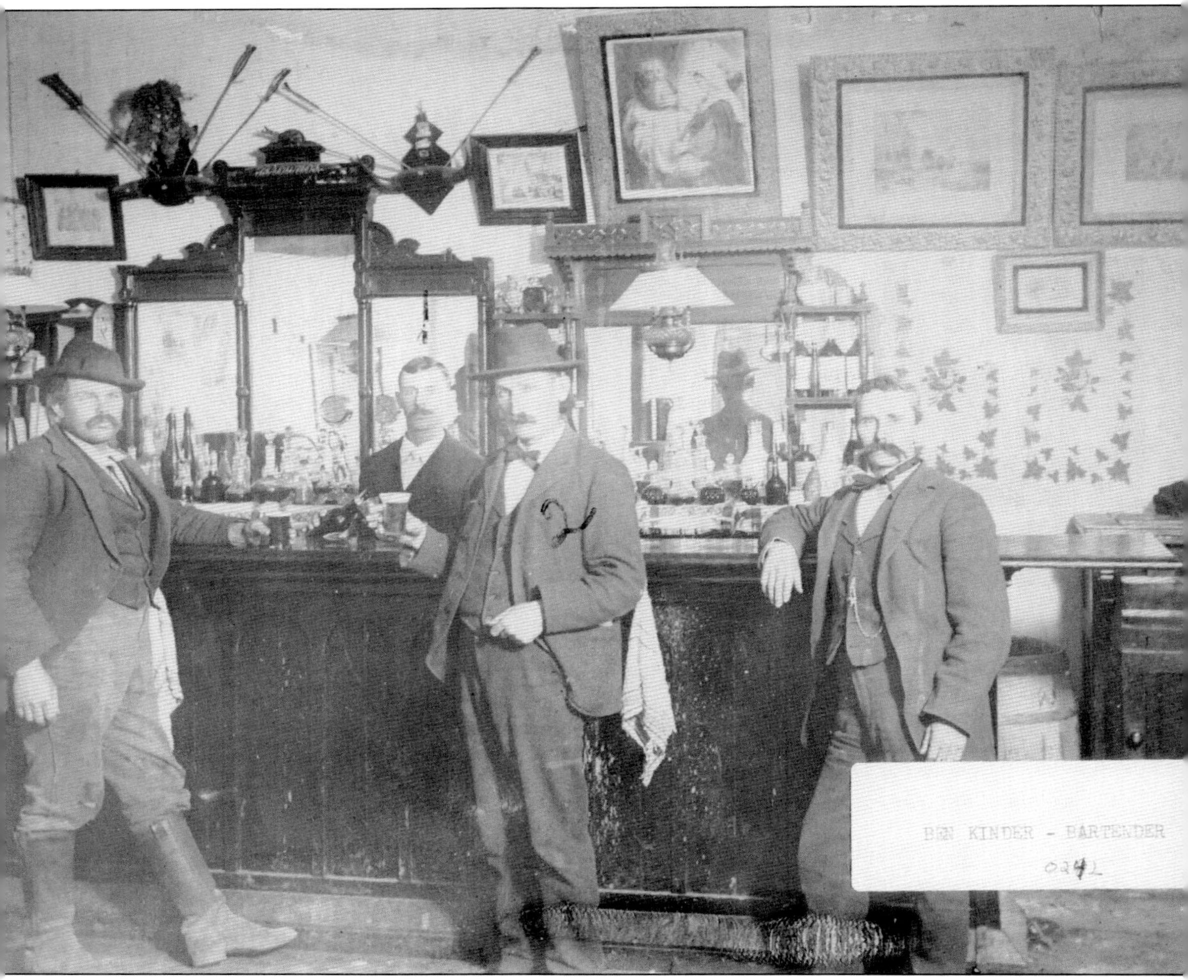

Ben Kinder, a bartender, is shown here with unidentified customers, although it is probable that they were prominent Beaver City men at the time. His saloon was on the first block of Douglas Avenue in the new town and sat just north of the present-day First Security Bank.

Two

Business in No Man's Land Grows

Beaver City in No Man's Land continued to grow as new businesses in town and cattle ranches in the surrounding area expanded. John Tuttle and Frank Chapman started a ranch near Beaver City called the CT Ranch. These two men worked out a more direct cattle route to Dodge City, Kansas, the closest shipping point. This route later became the Tuttle Trail, and the first head of cattle went up the trail to Dodge in 1870.

In Wichita, Kansas, a group of men had decided to locate a town site at the Beaver Crossing of the Jones and Plummer Trail in 1886. They platted a town site of 640 acres, and Beaver City was born.

According to Fred C. Tracy, the first business built was a livery stable constructed by D. R. Healy. The second business was a sod saloon built by Jim Donnelley just south of the Beaver River near what later became known as Old Main Street. Rube Chilcott and Frank Palmer erected the first dry goods store, selling mostly cowboy items. Other businesses followed, as well as dance halls, saloons, and residences. The first school was built in 1886 and the teacher was Mary Hunter.

Fred Taintor, whose ranch headquarters was on Taintor Creek located northeast of Beaver City, is said to have run as many as 30,000 head of cattle. His ranch was known as the GG Ranch.

With no law in No Man's Land at this time, a group of men formed what was known as the Beaver City Vigilantes. The vigilantes appointed A. N. Howe, who had come to the Neutral Strip (the official name of No Man's Land) in 1883 and was a pioneer cattlemen, to hold a young man accused of horse theft. After paying $125, the man was told he could go free. When the check cleared the bank, the vigilantes put a rope around his neck and hanged him from his own raised wagon tongue. It is believed that Howe was not a member of the vigilantes committee, but his pistol did have some notches cut into the handle.

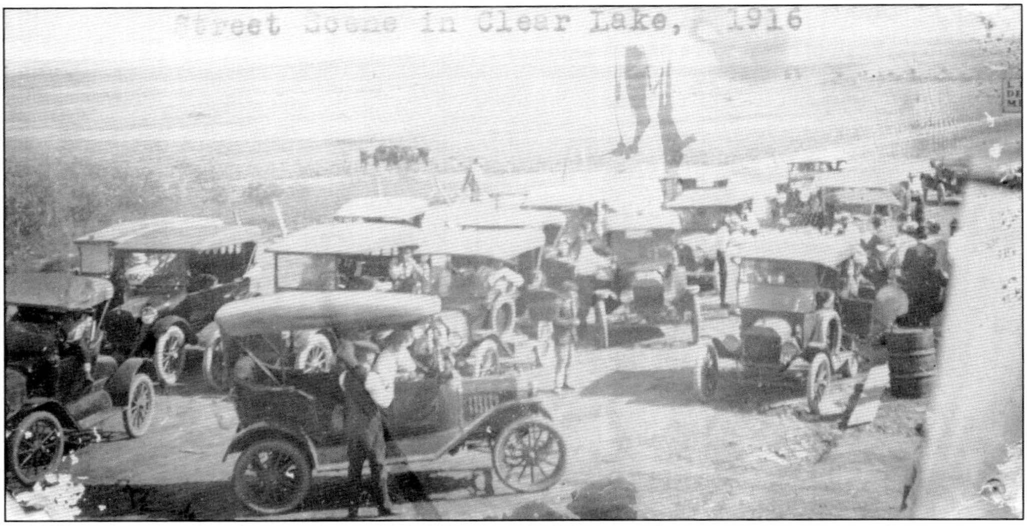

This street scene in Clear Lake in 1916 shows a traffic jam. The early town is now long gone.

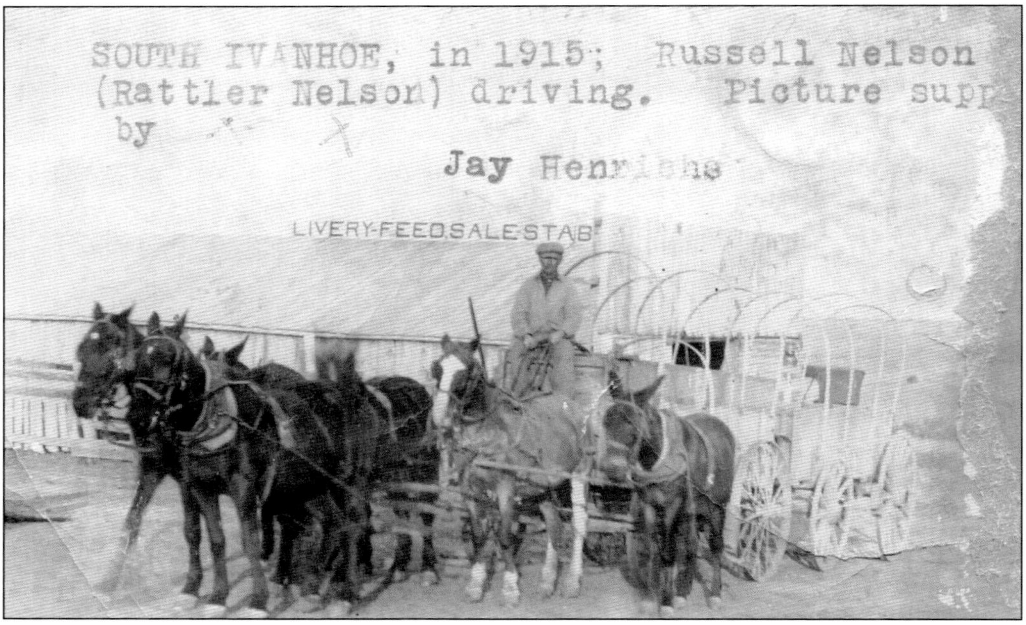

This is a street scene in South Ivanhoe. Russell Nelson is driving a freight team with the feed store and livery stable in the background. The town of South Ivanhoe was founded as a post office in 1887, then a school was added in 1890. In 1909, the new town was moved and called South Ivanhoe because a railway survey had caused a drive for money to build a roadbed and hopefully a railroad. When that scheme fell through, the Santa Fe Railway line from Shattuck, Oklahoma, to Spearman, Texas, came through just south of the Texas state line. The town was then moved to the new railroad town of Follett, Texas.

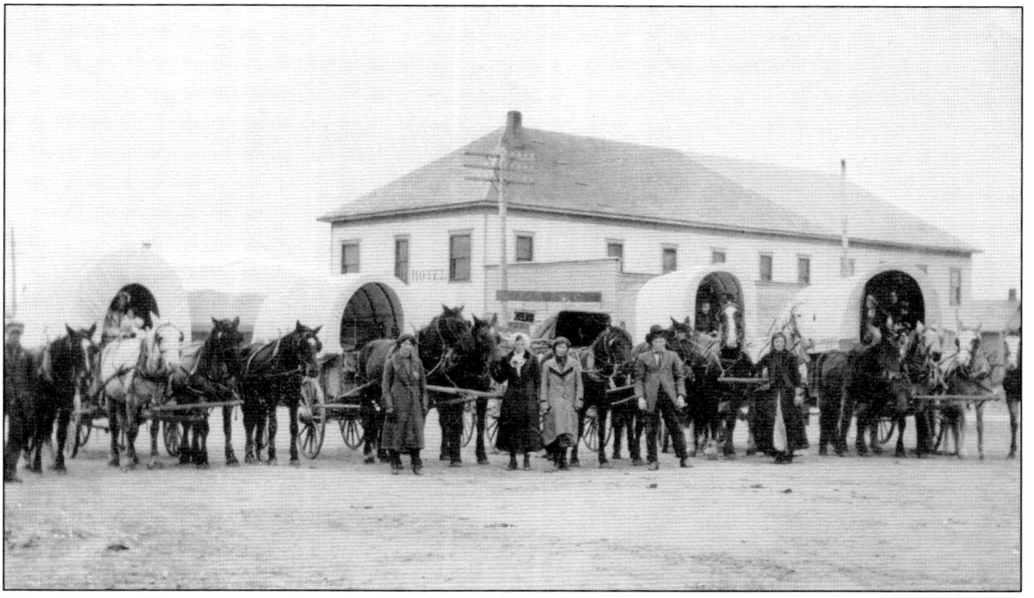

The Town of Forgan, seen here on April 2, 1915, was a new town and a bustling, busy place on the plains. By 1921, its population was nearly 1,900 hearty souls and it had many businesses, such as two banks, three grocery stores, two hardware stores, a lumberyard, two hotels, three cafés, a drug store, two doctors' offices, a dentist, two barbershops, and a telephone office. By the mid-1920s, it had five filling stations, a theater, a creamery, and two automobile dealerships. An unknown band from Minnesota played for the grand opening of the Chevrolet dealership, which featured Lawrence Welk, whom no one had heard of at the time. According to the dealer, he talked funny but came cheap.

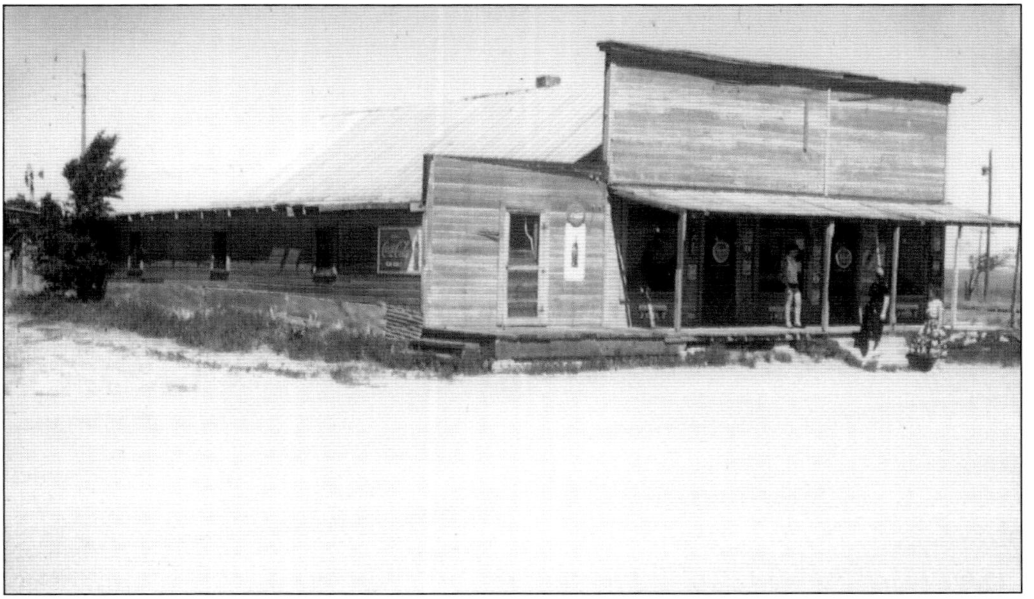

The Town of Balko is now a ghost of its original self. The school moved southwest and only a church and a few houses are left. The town was founded by a Mr. Ball and a Mr. Coe, hence the name. (HSK.)

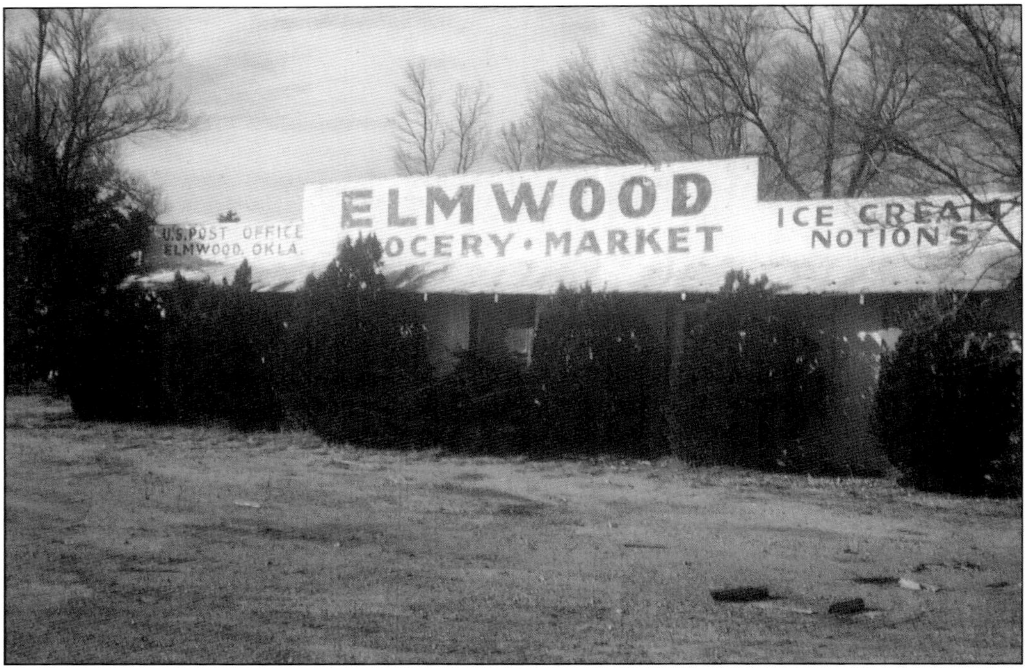

The site of the town of Elmwood was on the south side of what is known today as Highway 3. The north side of the road was called Hibbs' Corner until the post office was moved to the site and both sides became Elmwood. This site now is at the junction of Highway 270 and Highway 3, some 14 miles south of Beaver. (HSK.)

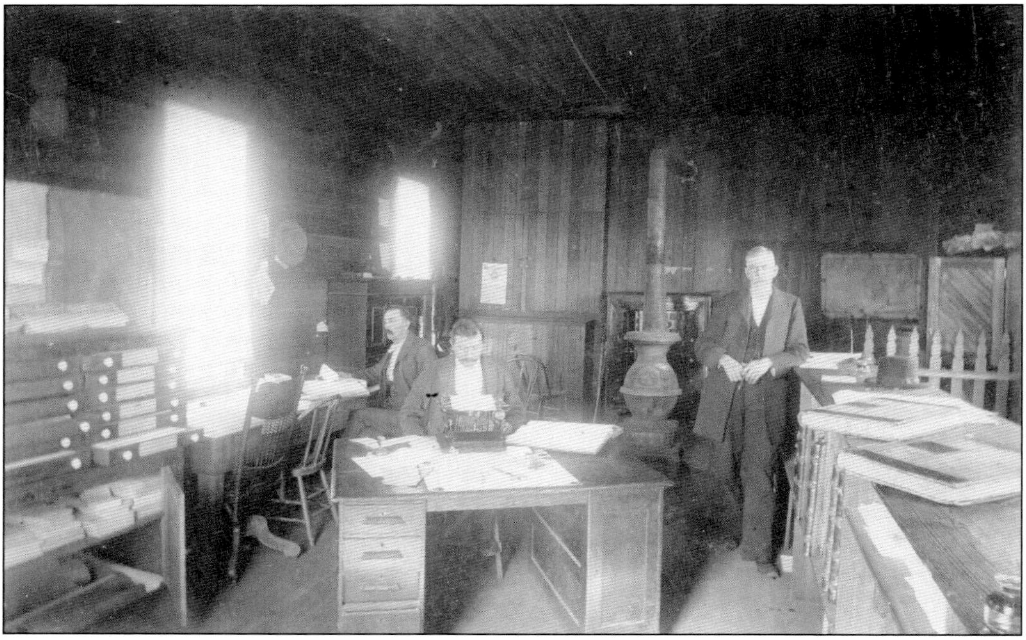

The early day land office was where new homesteaders claimed their stakeouts. These offices were essential since cattlemen and ranchers used the land before to run their herds, and because there was no government, no clear titles had been established for ownership.

Ben Kinder, an entrepreneur and businessman, became one of the most prominent and important men in Beaver City. However, when he decided to move his saloon from the first block to the second block of Douglas Avenue at the south end of the new town, several church ladies picketed both the existing business and the new site until he changed his mind. He learned that it was not wise to underestimate the ladies of Beaver City. Here Kinder is much older and, in 1959, was honored as Beaver County's oldest citizen.

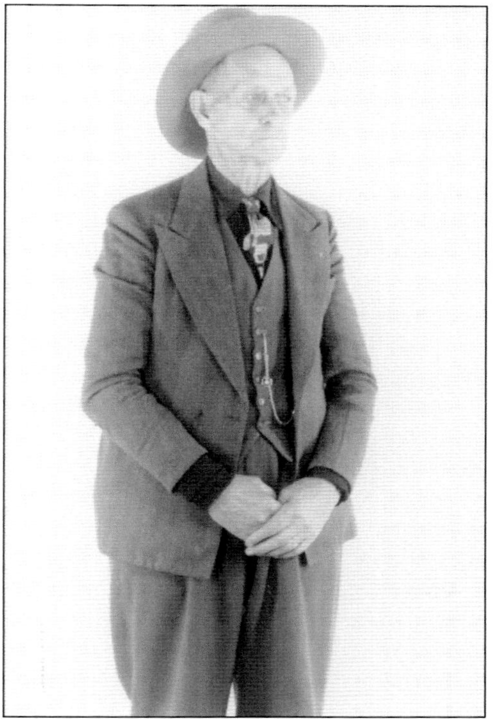

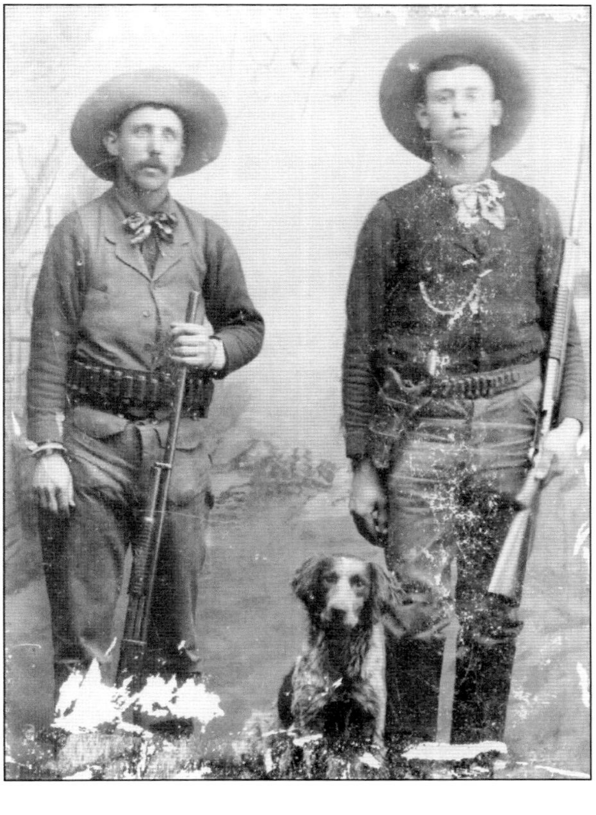

Ben Kinder (left) and G. W. Husted, pictured here in 1893, were business partners in various enterprises in the new town, other than saloons. Husted's descendants still live in the Gate/Knowles area.

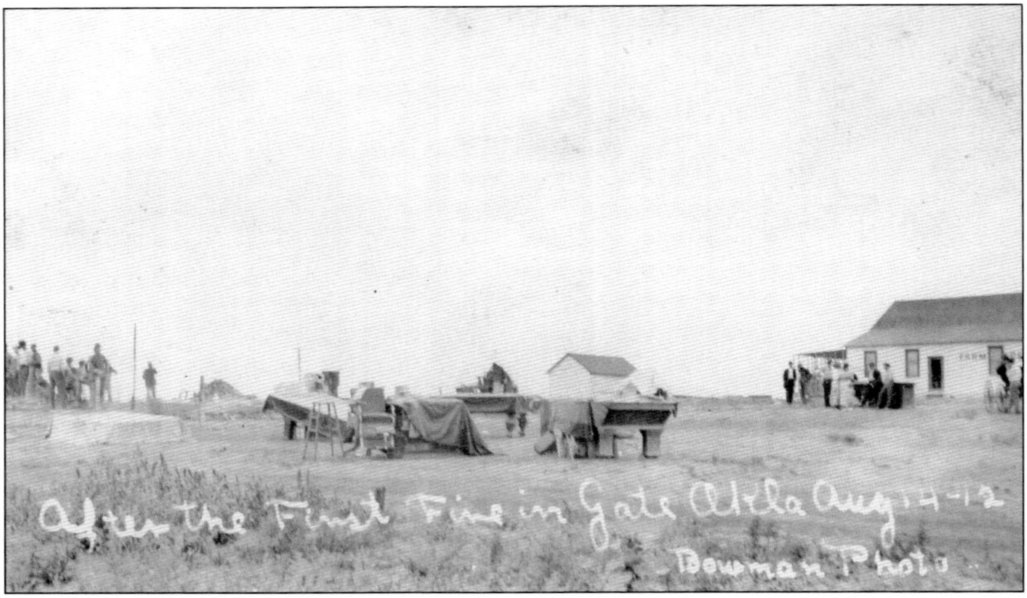

Gate City is seen here after the first fire destroyed much of town. The town had three locations, two prior to moving to its present site because of the railroad coming through the area.

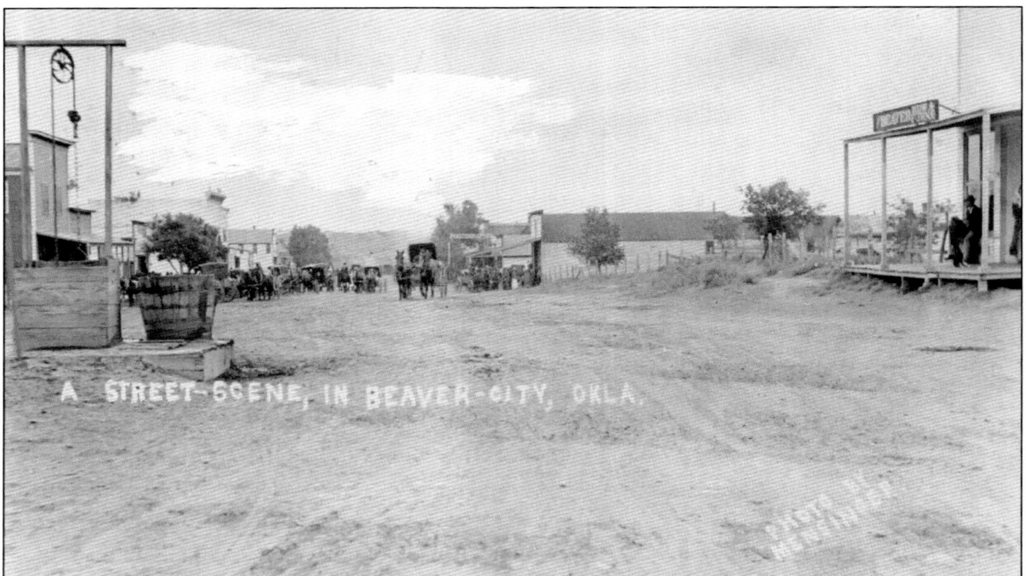

Pictured here is Beaver City in 1886 at the formation of the Cimarron Territory, which was an attempt to bring law and order to the area. If the two factions that helped form the territorial proposal could have agreed, it is likely that territorial status would have been approved and eventually the state of Cimarron would have been created. After all, the territory covered all of the area today known as the Oklahoma Panhandle and was larger than any of the five existing states of that time. Beaver City was the capital of the Cimarron, as well as the capital of the Seventh County later—which earned its name by being the seventh county formed in Oklahoma Territory.

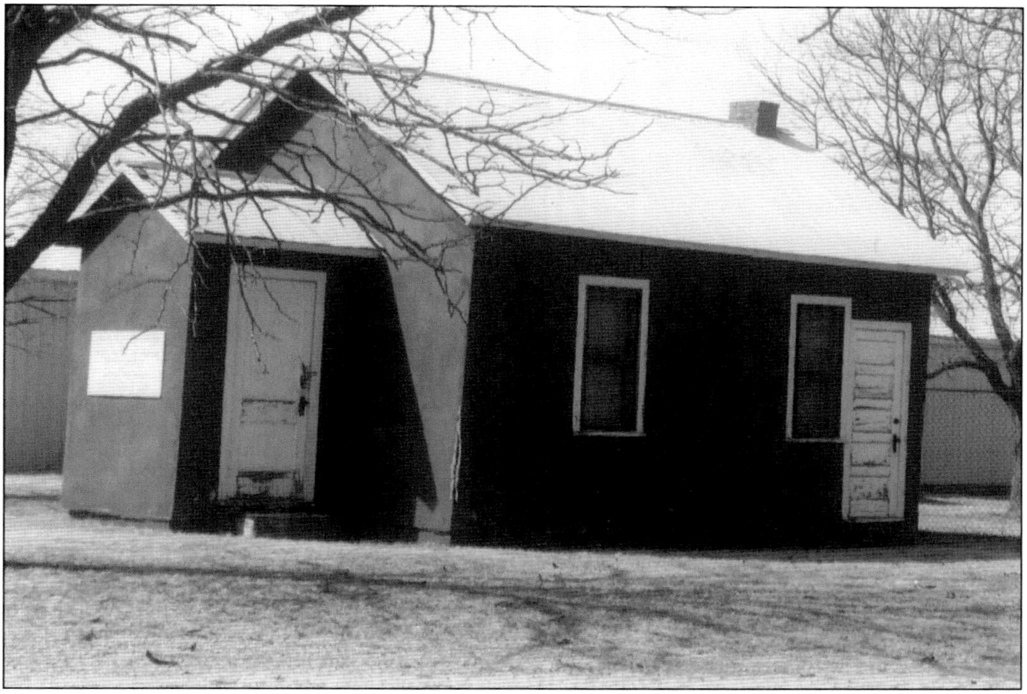

Sunnyside School, an early attempt to bring education to the area, was located on the Barby Ranch. In 1989, it moved to the site of the Jones and Plummer Trail Museum, where it was cleaned and restored by Della Poorbaugh, Ozella Hendricks, and Pauline Hodges. (JWL.)

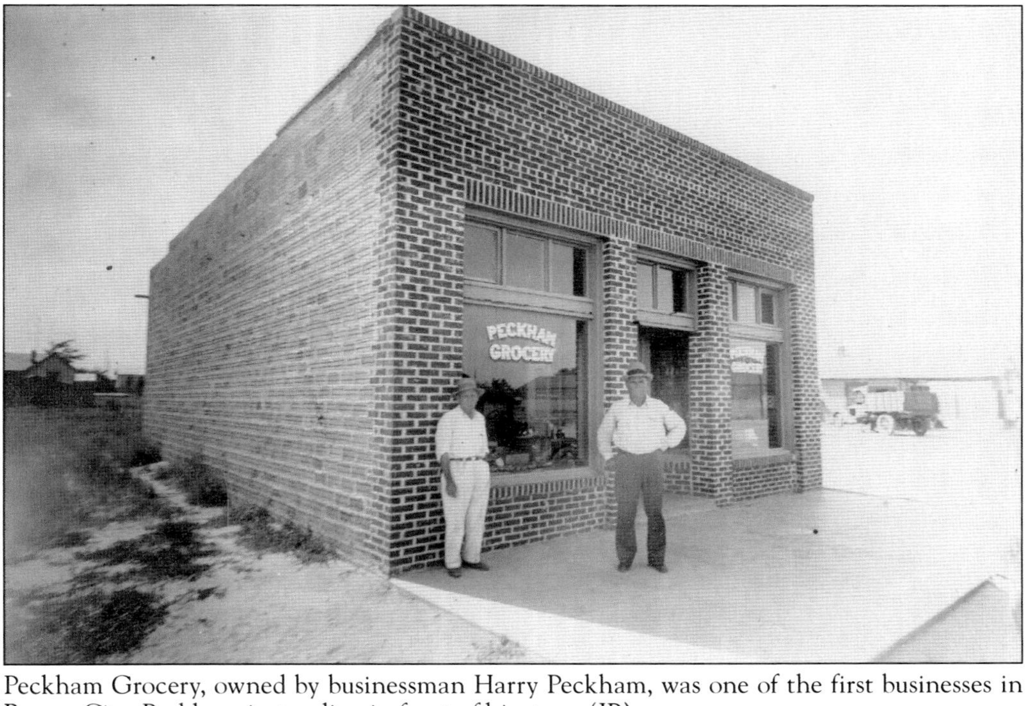

Peckham Grocery, owned by businessman Harry Peckham, was one of the first businesses in Beaver City. Peckham is standing in front of his store. (JP.)

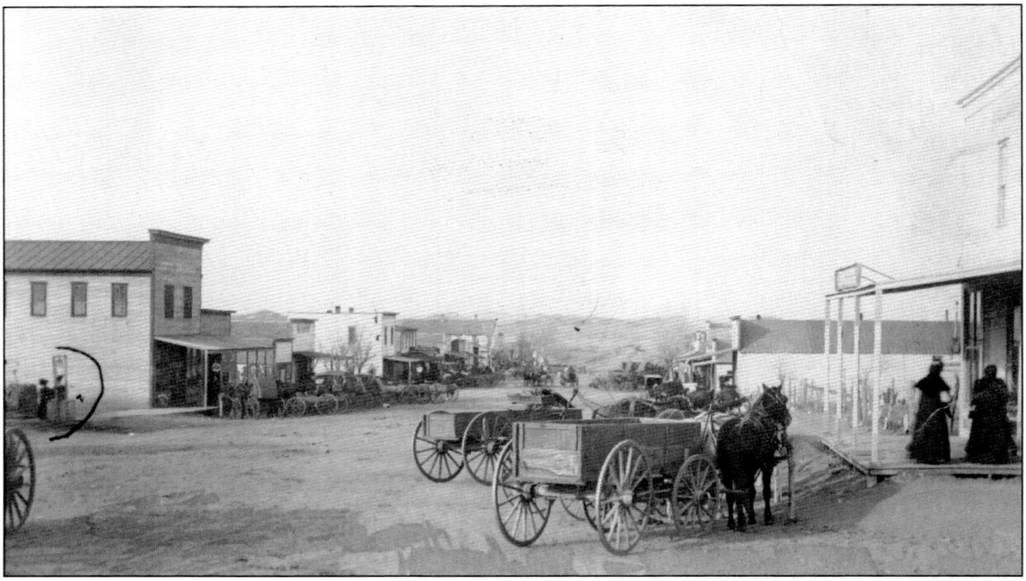

In Beaver City, the Goetzinger Grocery Store (foreground, left) was located on the ground level and the KP Hall, or Knights of Pythias Lodge, was located on the second level. The Willis and Leonard Goetzinger families not only owned the grocery store, but their parents, the John Goetzinger family, homesteaded southeast of Beaver City. Robert Goetzinger, one of the descendants, served as a county attorney for Beaver and Harper Counties, as well as a district attorney. Other descendants still living in Beaver County are Janell Edwards, a former teacher, and Peggy Morrison, a nurse.

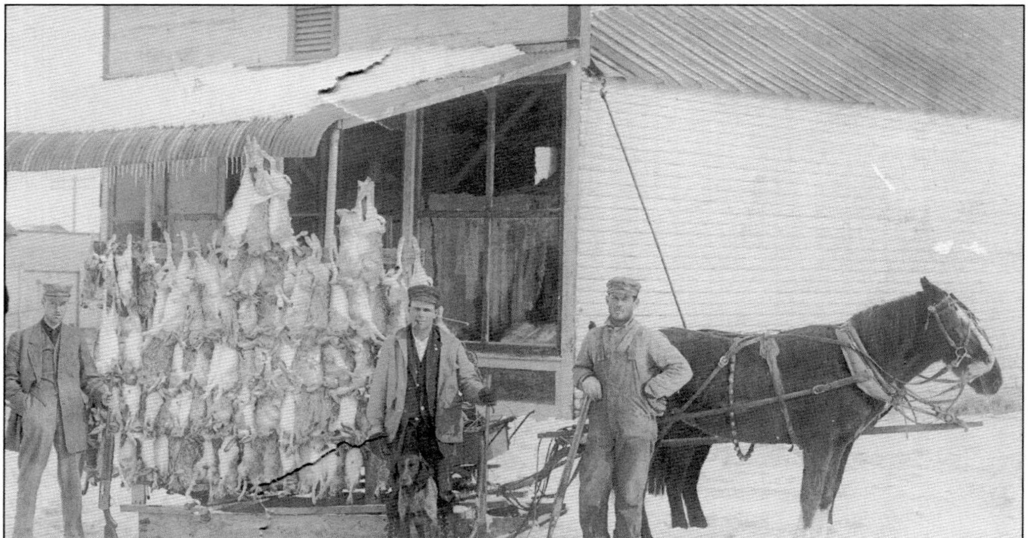

Jim Crabtree (left), Will Thomas (center), and Henry Garret are pictured selling rabbits, which were plentiful. These critters were also used for food, especially during the Dust Bowl when times were extremely hard and food was scarce. When folk came to homestead, rabbits were also a welcome dish on many tables.

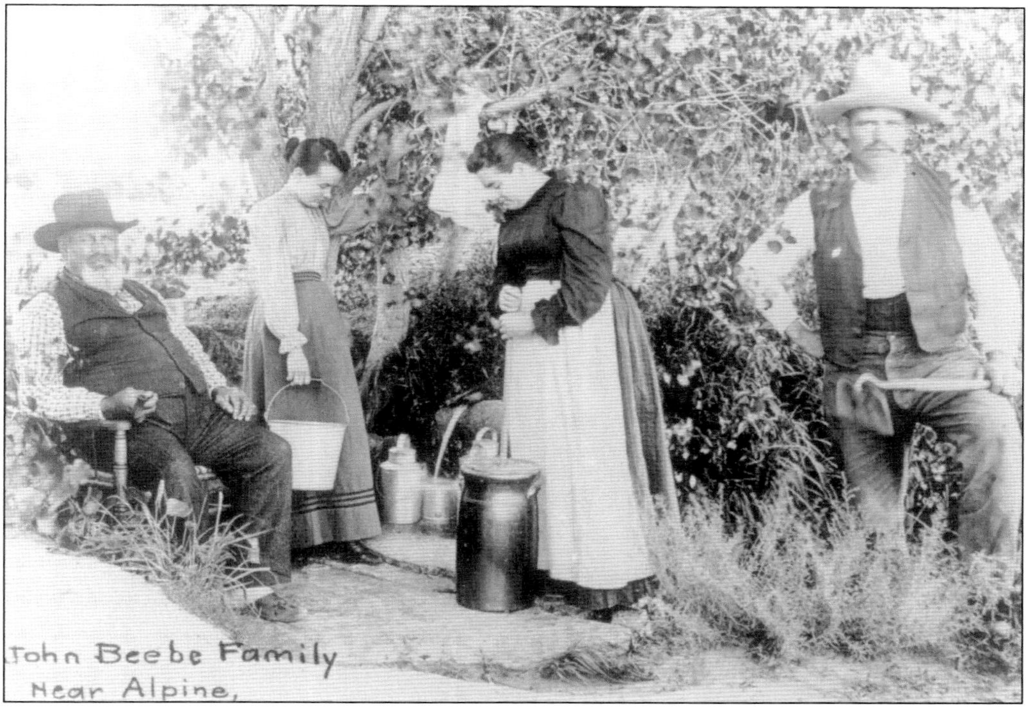

The Beebe family members, who were early day ranchers, are pictured here. Otto Barby Sr. married May Beebe, the daughter of prominent ranchers east of Beaver City, and was later the owner of the ranch. His descendants still own the ranch, along with other acquired properties.

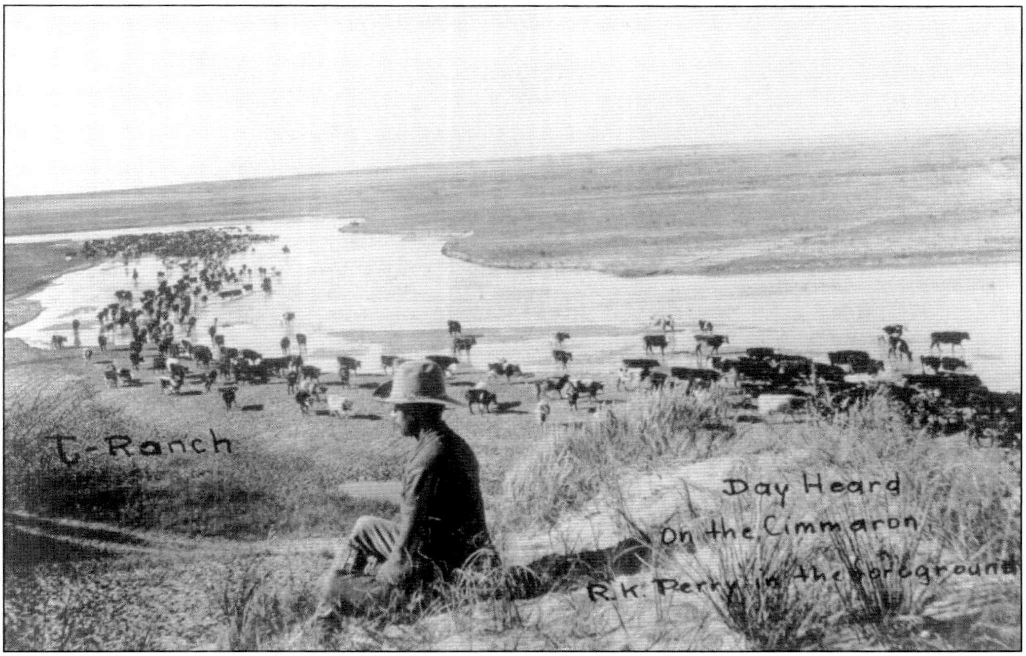

Cattle graze on the Fred Taintor ranch, which is near the Cimarron River. It was one of the first ranches in the area.

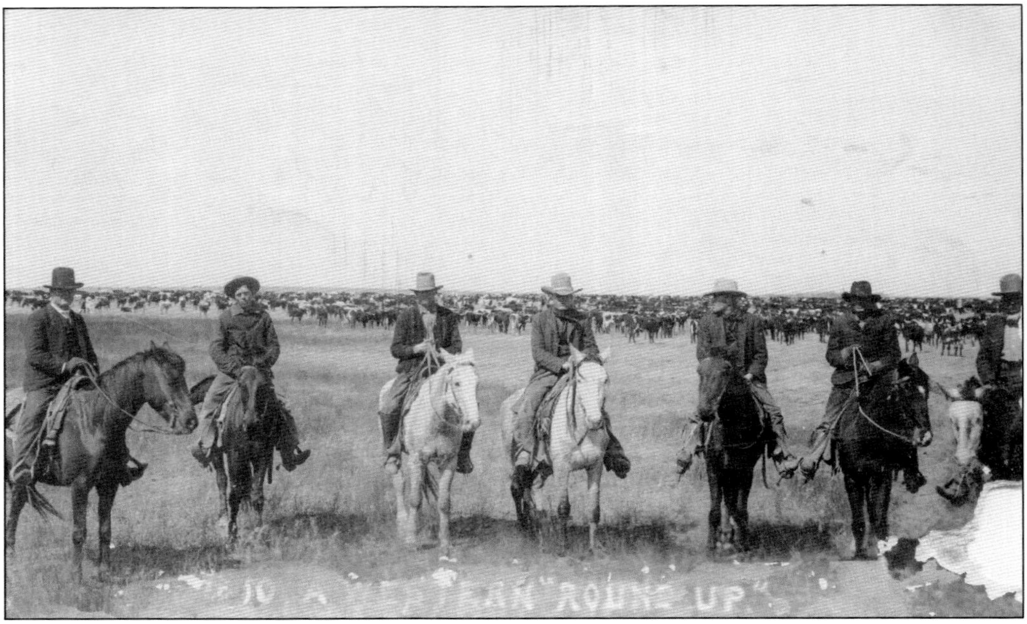

This is the "western roundup" crew in eastern Beaver County pictured prior to shipping cattle to Dodge City and points north in Kansas.

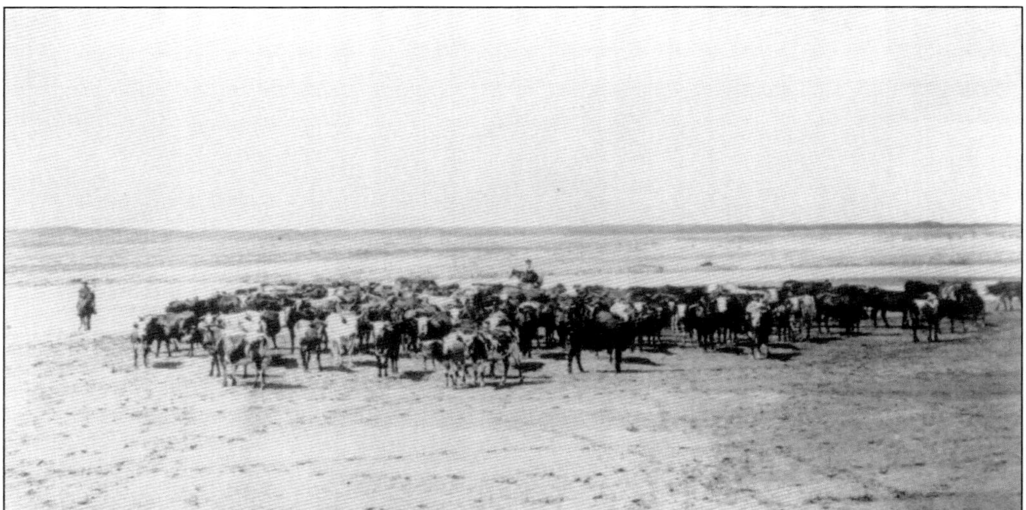

This herd was photographed on Sharps Creek in western Beaver County. Sharps Creek was well-known as a stopping place on cattle trails, as a picnic area for settlers miles around, and today as a park and recreation area.

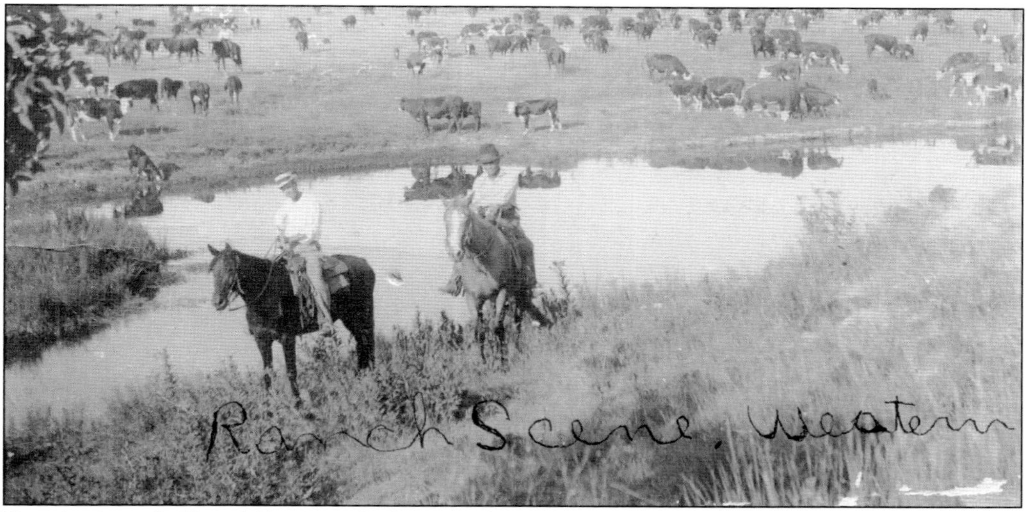

Doc Anshutz (left) and Shy Staniford run cattle on the Cimarron River, which served as a crucial point for early ranchers and settlers and borders Beaver County on the north. These two fellows were some of the early ranchers in the area.

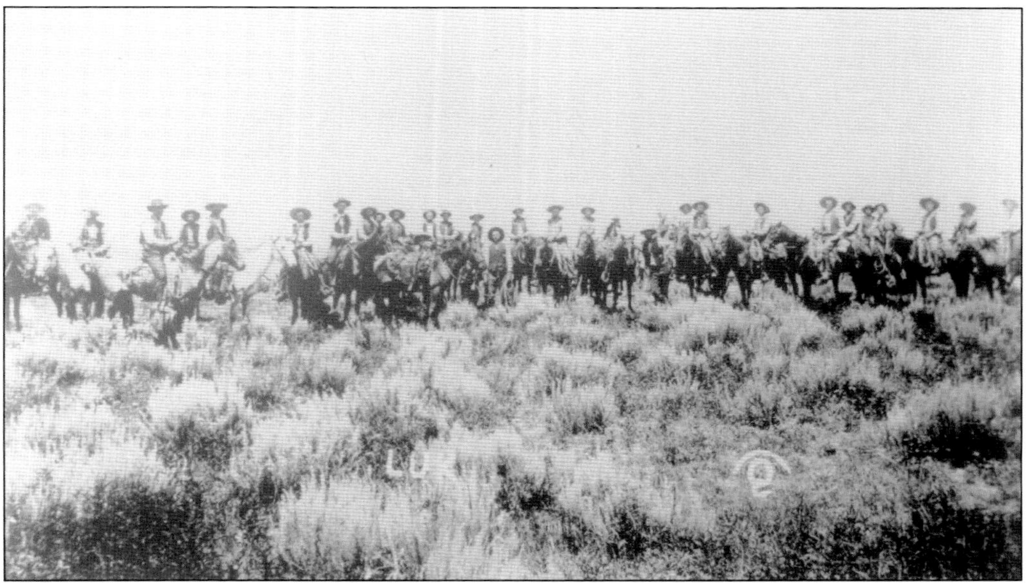

Cattle were put into a circle to keep them together, as there were no fences for hundreds of miles. Kramer and Sons Outfit, pictured here in 1885, are "ready for the circle" at roundup time.

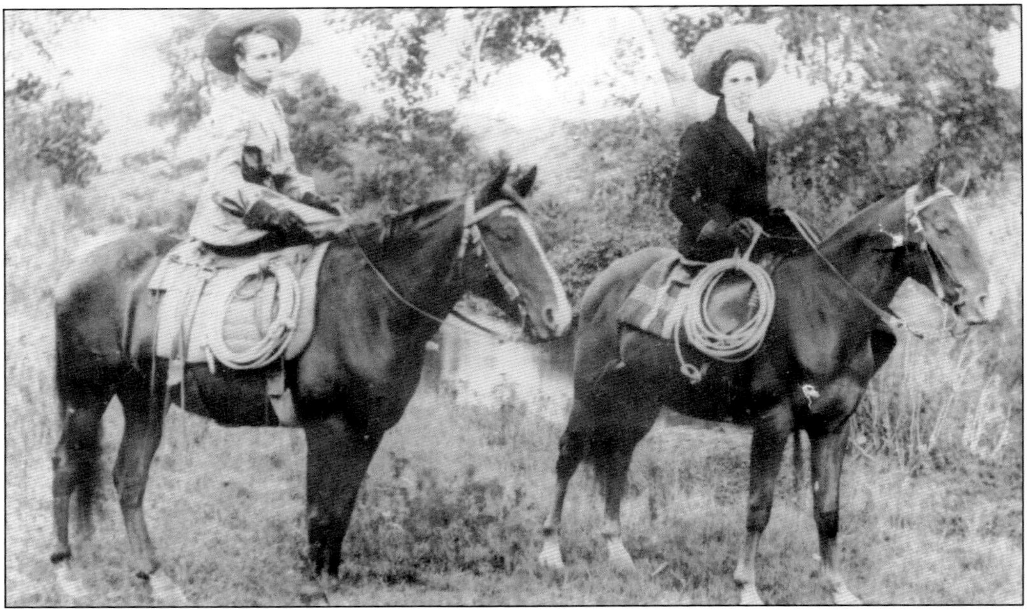

Ida (left) and Venal Kinder, two Beaver County women, are pictured here in 1902. These ladies were the wife and daughter of businessman Ben Kinder and were leaders of the community in their own right.

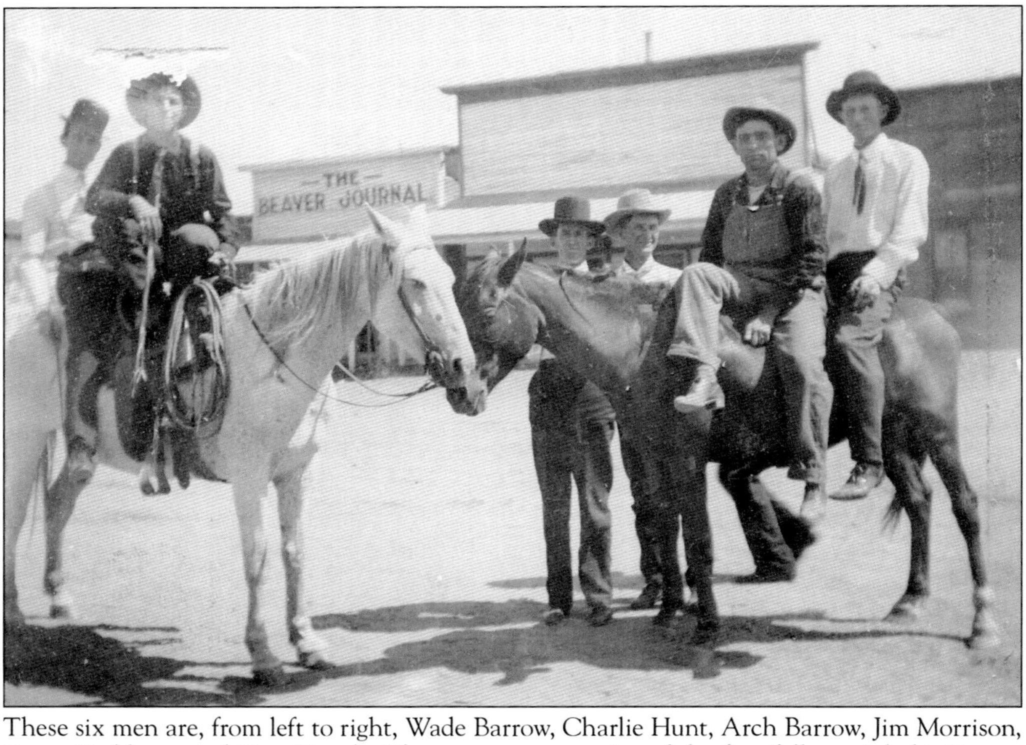

These six men are, from left to right, Wade Barrow, Charlie Hunt, Arch Barrow, Jim Morrison, Harry Peckham, and Tom Dowdy. They are representative of the first folks to inhabit Beaver County; they were businessmen, ranchers, carpenters, and later, farmers.

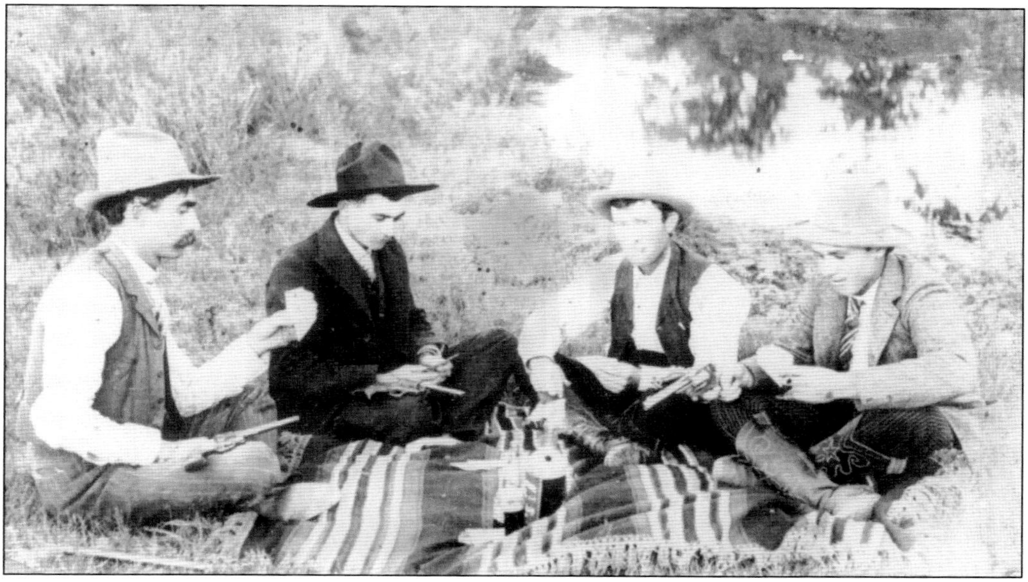

This congenial group on Kiowa Creek in 1902 was made up of, from left to right, Norval Earl, father of Ralph Earl; Charlie Ford, brother of Bob Ford, who shot Jesse James; Charlie "Shorty" Harris; and Charley Aikens.

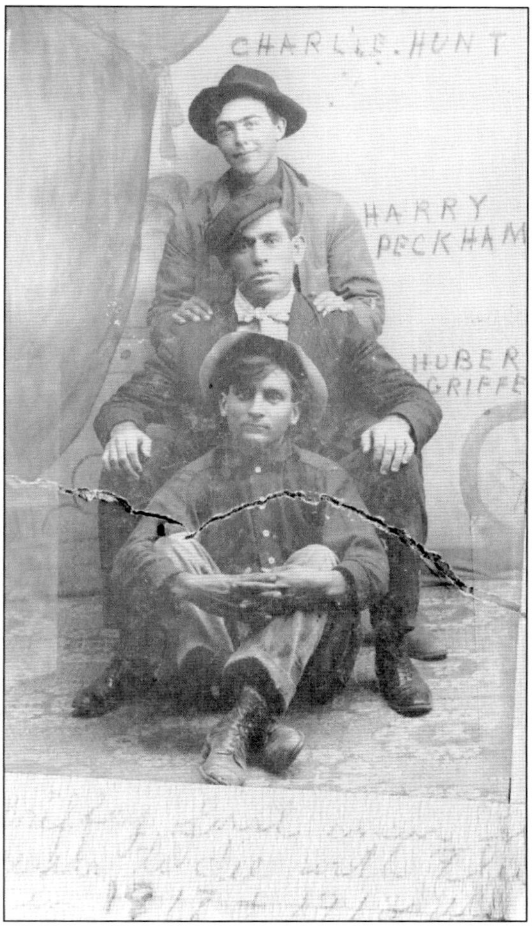

Charlie Hunt, Harry Peckham, and Hubert Griffey were three young men who helped bring civilization and government to No Man's Land.

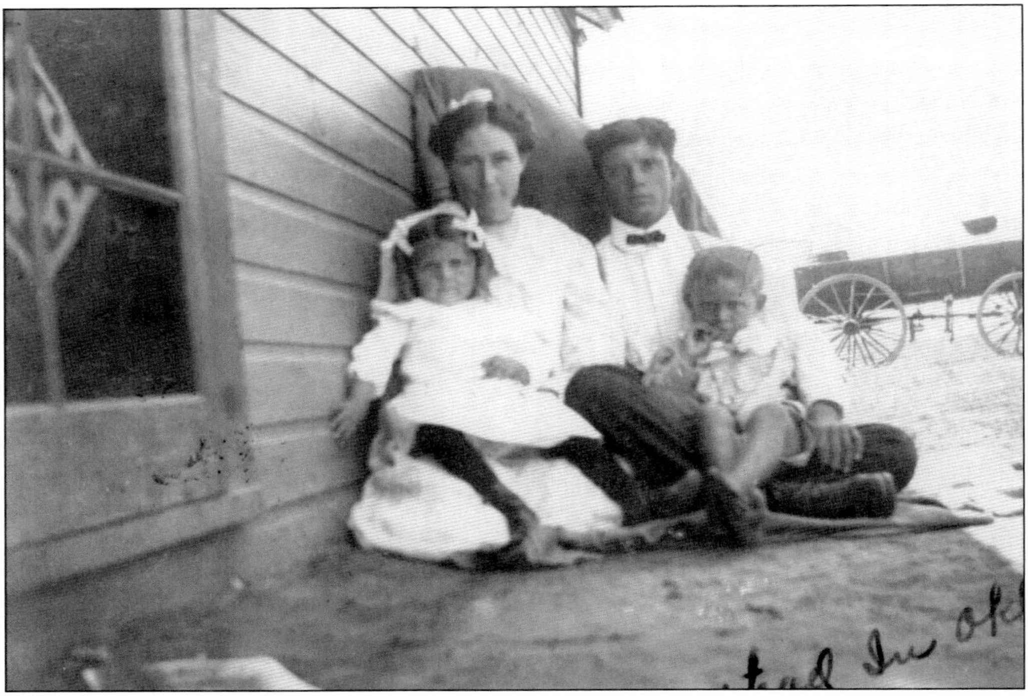

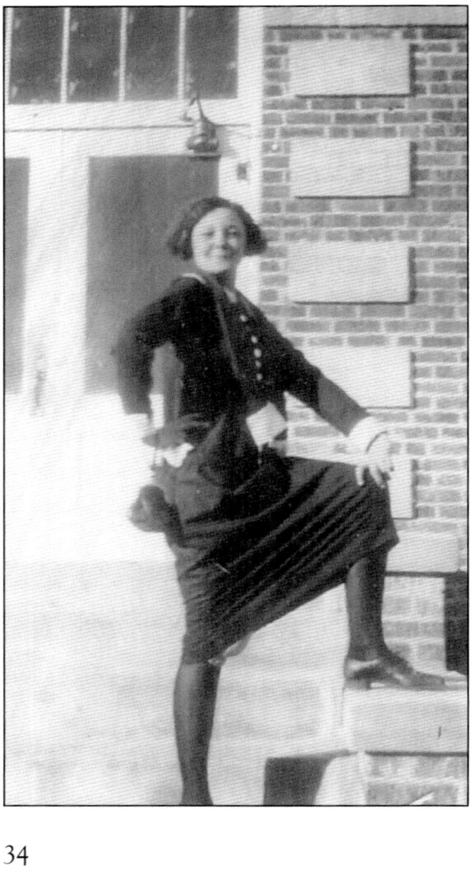

The Whisenant homestead north of Forgan was claimed by Allie and Rufe Whisenant, who are pictured with their children, Clayda and Cull. Rufe Whisenant was a farmer, merchant, hotel owner, and entrepreneur. He ran the Elk Hotel (later called the Commercial Hotel), as well as had an interest in a hardware store, funeral parlor, and a grocery store in the new town created by the railroad. (RJK.)

Faye Harrington Day is on the steps of Beaver High School in 1927, her senior year at Forgan. She lived in or near Forgan until her death in her late 90s and was one of the community members who frequented numerous functions such as ball games, plays, and so on, until her health failed in the early 2000s. (IHL.)

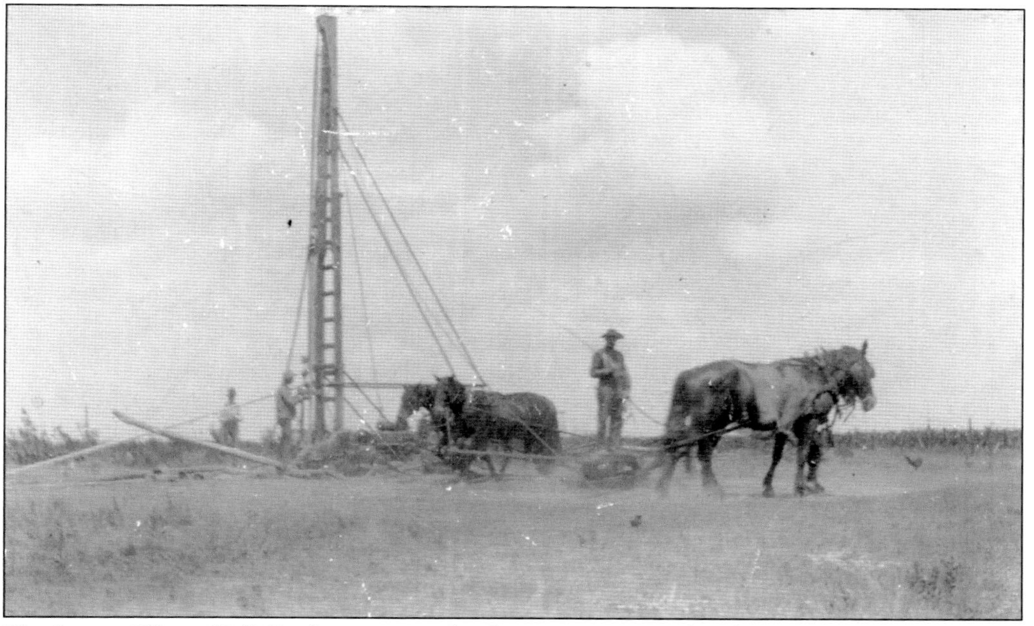

The Larson Water Well Outfit was critical to bringing water to families.

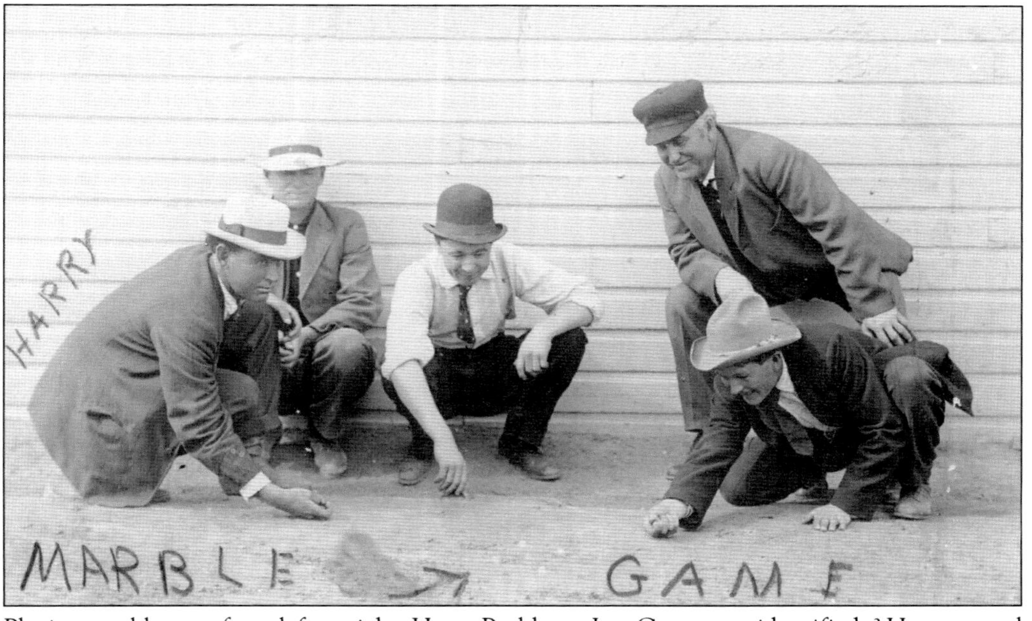

Playing marbles are, from left to right, Harry Peckham, Lee Gosney, unidentified, ? Hogsett, and Ed Gardner. These were young men who would someday lead the county.

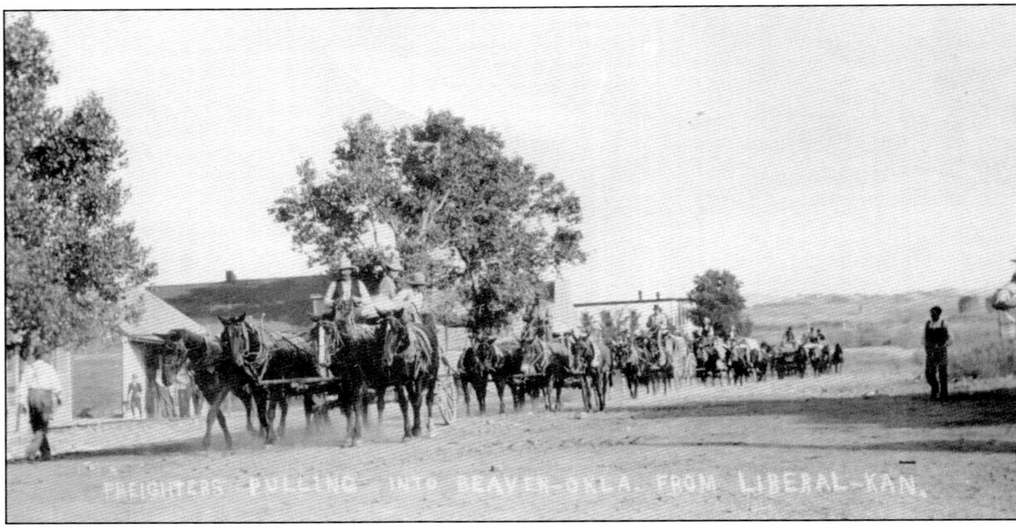

This freighter is pulling into Beaver City from Liberal, Kansas, where lumber and other supplies were purchased until such businesses could be established in the new towns that were springing up.

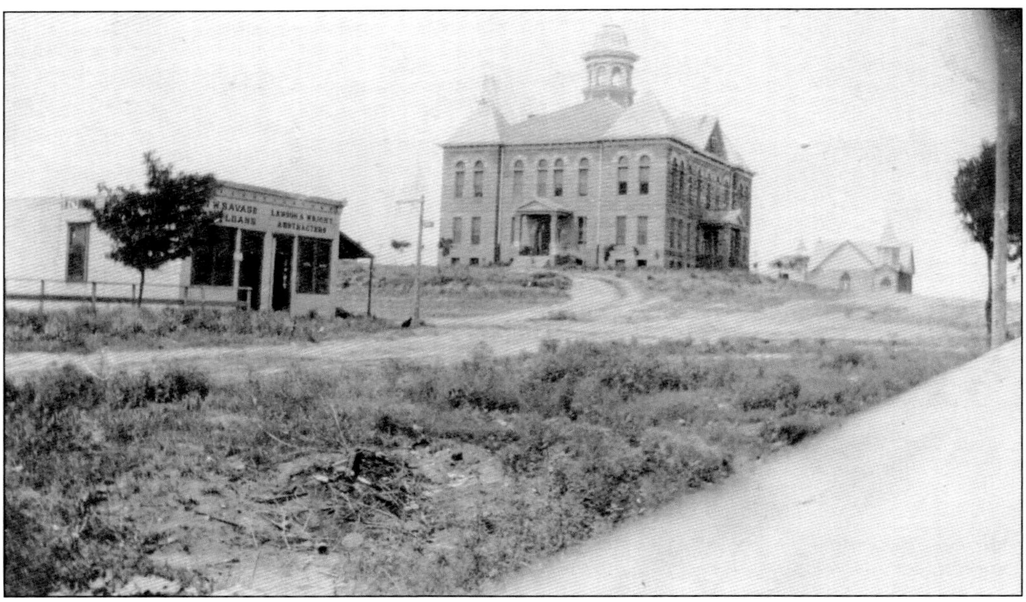

The Beaver County Courthouse and Fickle Abstract Company served as vital parts of the new settlements coming into the county. Recording deeds and abstracts was critical as homesteads were filed for or were relinquished and re-filed for. This was the second courthouse, as the first one burned in 1910. The Beaver First Methodist Church is on the hill behind the courthouse.

Dr. Lindsey L. Long, seen here in 1898, was an early Beaver City physician. He operated his practice out of his home and had S. S. Strong build a new residence to house his doctor's office on the first street west of Douglas Avenue. This new location was convenient for his patients since there was not a hospital in Beaver City until 1929.

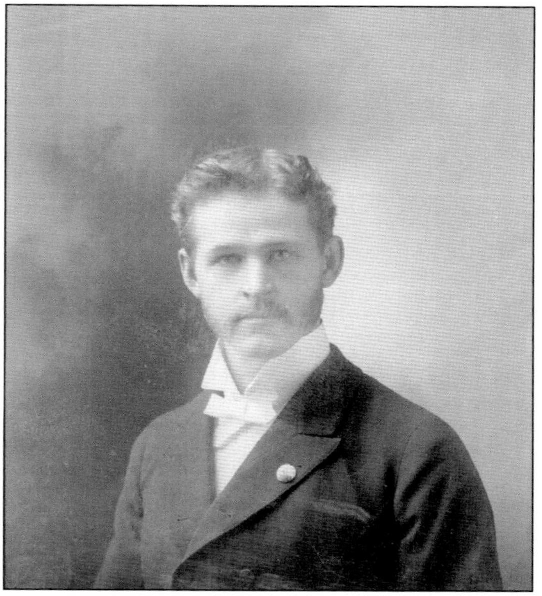

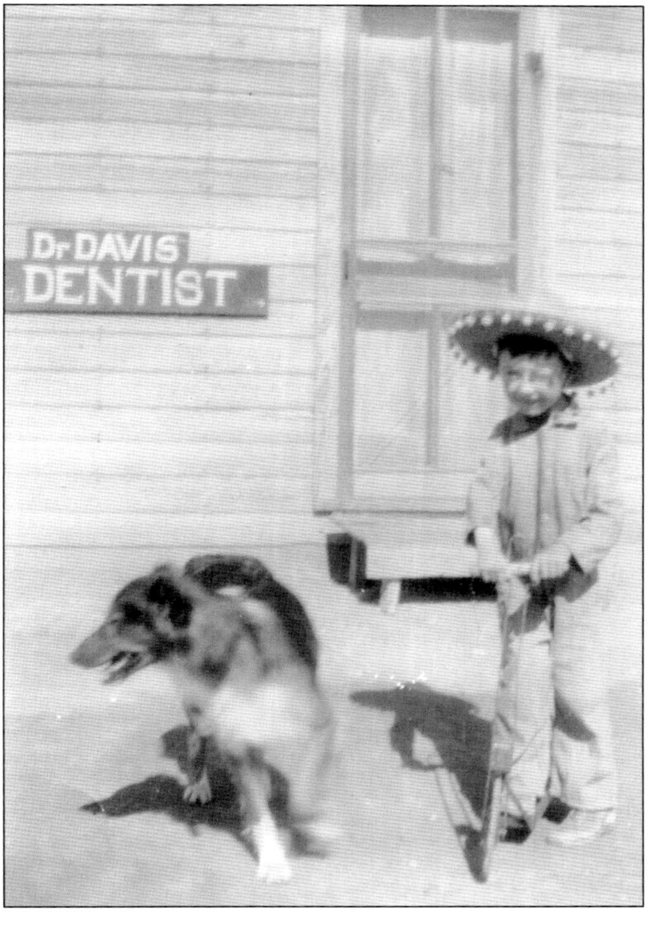

Dr. Earl T. Davis' dental office, which served settlers, was located first on his farm south of Beaver City. It was later moved to the new town. His son Earl is standing in front of the office.

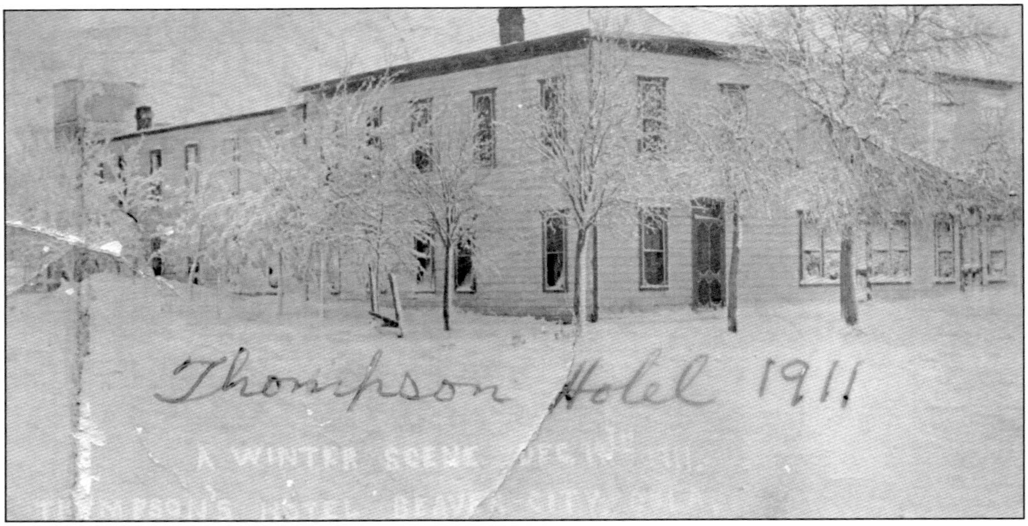

The Thompson Hotel in Beaver City, pictured here in 1911, was one of the most successful businesses in the new town and operated for many years.

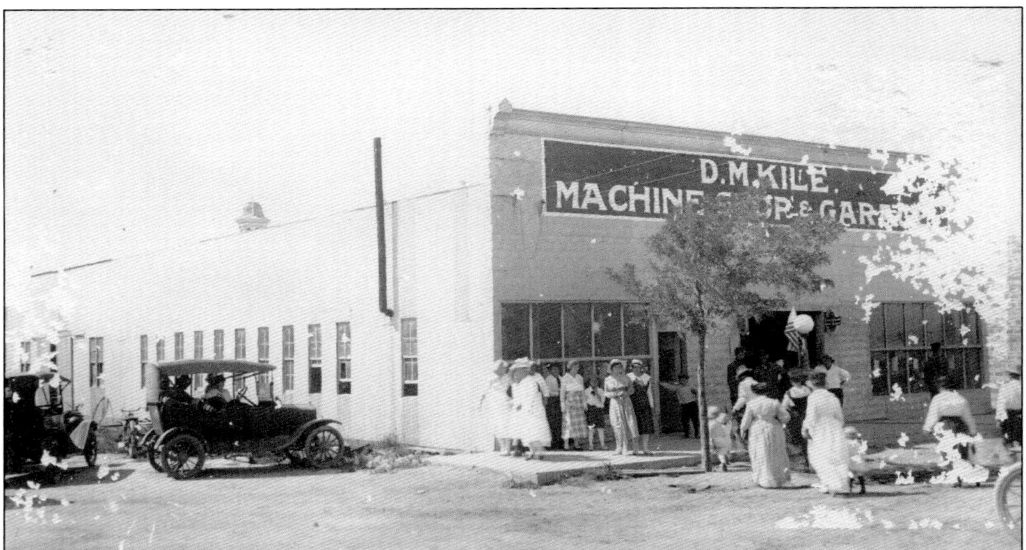

The D. M. Kile Machine Shop and Garage in Beaver was essential to serving the advent of new machines for farming and ranching, as well as the new automobiles coming to town during the early 1900s. Note the different styles of dress by the women; some of them are wearing 1920s attire and some are dressed in 1910s style with long skirts.

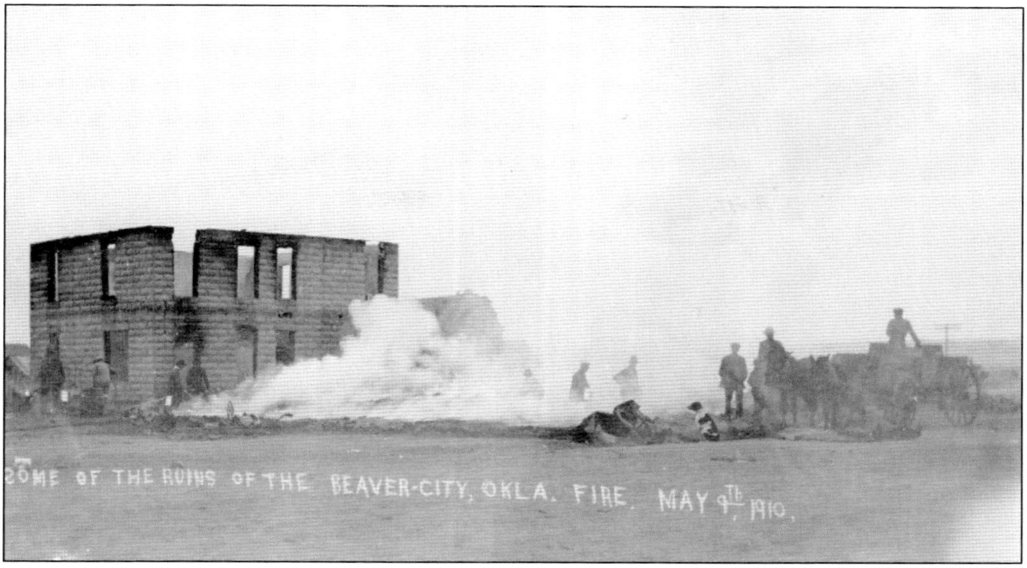

The courthouse fire of 1913 is seen here. This and the following picture are erroneously labeled as 1910. However, the 1910 fire destroyed the wooden courthouse that sat on Douglas Avenue and was in all probability caused by a pipe, cigar, or cigarette left burning in the card room behind a local barbershop a few doors down the street. The courthouse remains in the picture are from the new building erected on Second Street after the 1910 fire.

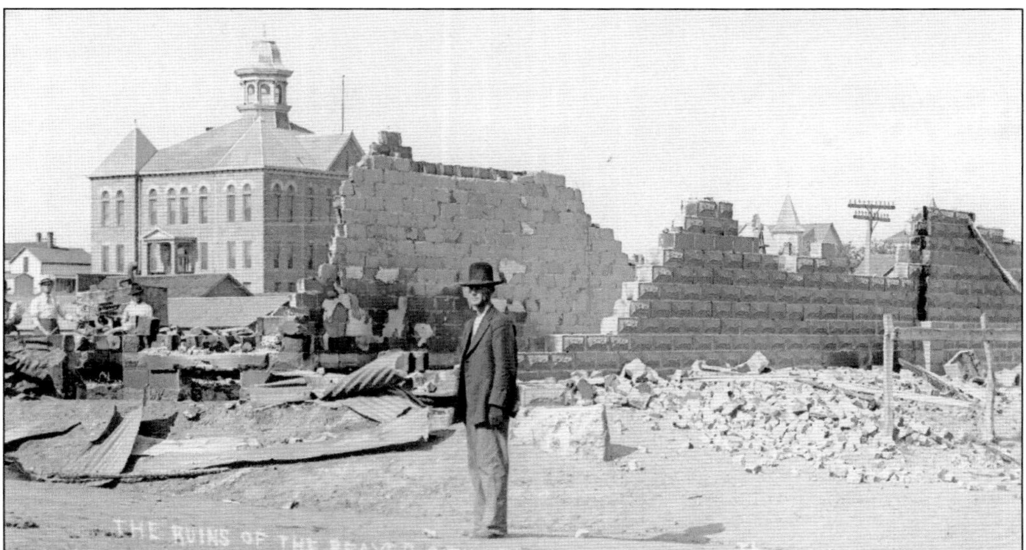

This image also shows the courthouse fire of 1913 with Jacob Lebo in the foreground. The town had a previous devastating fire in 1910. The first fire burned the west side of Douglas Avenue, and in 1912 one burned the east side of the main business street.

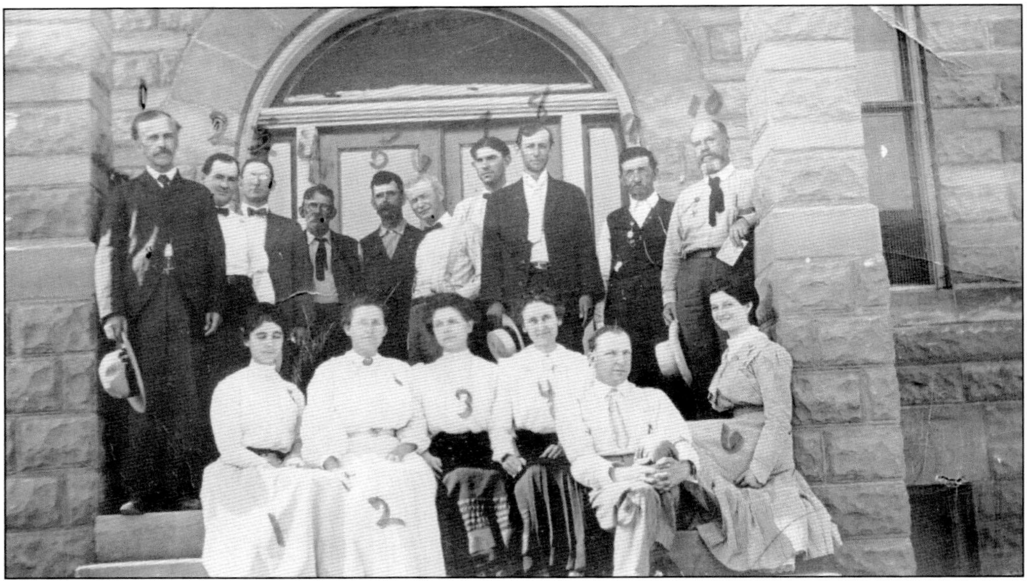

Early day Beaver County officers are pictured here after statehood. Until becoming a part of the Oklahoma Territory, Beaver County had no legally elected officers, although some had been elected for the Cimarron Territory.

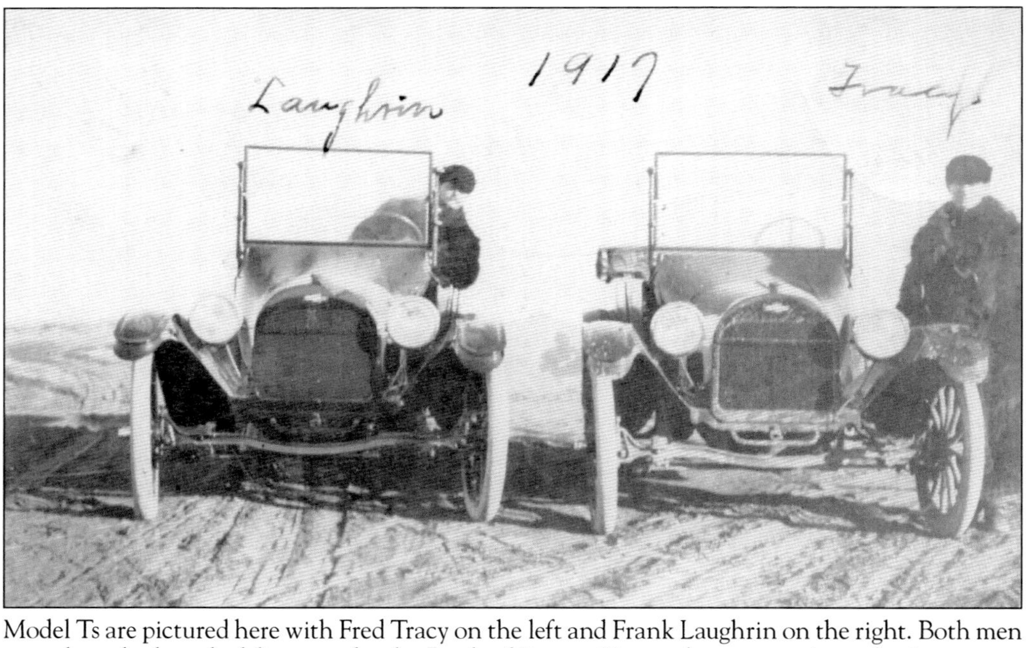

Model Ts are pictured here with Fred Tracy on the left and Frank Laughrin on the right. Both men served on the board of directors for the Bank of Beaver City and were prominent businessmen.

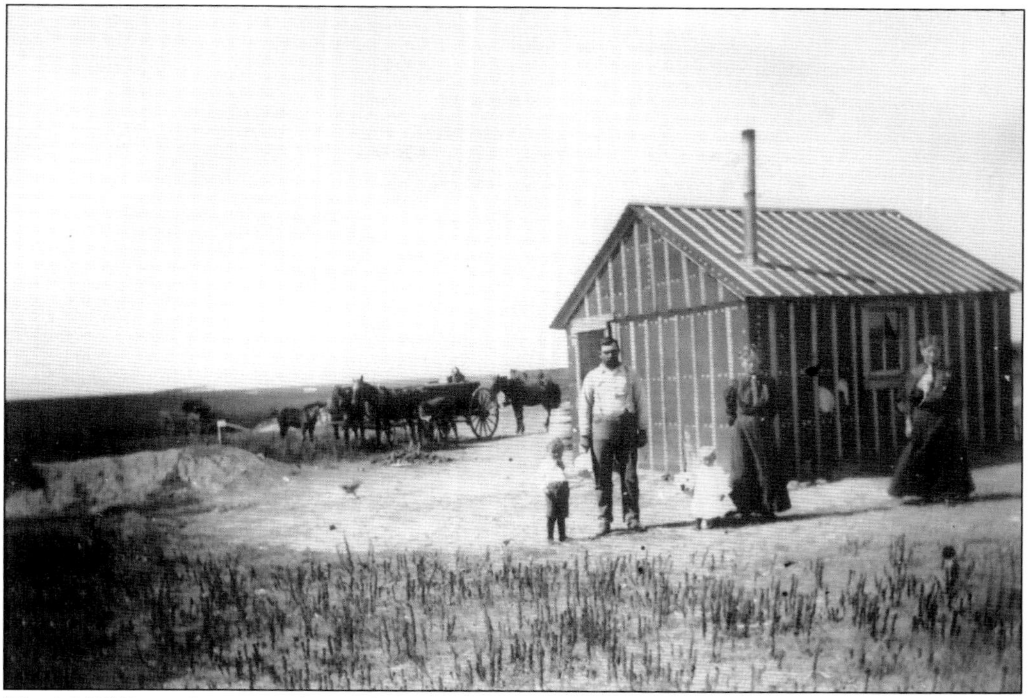

The McWilliams homestead near Gray was claimed in 1907 by Abe McWilliams and Estelle McWilliams, who are shown here with son Joe and Estelle's sister Edna. At that time, Gray was an enterprising young town, but with the coming of the railroad to Ochiltree County, Texas, just a few miles south, Gray was moved to a newly created railroad town called Perryton. (RJK.)

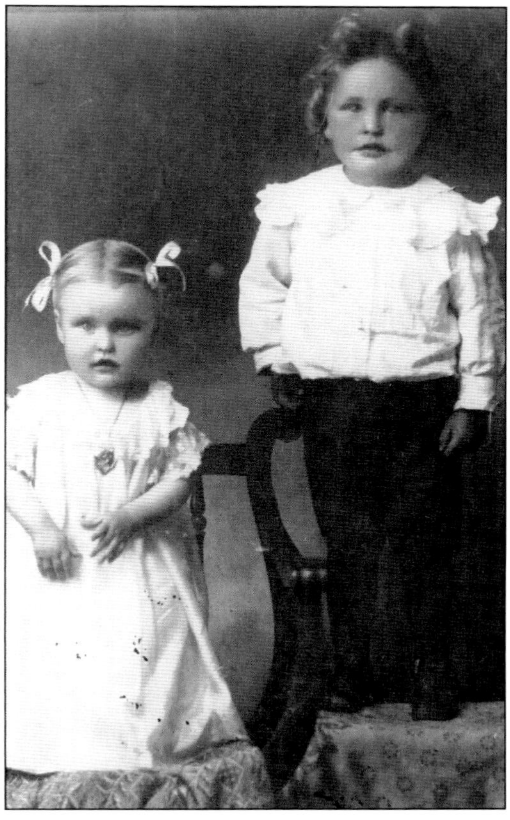

Alice McWilliams and Joe McWilliams, pictured here, were the children of Abe and Estelle McWilliams. Alice married Cull Whisenant of Forgan and lived on a farm east of Turpin before moving to Liberal. Cull was the son of Rufe Whisenant, an early Forgan businessman. (RJK.)

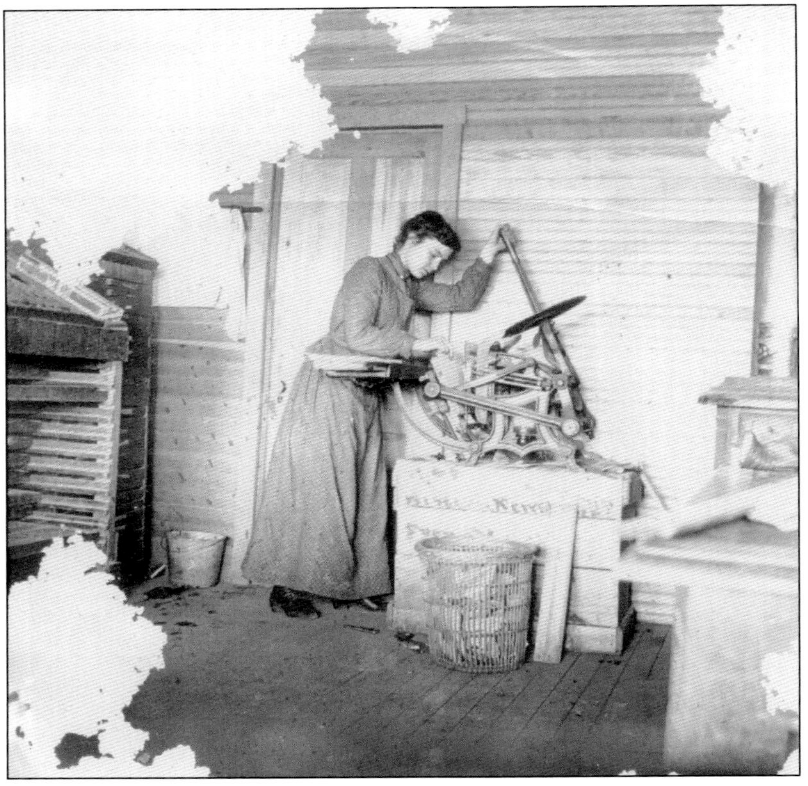

Maude O. Thomas was the owner of the *Beaver Herald*, and is pictured here in her office. She was a businesswoman, politician, and civic leader. (JWL.)

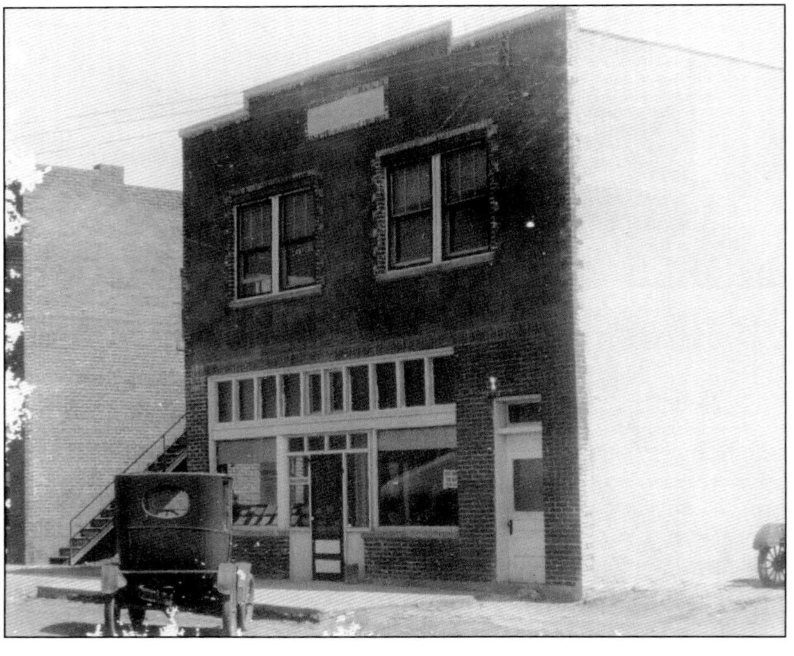

The *Herald Democrat* office, seen here, was the successor to the *Beaver Herald*. This paper continues to be the only Beaver County newspaper. Willis Lansden purchased the paper from L. L. Hubbart and it is still published by the Lansden family. (JWL.)

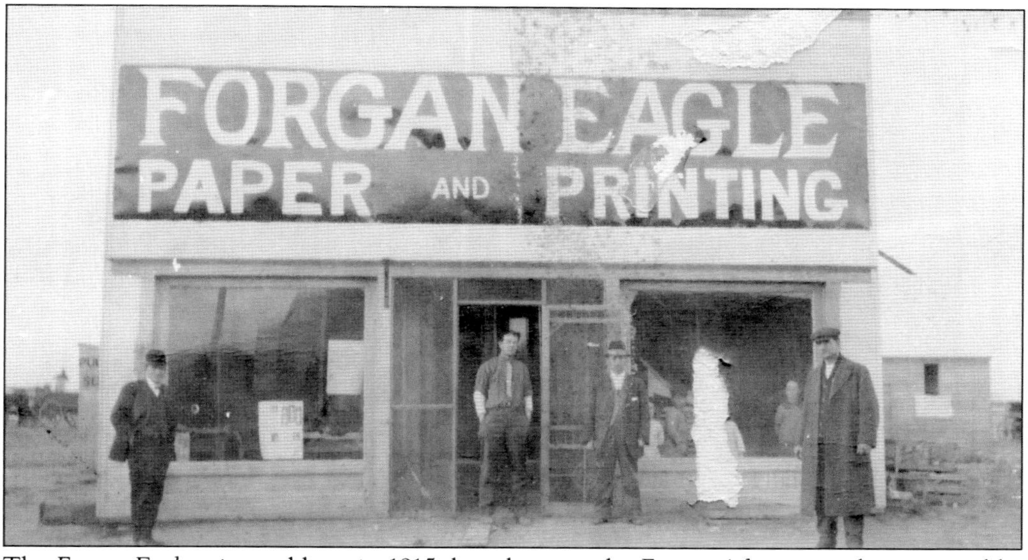

The *Forgan Eagle*, pictured here in 1915, later became the *Forgan Advocate* and was owned by L. L. Hubbart and later by Willis Lansden. (JWL.)

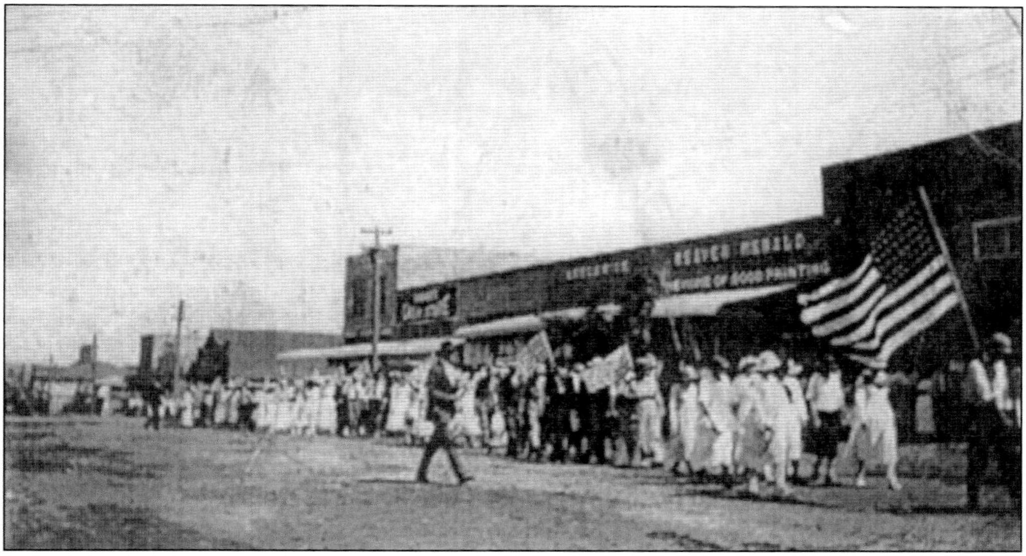

Jim Herron, left, was elected the first sheriff of the Cimarron Territory and later of Beaver County, Oklahoma Territory. He was a rancher, hotel owner, saloon owner, and lawman. He was accused of taking strays from trail herds (called "cattle rustling"), which was a common practice. He and Jack Rhodes were tried at Meade, Kansas, but Herron escaped and lived in Arizona and Mexico for 50 years. He tried several times, with the aid of lawyer Temple Houston and other Beaver lawyers and businessmen, to get his named cleared but to no avail. His life story is told in *Lost Trails of the Cimarron* by Harry Chrisman. (JWL.)

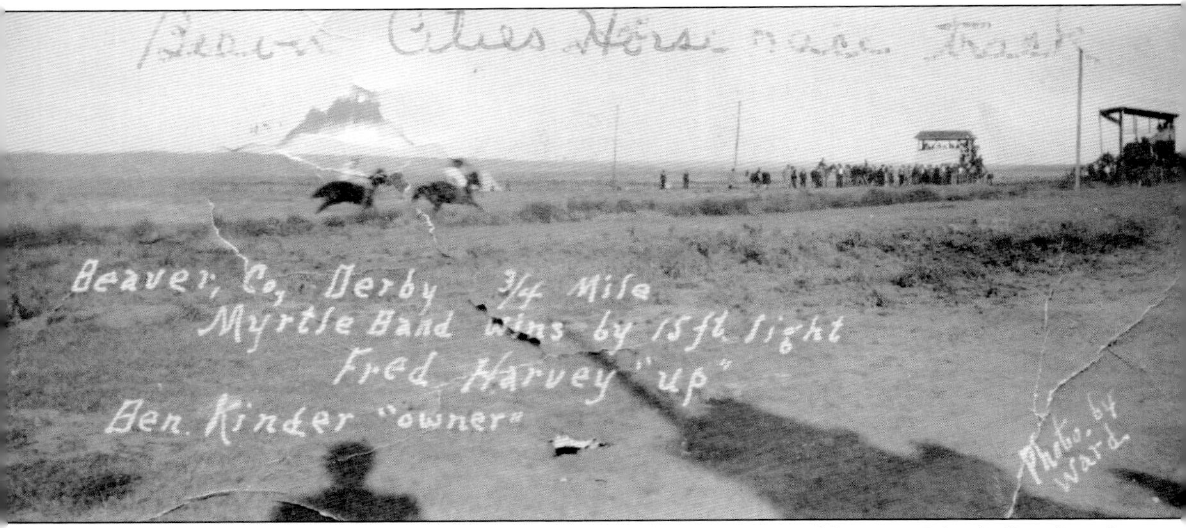

The Beaver County Derby was a three-quarter-mile race. Pictured here are Myrtle Bond in the lead and Fred Harvey behind.

Three

Attempts at Establishing Law and Order

The Cimarron Territory was the name of the area known as No Man's Land during the attempt to bring law and order to the territory when no state or government claimed the land. Through the years, the area had officially been under the flags of Spain, France, Mexico, and the Republic of Texas, until Texas became a part of the United States. For 70 years, no government entity had recognized the area today known as the Oklahoma Panhandle. After all, it was sparsely populated and, in the opinion of the surrounding government entities, held few resources worth claiming.

By 1885, lawbreakers and outlaws threatened the relatively few folks who had settled the area. Since there was no legitimate claim to land titles and no official law officers, the settlers could not get bank loans, legally keep the land they settled on, or have protection from outlaws. An effort was made by U.S. representative D. W. Vorhees of Indiana to get a bill passed in Congress that would attach the area to Kansas. However, Pres. Grover Cleveland let the bill die because of pressure to open public lands for settlement.

Therefore, 30 men from Beaver City began an effort to form a territorial government. The group—led by Dr. D. O. Chase, J. C. Hodge, and Dr. J. A. Overstreet—formed a territorial government and sent a petition to Washington, D.C., to form a legitimate territory, a land office, a land survey, and a federal court. Chase was elected as the Washington representative, but not all agreed with his appointment and they formed another group and elected John Dale as the representative. Both went to Washington. However, the request was tabled and died. Finally, in 1890, the area was attached to the newly created Oklahoma Territory and became known as Seventh County, being the seventh county of that entity.

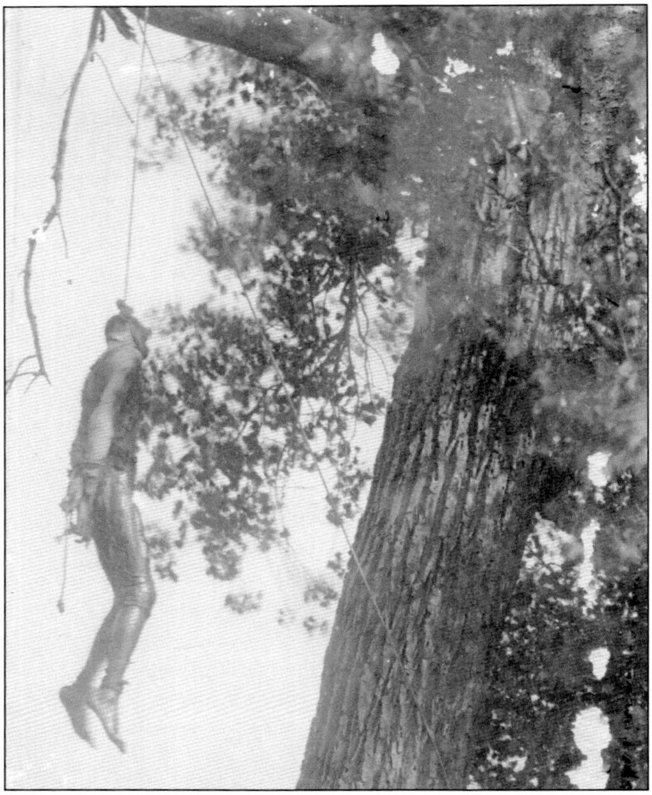

The hanging tree at Gate City was part of an attempt to bring law and order. It mostly was used by the vigilantes committee before any legal government was formed.

This is the seal of the Cimarron Territory, known earlier as No Man's Land. Its renaming was the first attempt at government in the area. For 70 years, the land had belonged to no one legally, so residents had no rights or protection. (HSK.)

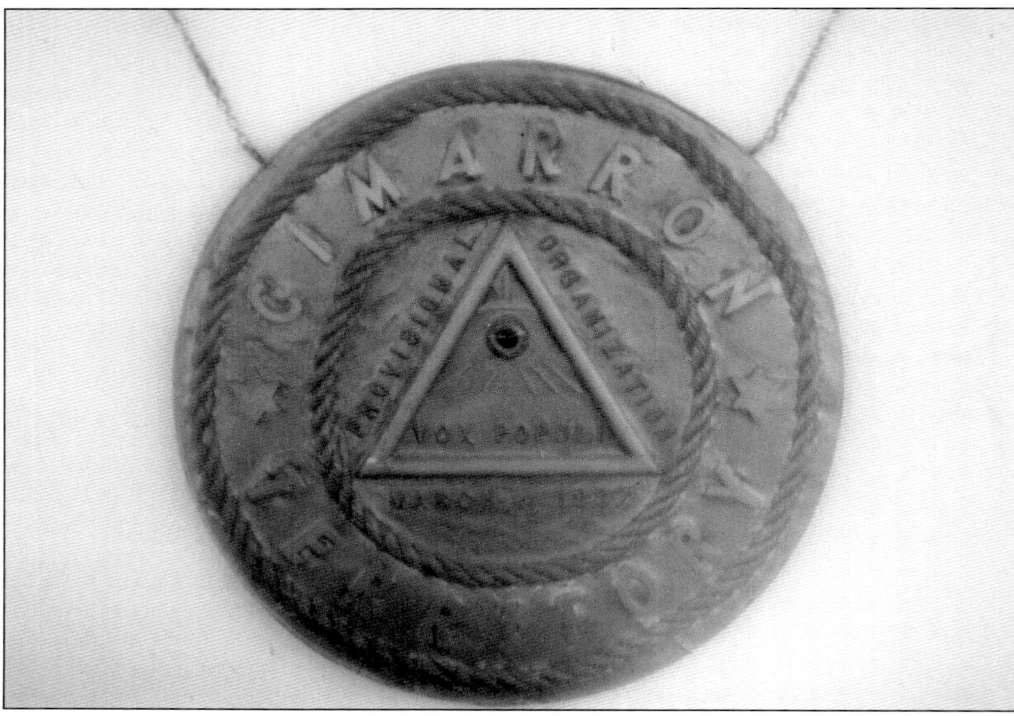

The book of minutes for the Cimarron Territory recorded the meetings and attempts to send a delegation to Congress to gain recognition for the newly formed government in the area that is known today as the Oklahoma Panhandle. (HSK.)

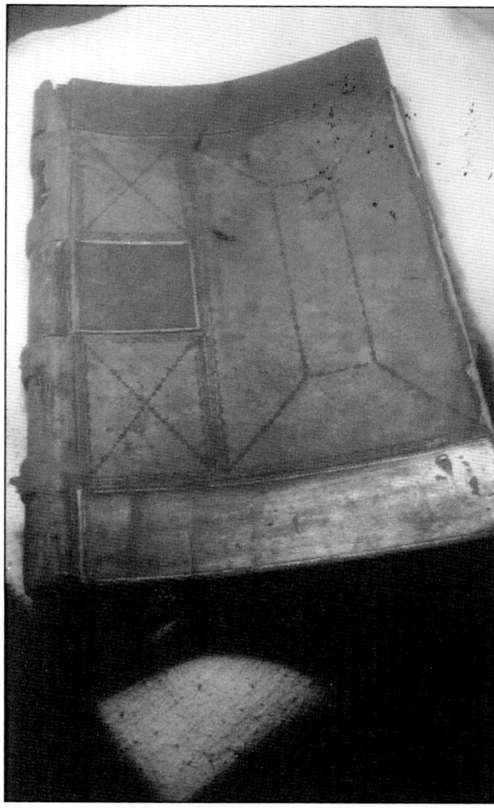

This copy of the minutes for the Cimarron Territory shows the dissension among the delegates that resulted in two different delegations going to Washington. (HSK.)

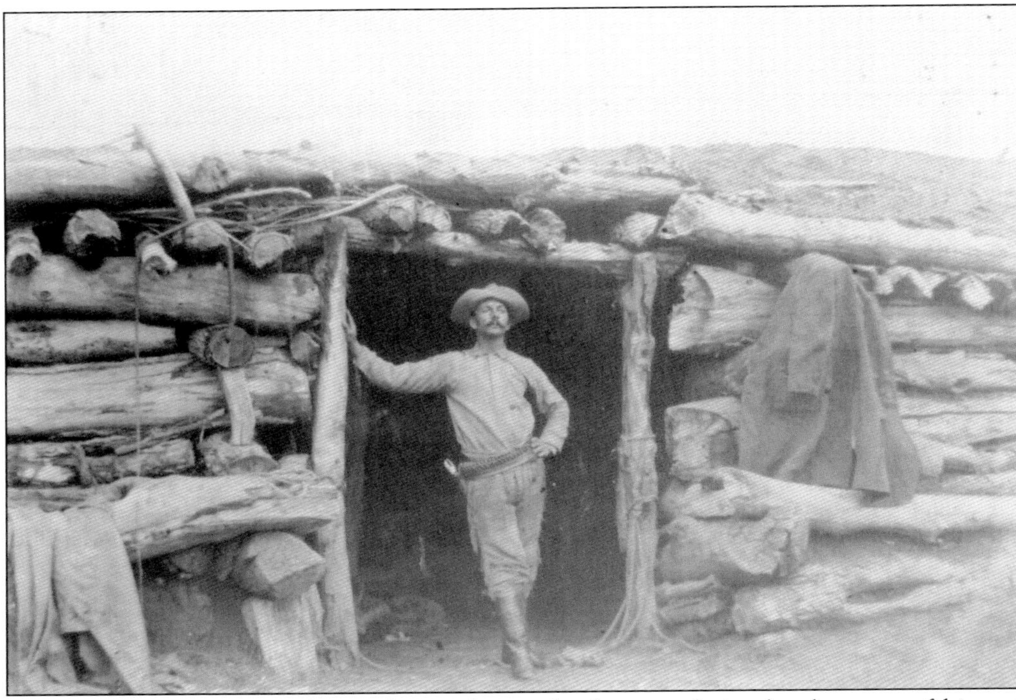

Frank Dale Healy, an early rancher and civic leader, stands in the doorway of his sod ranch house. (FDHIV)

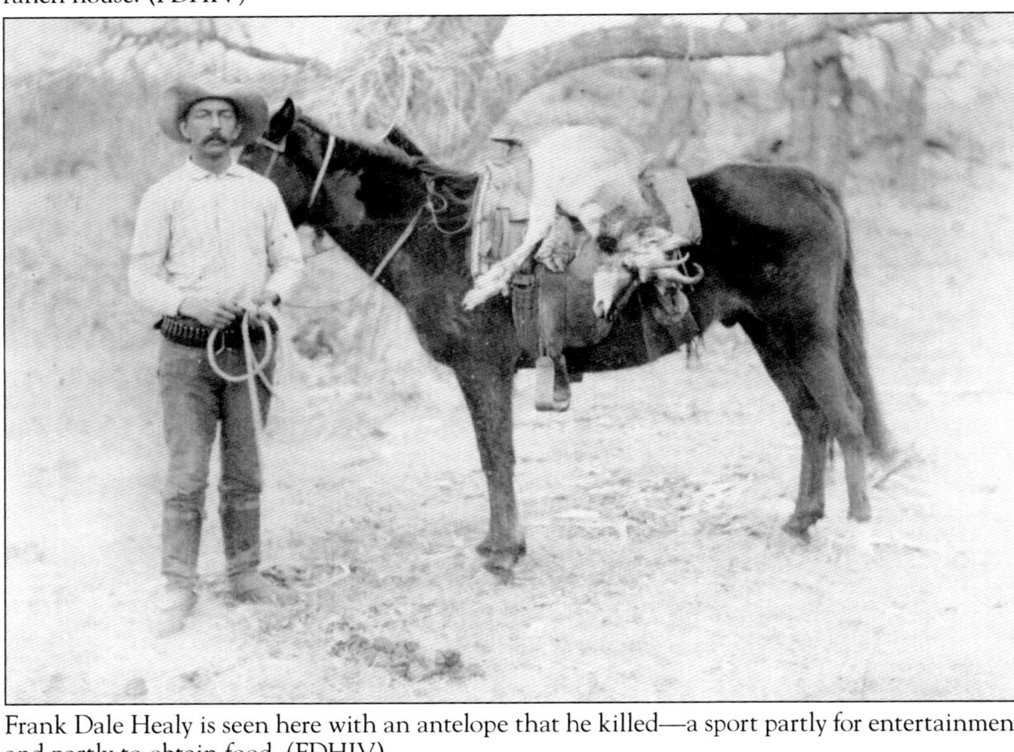

Frank Dale Healy is seen here with an antelope that he killed—a sport partly for entertainment and partly to obtain food. (FDHIV)

Pictured here is William Robert of the XI Ranch, which was later owned by the Adams family. The ranch still exists along the Cimarron River.

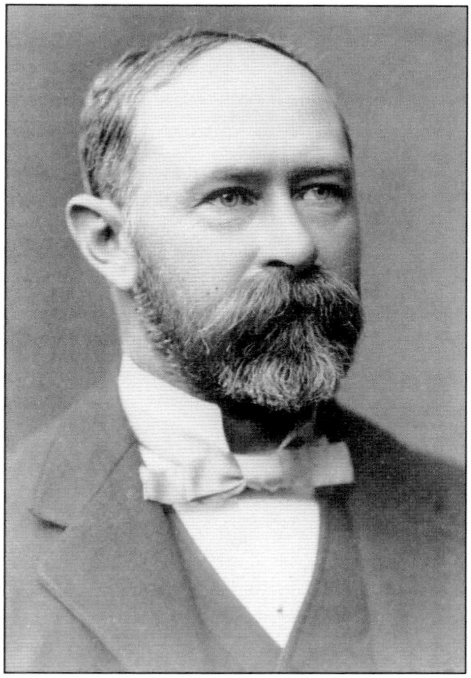

This is the county jail building. The fellow in the tuxedo is unidentified, but it is unlikely he is the jailer.

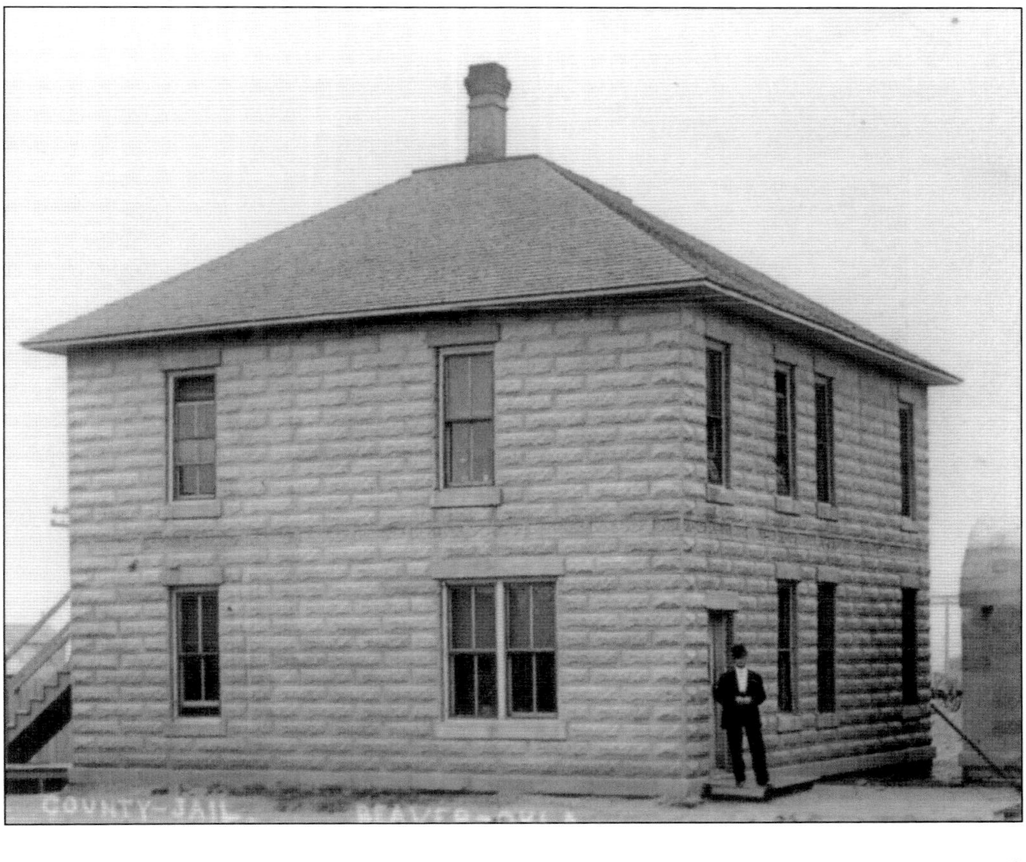

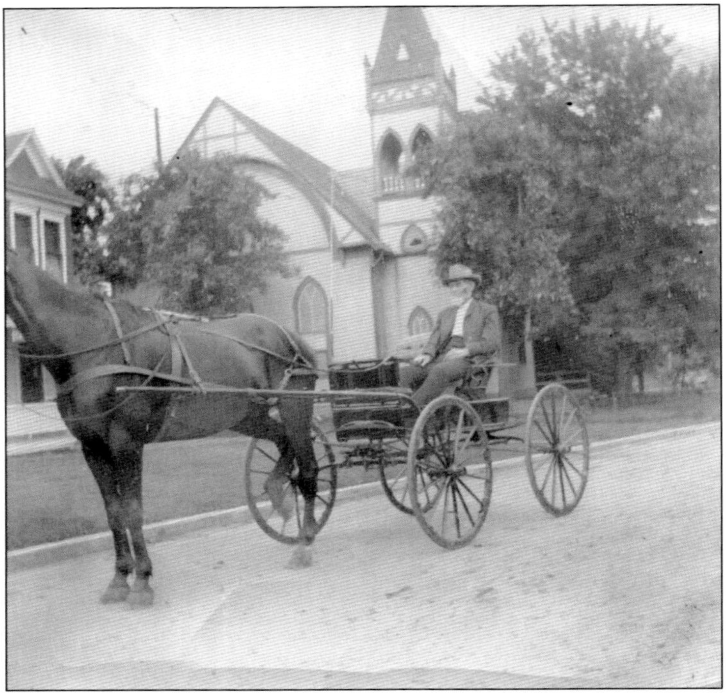

Judge Carter Tracy moved to Beaver in early 1891 from Gate City, where he had a store in the original town. Previously he had a store in Englewood, Kansas. His original home was in Rochester, Illinois.

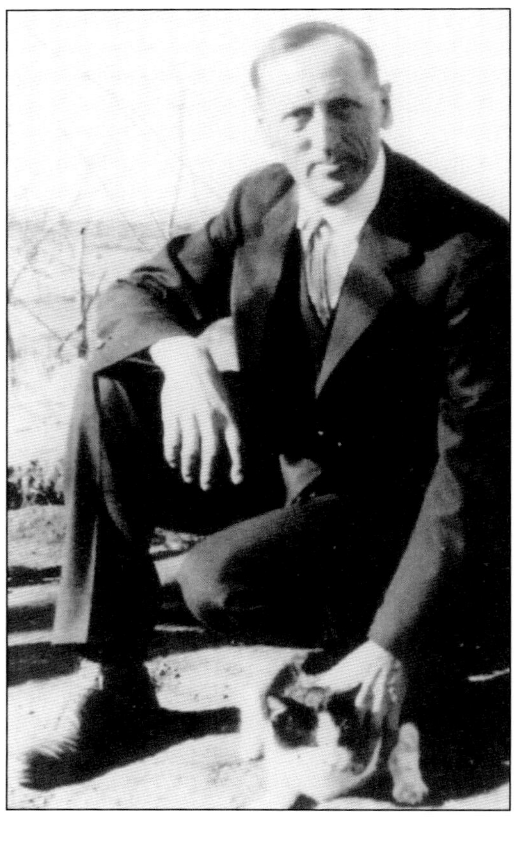

Judge John Spohn was an early homesteader in Beaver County. His daughter Alice Spohn Newton returned to Beaver in the 1970s and maintained his legacy as long as she lived, which was into her late 90s.

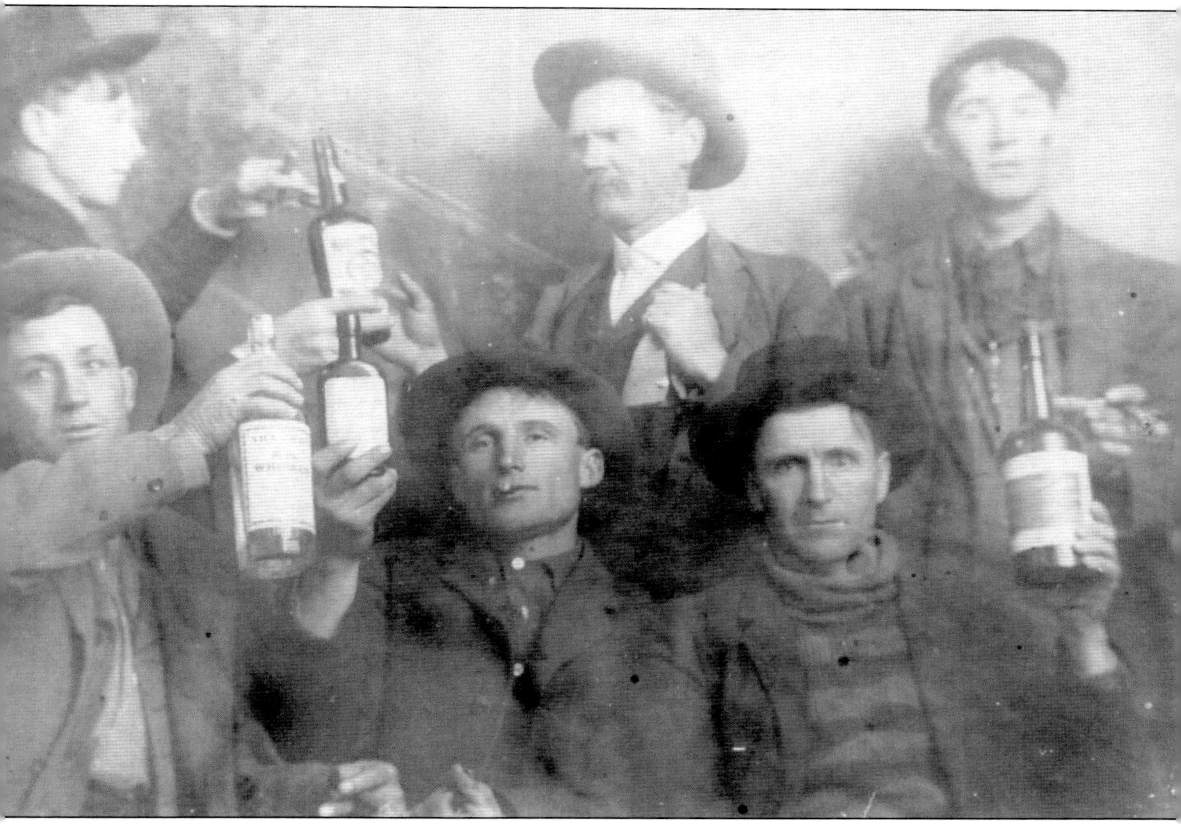

Law and order was established first with the area becoming part of the Oklahoma Territory in 1890, then part of the State of Oklahoma in 1907. These men were duly elected officers of Beaver County, Oklahoma. From left to right are (first row) Edd Hanson, Charlie Dixon, and Andy Dixon; (second row) Tom Shelton, Sheriff Shelton (Tom's father), and Otto Lastro.

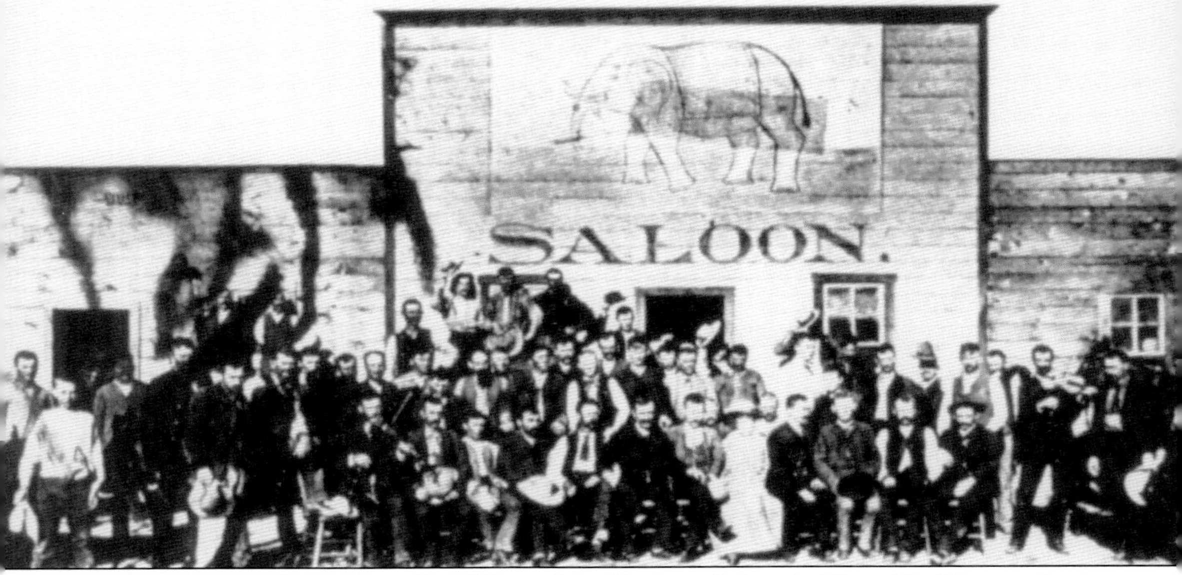

This photograph from June 25, 1888, is of the Elephant Saloon in "Beer City." It was a business located in this prairie haven of rest and relaxation for the cowboys of No Man's Land, called "the Sodom and Gomorrah of the Plains." The name of the town was White City because most of the buildings were tents, except for a few saloons and "hotels." Beer was hauled from the trains in Liberal, a town in Kansas—a dry state—located just north of the tent city. The beer was stashed behind the tents, and thus it became known as Beer City. Amos Bush, who was shot to death by Madam Pussy Cat Nell, sits next to the standing fiddler. Bush was the self-appointed sheriff in this tent city just across the line from Liberal, Kansas. He was buried in Ashland, Kansas, where he had lived before coming to Beer City.

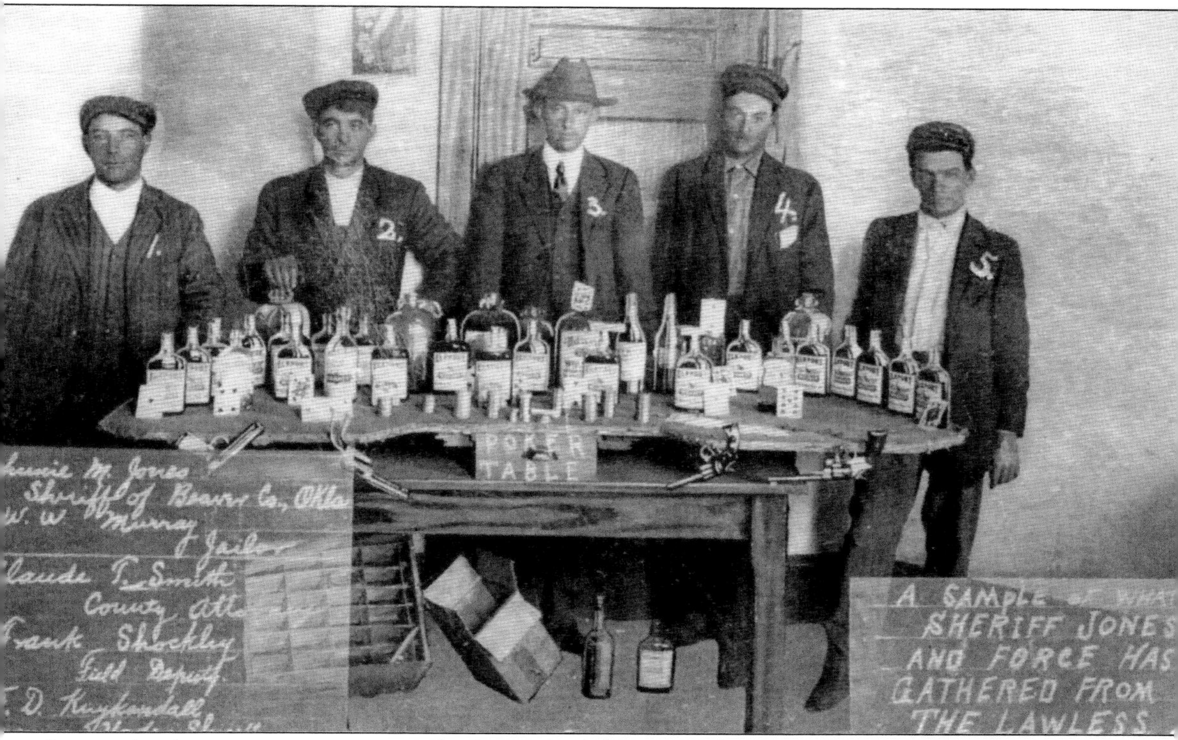

Law and order was not easy to come by during Prohibition, so the importance of county officers was evident. They were, as numbered above, sheriff John Jones, jailer W. W. Murray, county attorney Claude Smith, field deputy Frank Shockley, and undersheriff F. D. Kuykendall.

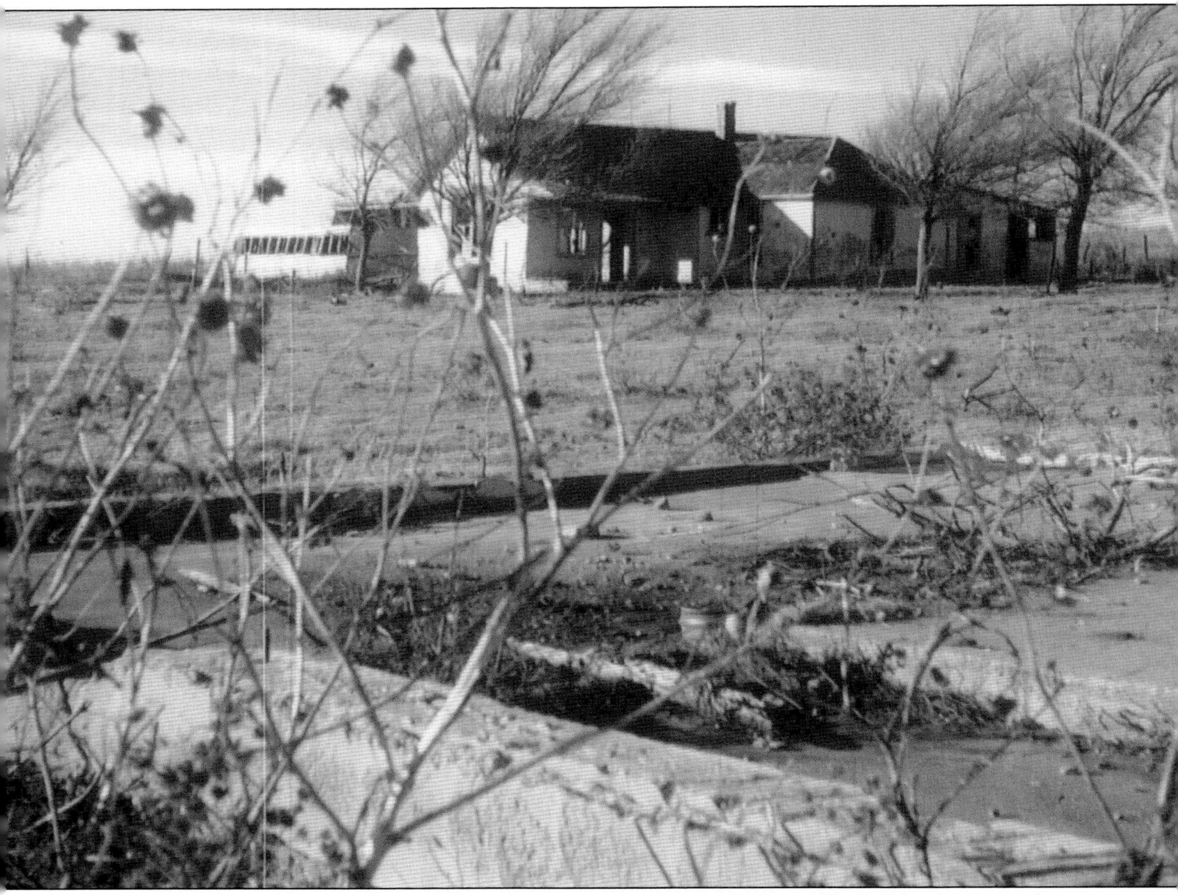

This photograph may show a bootlegger's sod house. The large sod house had a tunnel running from the bedroom to the cellar, which made doing business convenient. (HSK.)

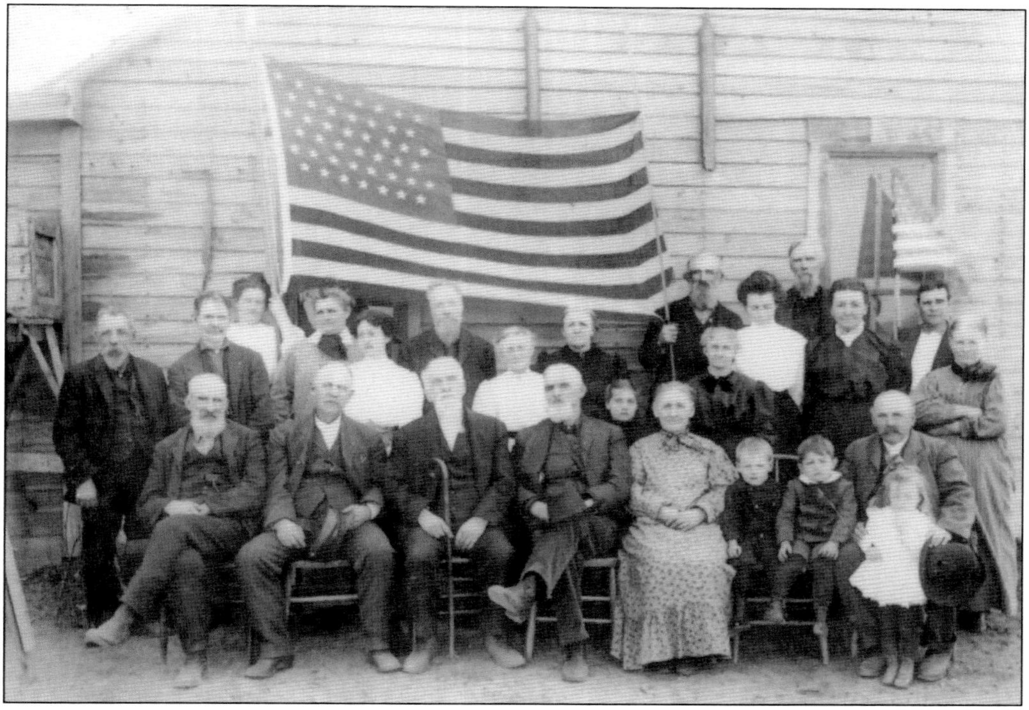

A meeting of the Grand Army of the Republic was held at the J. R. Quinn homestead. Some of those at the meeting were J. R. and Ada Quinn, Mary Jane Coombe Thomas, Mother Hanson, Wesley Hibbs, Rev. Davidson, J. R. Thomas, Amos Hibbs, Claude Mansfield, I. S. Drummond, and Jim Crabtree. J. R. and Ada entertained often and were leaders in the Beaver County community, not just in Beaver City.

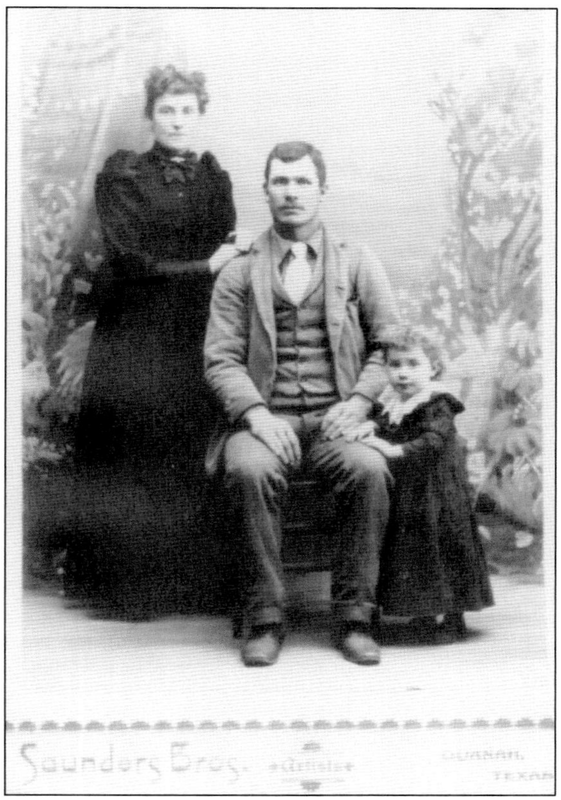

Pictured here are Sarah Ellen Bogue, born in 1873; Elias Ellsworth Bogue, born in 1866; and Mildred Ellen Bogue Broadfoot, their daughter, born in 1893. They were a very prominent family in southeast Beaver County. Later Elias and Ben Bogue operated a hotel and livery stable, as well as other businesses in Beaver. (JO'R.)

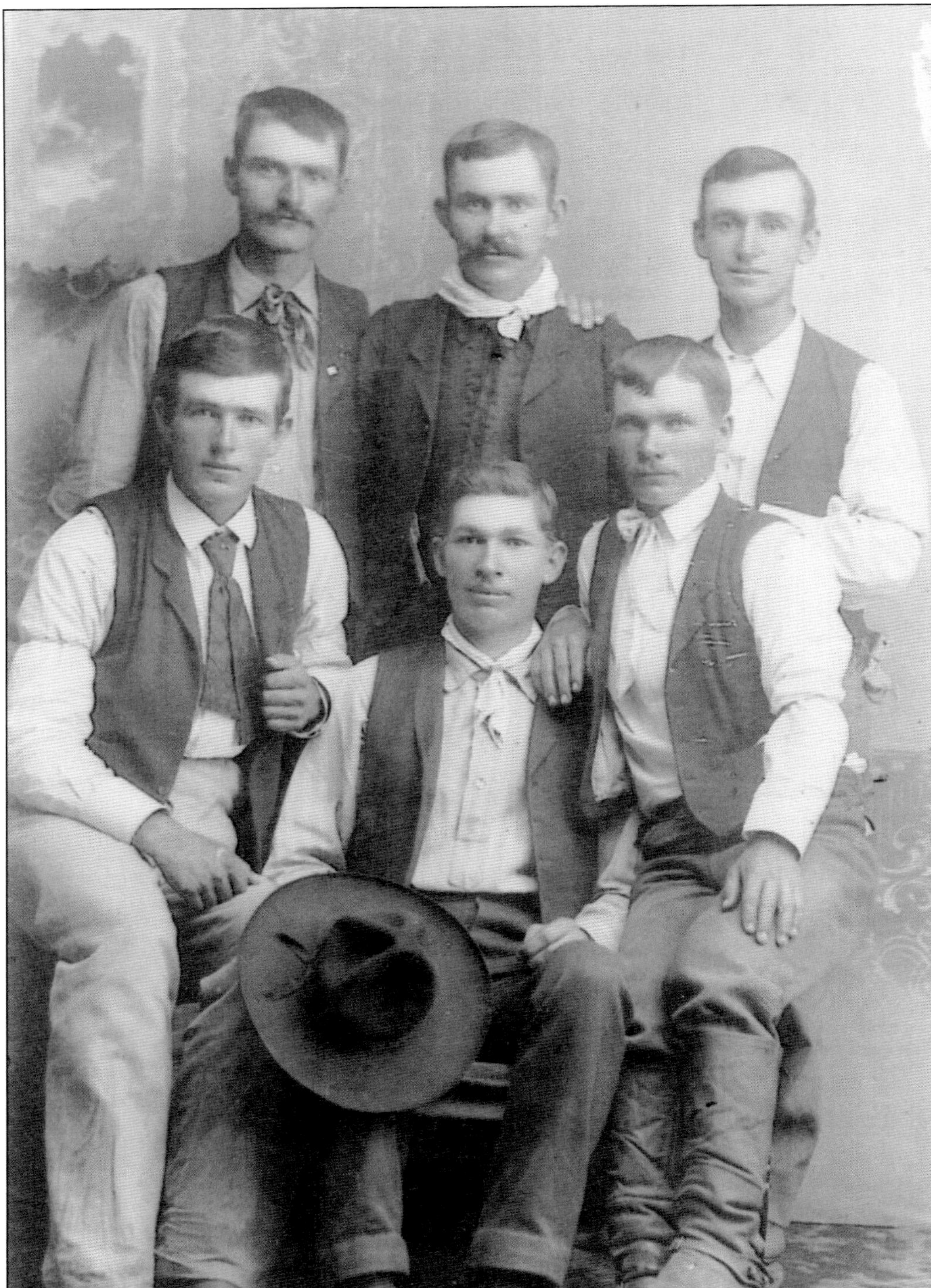

Ranching was the first business enterprise undertaken in Beaver County. Among those early ranchers are, from left to right, (first row) Emmet Gardner, Ben Bogue, and Perry Hibbs; (second row) Jake Redemer, John Hibbs, and Frank Bogue. (JO'R.)

Four

Beaver County Becomes Part of Oklahoma

Beaver County became a part of the Oklahoma Territory by default since no one in the territorial legislature seemed to realize that people were "out there." To complicate matters, political leaders in No Man's Land proposed to Congress that creating a new territory would provide law and order. Unfortunately these leaders formed themselves into not one, but two delegations to support the proposed new Cimarron Territory. Since they could not agree among themselves, Congress then "tacked on" the land to the new Oklahoma Territory as the appropriately named Seventh County. When Oklahoma Territory achieved statehood in 1907, Beaver County became one of the three new counties in what is known today as the Oklahoma Panhandle. The rest of the area became Texas and Cimarron Counties. Beaver City remained the county seat, but now it was only for the easternmost county in what was once No Man's Land. Had the Cimarron Territory come into being, it is likely it would have eventually became a state in itself. After all, it is geographically larger than any of the five New England states established at that time.

Beaver County was fortunate to have one of its very own prominent citizens to serve on the Constitutional Convention. Fred C. Tracy, whose family had come to Beaver City in the early 1890s, had that honor, and he and his family continued to serve the county well. Tracy was the county attorney, as well as a businessman, postmaster, bank director, and an active citizen of the area. His father had established a hardware store, a general store, and a bank. Tracy's sister-in-law, Maude O. Thomas, was a prominent newspaper woman who was active in politics and served on the first state highway commission—a feat unheard of for a woman during those times. Tracy was later instrumental in obtaining financing for building a railroad spur to hook up with the new railroad coming through Gate, Knowles, Mocane, and Forgan, and thereby to the newly created towns of Floris and Turpin, connecting all of these towns to Hooker. This was critical in providing the farmers south of Beaver a place to sell and ship their crops.

Even though there have been some attempts by the three panhandle counties throughout the last century to secede from Oklahoma and annex to Texas—or to form a new state with southwest Kansas, the Texas Panhandle, and southeast Colorado—nothing has come of the proposals. Sometimes those in Beaver County, as well as the other two counties of the panhandle feel like unloved, unrecognized stepchildren, but so far they have survived and, in fact, have done better than many of the other counties in the state. Often these panhandle counties have the highest literacy rates and highest per capita income levels in the state. They are a proud people who inherited that trait from the early pioneers who survived many hardships.

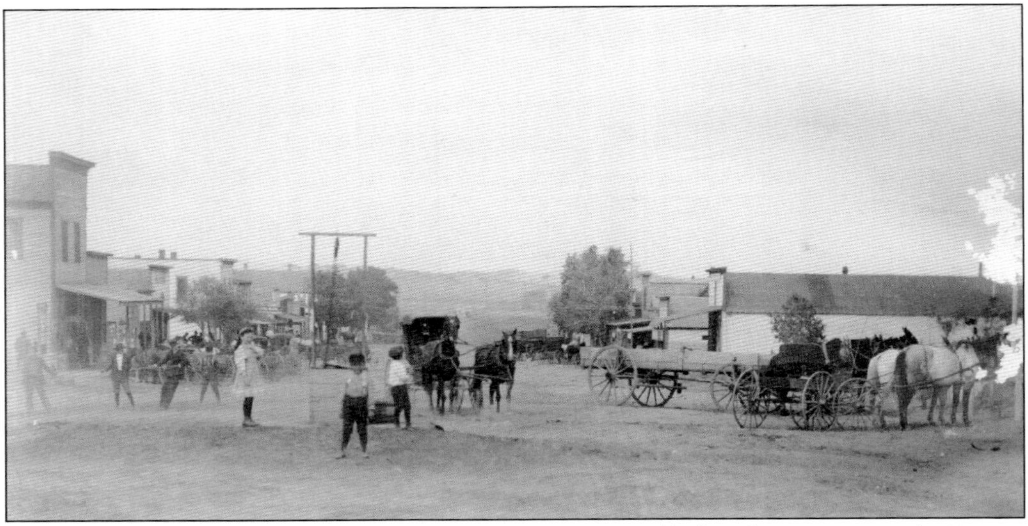

This Beaver City view from 1893 looks north toward the sand hills. The town was only 14 years old but had made progress.

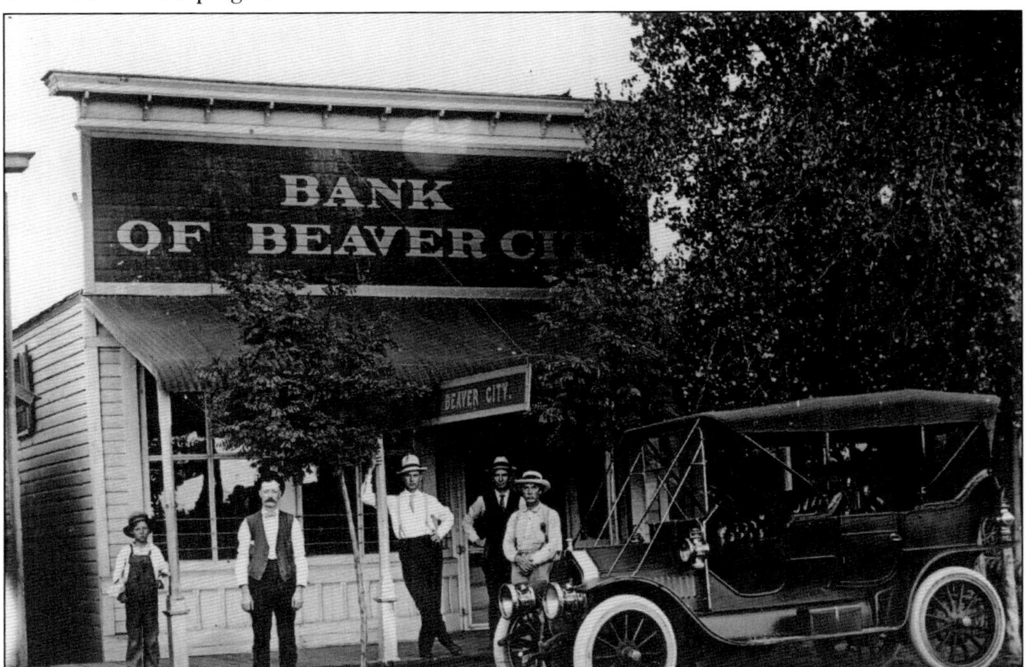

The Bank of Beaver City was established in 1902 by, from left to right beside an unidentified boy, directors R. H. Loofburrow, F. C. Tracy, W. H. Thomas, and R. W. Maple and was called the First State Bank. Two of the founders were Carter Tracy and Frank Laughran. When the First State Bank at Forgan was purchased by O. H. Cafky, R. W. Maple, and W. E. Hocker—who also bought controlling interest in the bank at Beaver—they changed its name to the Bank of Beaver. The Cafky family operated both banks until the 1950s with sons George Cafky taking over the Bank of Beaver and John Cafky operating the Forgan Bank after the death of their father, O. H. Cafky.

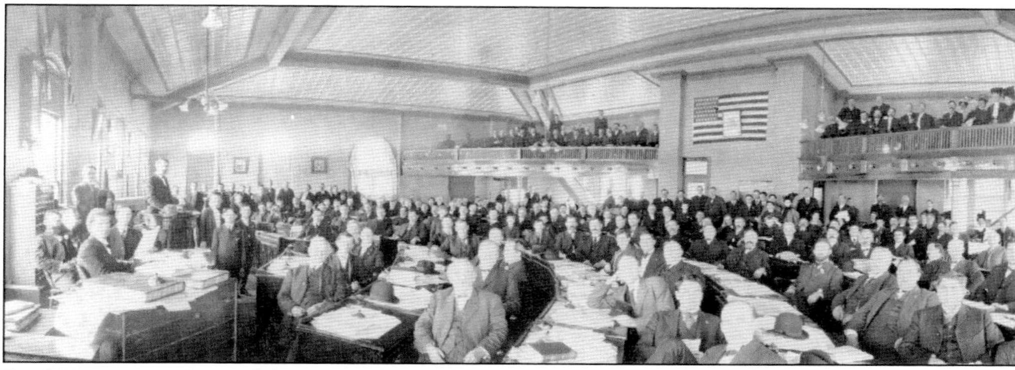

Fred Tracy served as a delegate to the Oklahoma Constitutional Legislature (above). Tracy was the son of Carter Tracy, one of the first businessmen in Beaver City and with whom Fred was a partner.

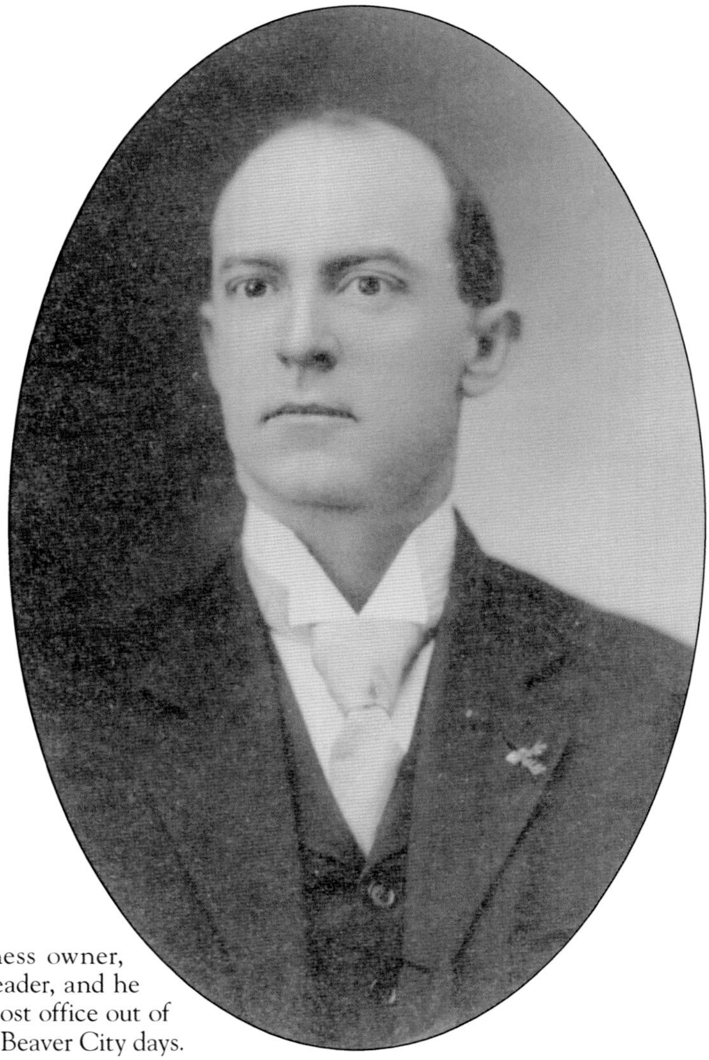

Fred C. Tracy was a business owner, county attorney, and civic leader, and he operated a pharmacy and a post office out of his department store in early Beaver City days.

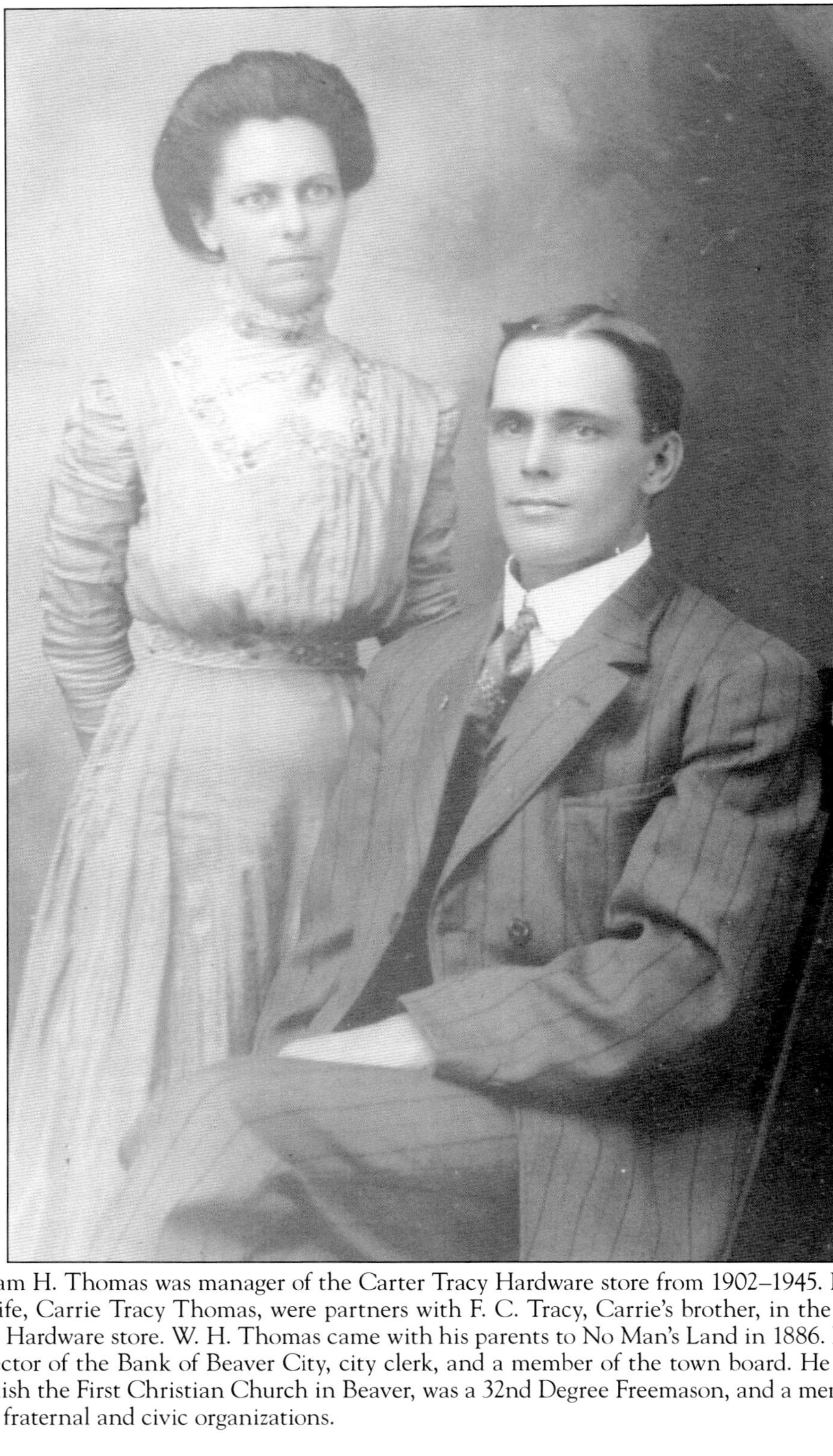

William H. Thomas was manager of the Carter Tracy Hardware store from 1902–1945. He and his wife, Carrie Tracy Thomas, were partners with F. C. Tracy, Carrie's brother, in the Carter Tracy Hardware store. W. H. Thomas came with his parents to No Man's Land in 1886. He was a director of the Bank of Beaver City, city clerk, and a member of the town board. He helped establish the First Christian Church in Beaver, was a 32nd Degree Freemason, and a member of other fraternal and civic organizations.

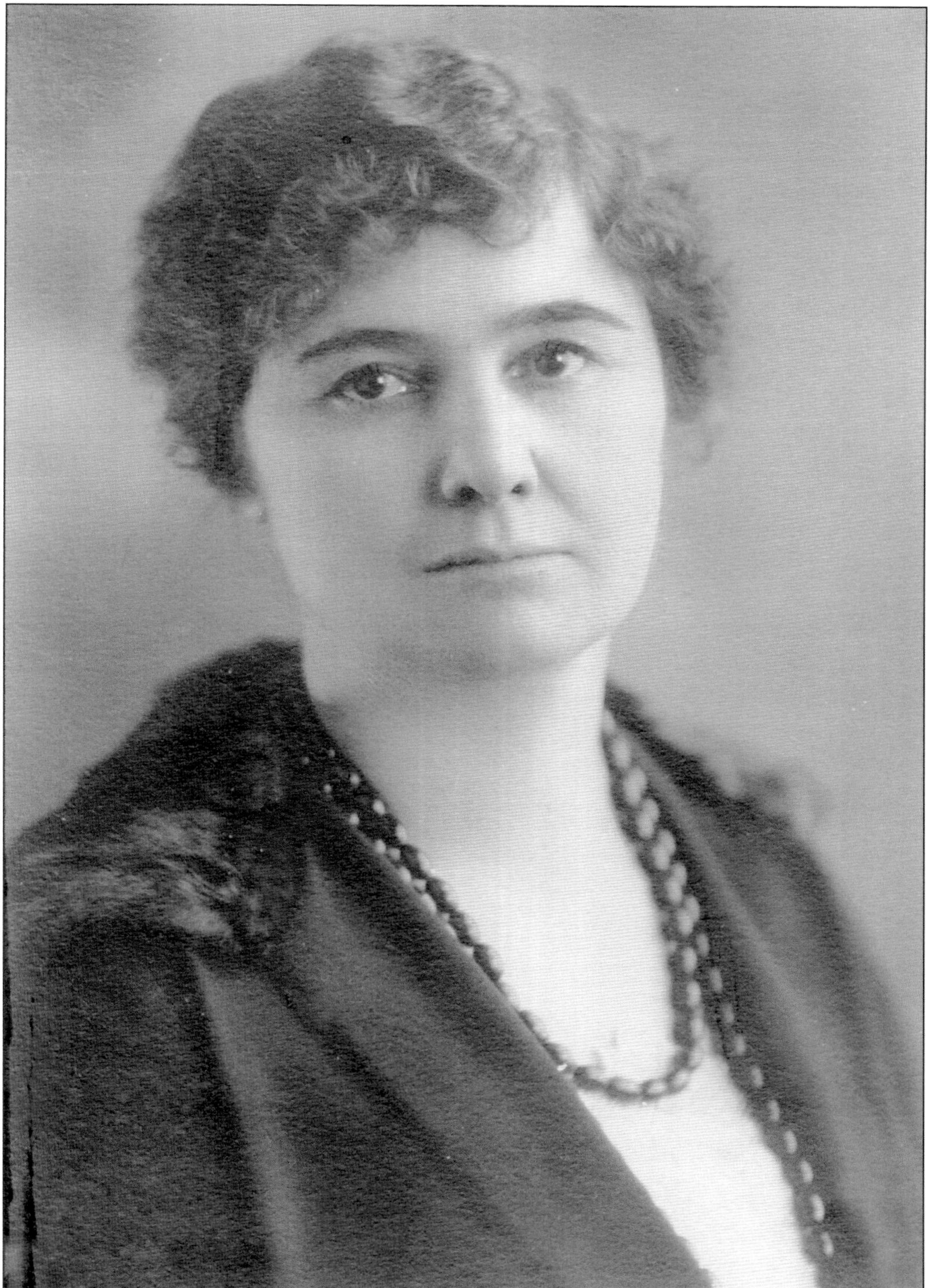

Maude O. Thomas, a newspaper businesswoman and member of first Oklahoma Highway Commission, was definitely a woman ahead of her time.

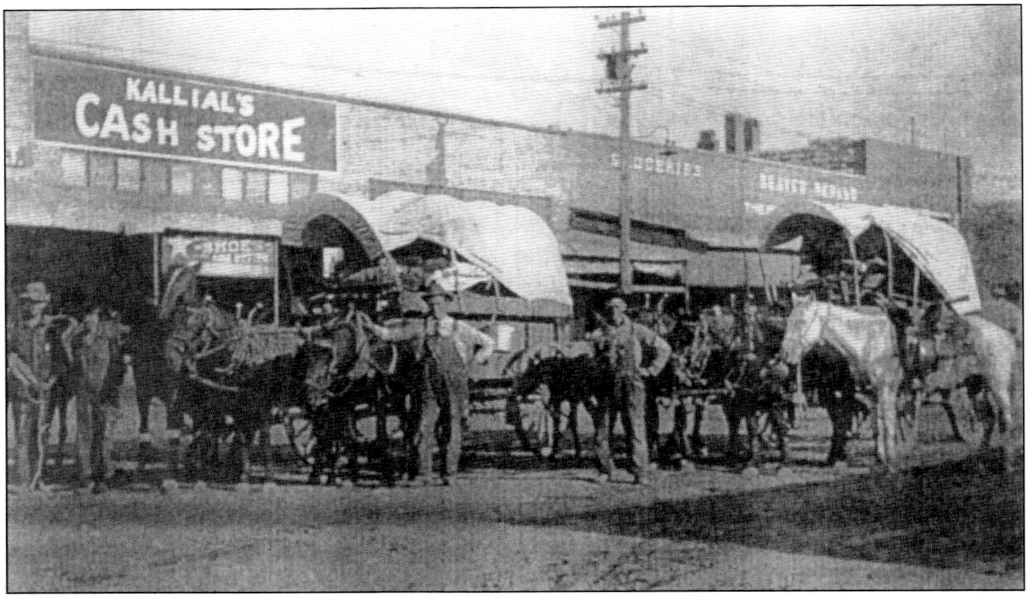

The Cash Store, selling only a few items, was the means of livelihood for many settlers and was a source of supplies for the folks living on the prairie many miles from a town.

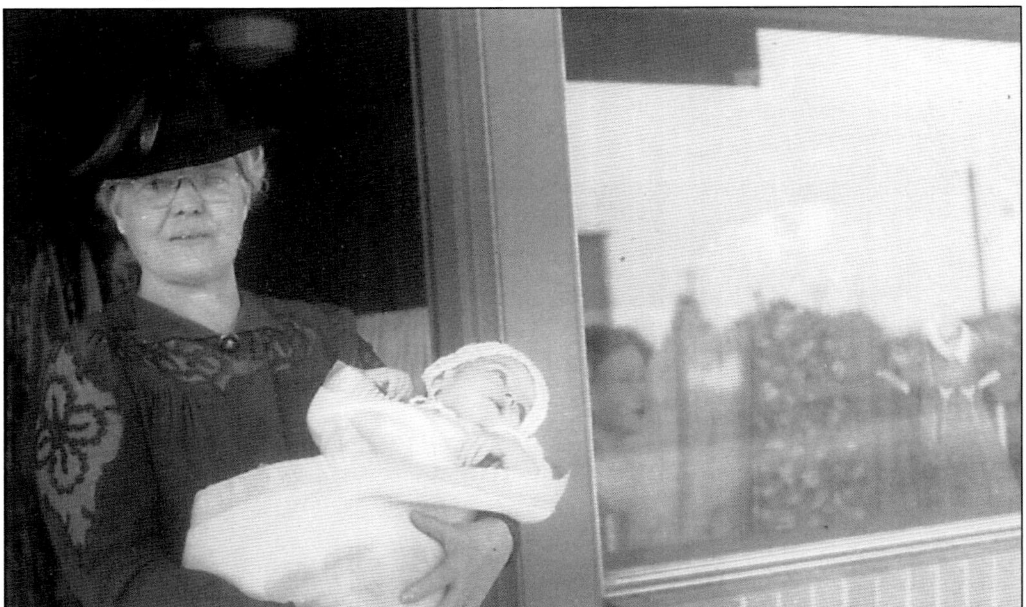

Mary Elizabeth Rich Leonard was a leader in Beaver City, especially in the First Presbyterian Church where her husband was a minister and she was the Sunday school superintendent. She was also the principal of the Beaver High School for several years. She later owned the Frock and Bonnet Shop in Beaver. One of her sons, Dwight, became a farmer, lawyer, and senator from this area. Her son John helped her manage the farm after his retirement from Southwestern Bell Telephone Company in St. Louis, Missouri. Her son Leonard Rich was a sales manager for the Veedol Oil Company, later acquired by Standard Oil and J. Paul Getty. The baby in the photograph is William Leonard, the son of Dwight and Mary Evelyn. (WLL.)

Five

Homesteaders and Punkin' Rollers

The coming of the new pioneer settlers was the beginning of the last of the open ranges and ranches. The ranchers had claimed large areas of unfenced pastures. The homesteaders brought with them that so-called "hell rope," barbed wire. The plow also came, which was later blamed for the Dust Bowl because thousands of acres of native grass was plowed up and planted with wheat, broomcorn, oats, and milo.

Many of the new families first made a dugout, or half-dugout, to live in and hold their claims. Some made a little money by picking the immense number of buffalo bones left by the hide hunters and selling them. There were other ways people made money, such as in Beer City with "Brushy" Bush, the self-appointed sheriff and "tax" collector; Pussy Cat Nell, who operated the Yellow Snake Saloon and was the local madam; and others who profited by betting on fist fights. This disreputable settlement in No Man's Land, just south of Liberal, Kansas, operated from 1888 to 1890.

As the homesteaders grew in number, the need for some form of government and law became apparent. The settlers succeeded in electing a representative to the Oklahoma Territorial Legislature meeting in Guthrie, Oklahoma Territory, for the 1904 election. The settlers were also candidates for county offices in the 1904 campaign, but they failed to get nominations on either the Democratic or Republican tickets. They blamed the cattlemen for manipulating the elections.

This group then seceded to form an independent party known as the Punkin' Rollers. The Punkin' Rollers convention was held at Beaver City, and it was there that the party withered on the vine.

The cattlemen and farmers grew to become friends in later years. They lived in peace and helped one another through hard times. Ethnic groups seemed to settle together, such as the Germans near Balko and Turpin and the Quakers at Gate. Today the Mennonite churches at Balko and Turpin, as well as the Friends Church (of the Quaker denomination) at Gate are a testimony to these hardy immigrants.

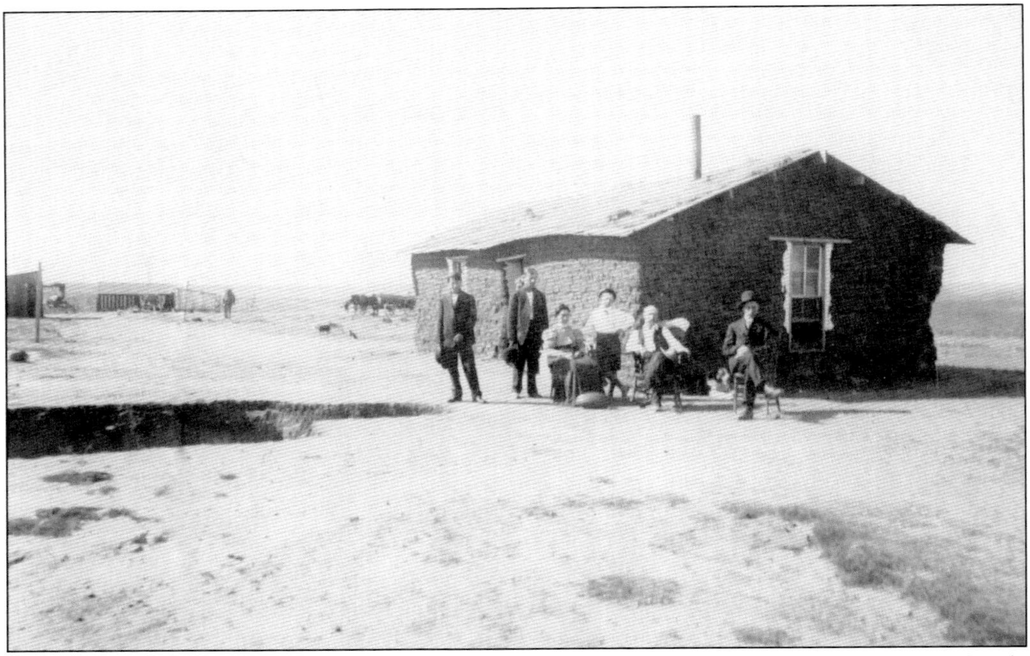

This "soddy" near Balko, pictured with the beginnings of a storm cellar, was indicative of early housing by settlers since there were no native trees to cut for lumber. Although the folks in the photograph are not identified, they are typical of rural families at the time that had several generations living under one roof.

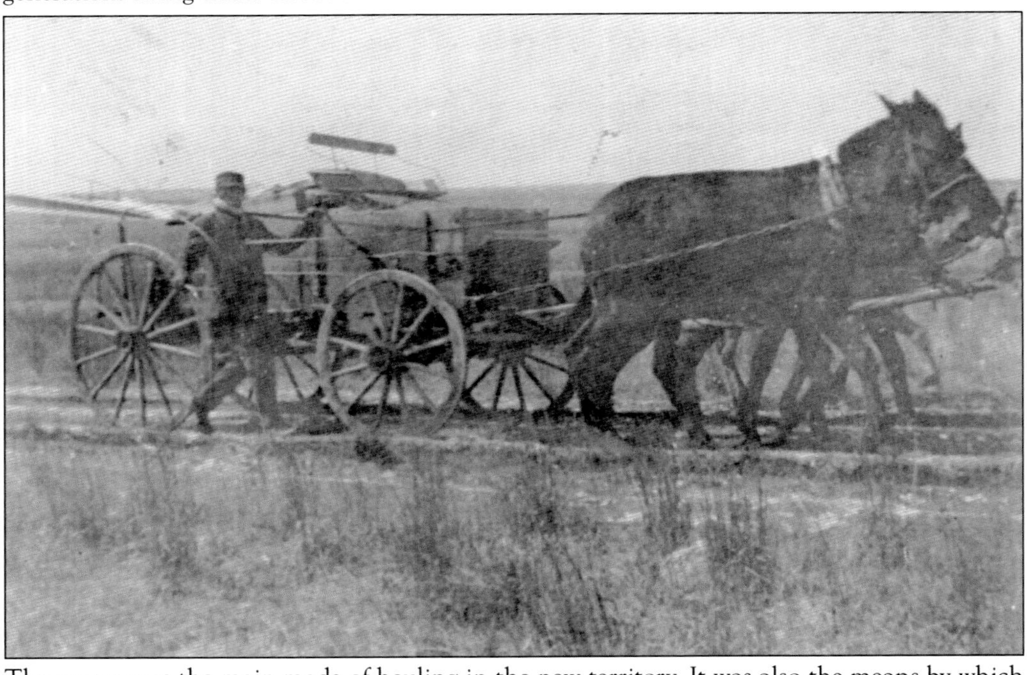

The wagon was the main mode of hauling in the new territory. It was also the means by which homesteaders came to the Neutral Strip to claim land and make a new life. The sparse vegetation beside the wagon reminds the settlers that it really is a desert out there in No Man's Land.

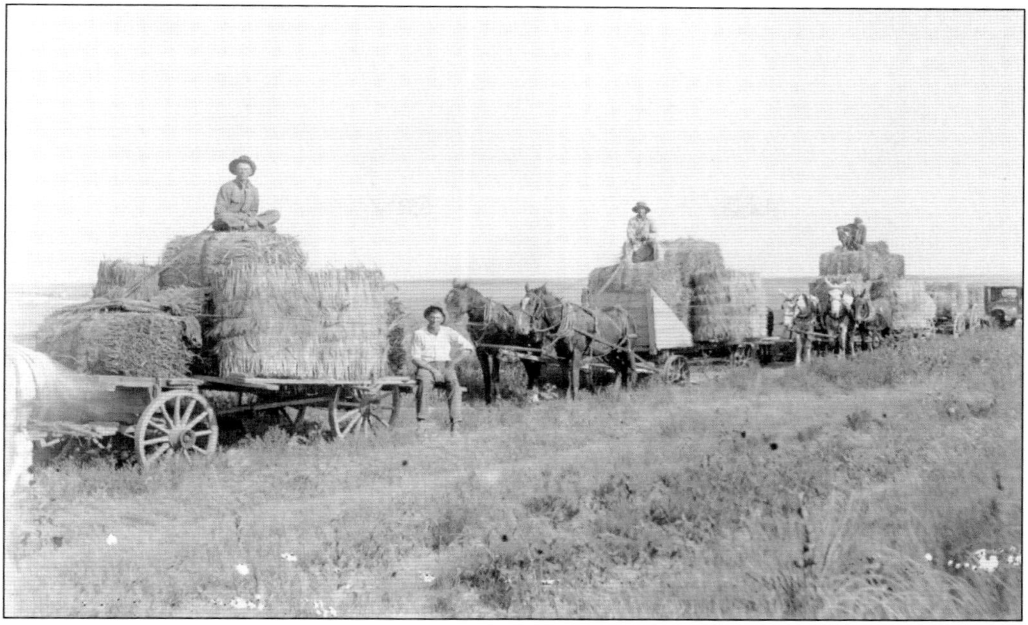

This 1910 photograph shows broomcorn bales, the popular crop of early homesteaders.

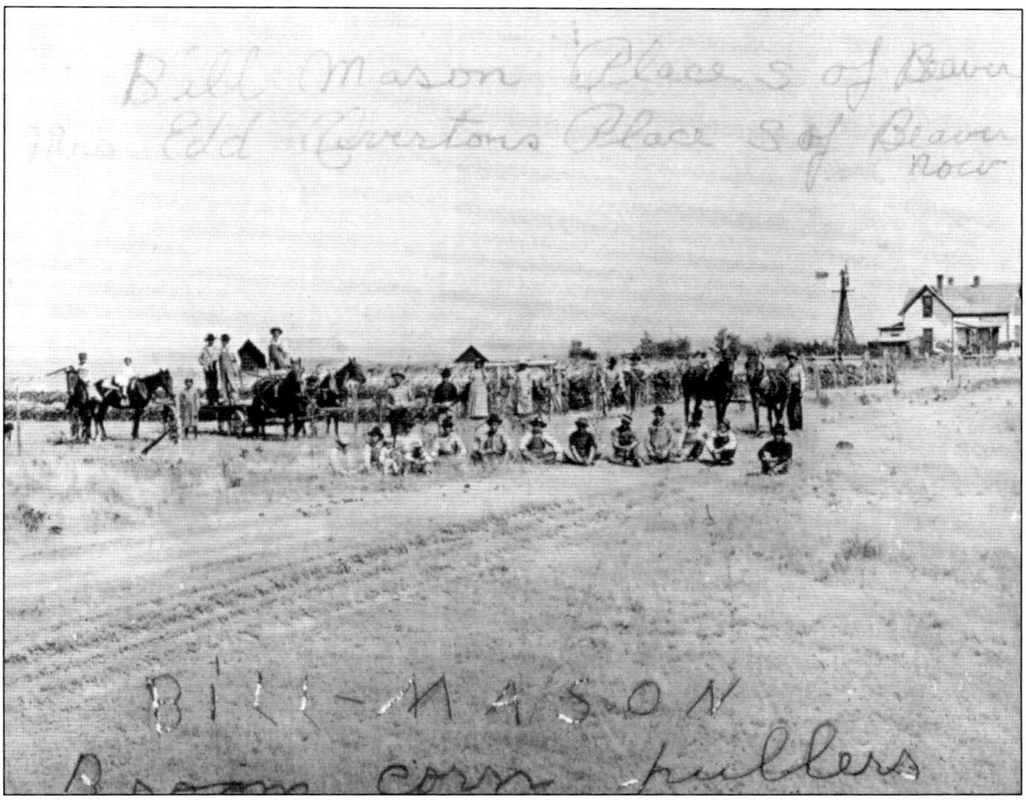

Broomcorn pullers are pictured here at the old Mason house built in 1917 by the Mason family, bricked in 1928 by S. S. Strong, and now owned by Harold and Joan Kachel.

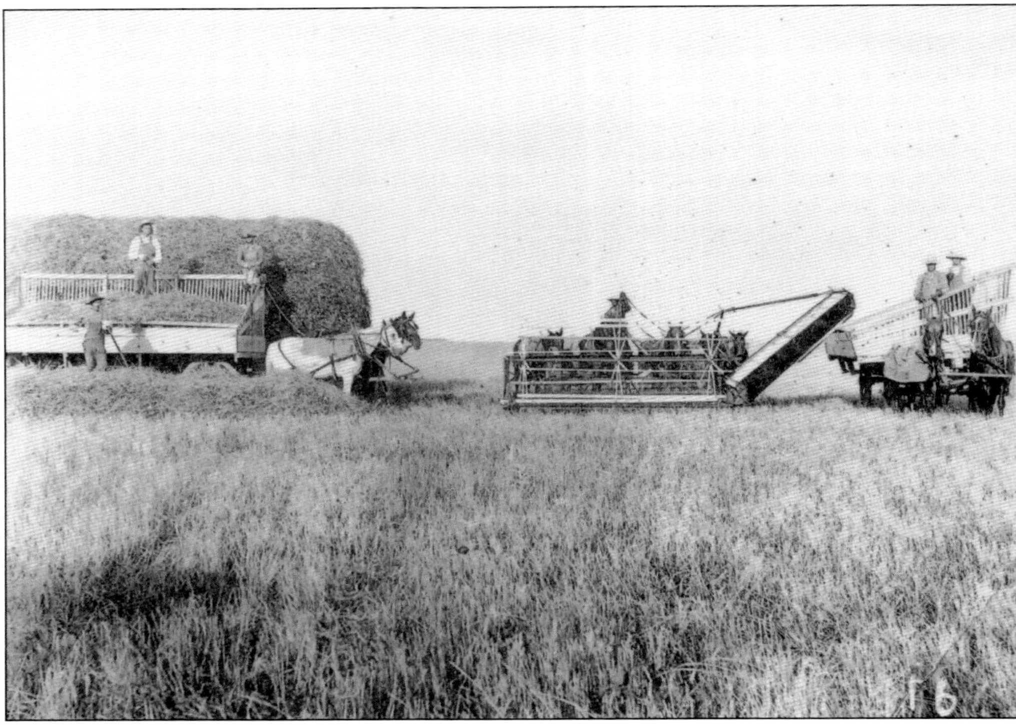

Harvesting at Harry O. Evans's place took the help of family and neighbors to complete.

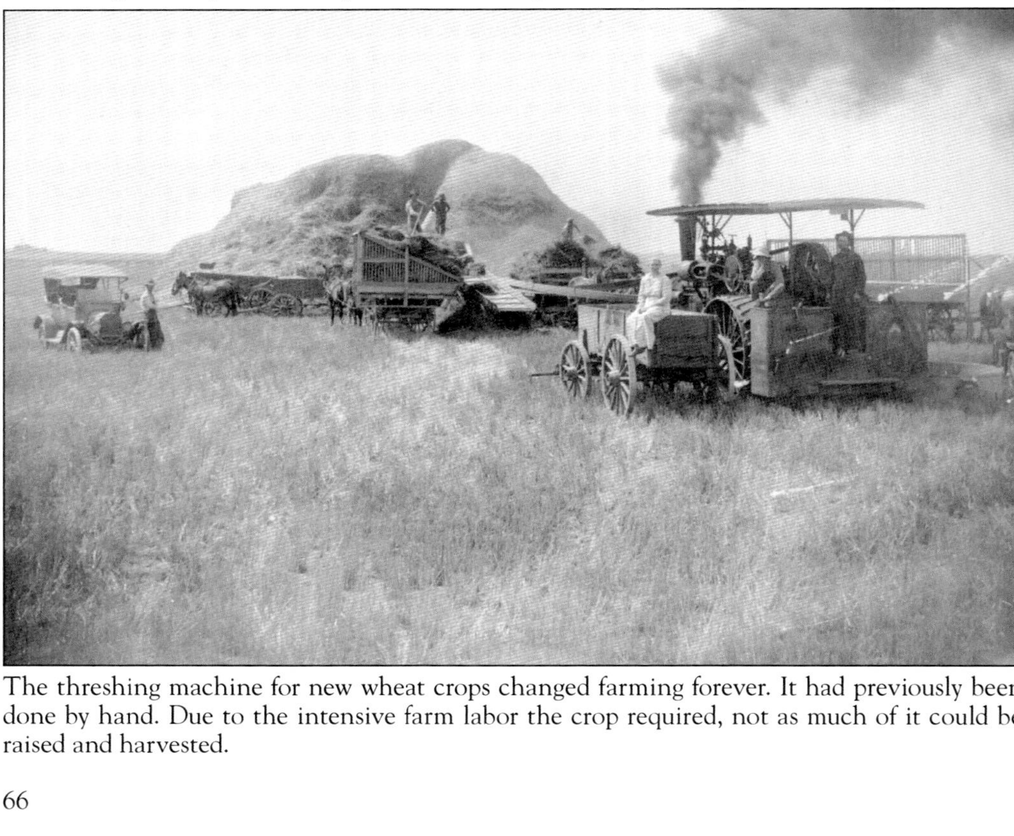

The threshing machine for new wheat crops changed farming forever. It had previously been done by hand. Due to the intensive farm labor the crop required, not as much of it could be raised and harvested.

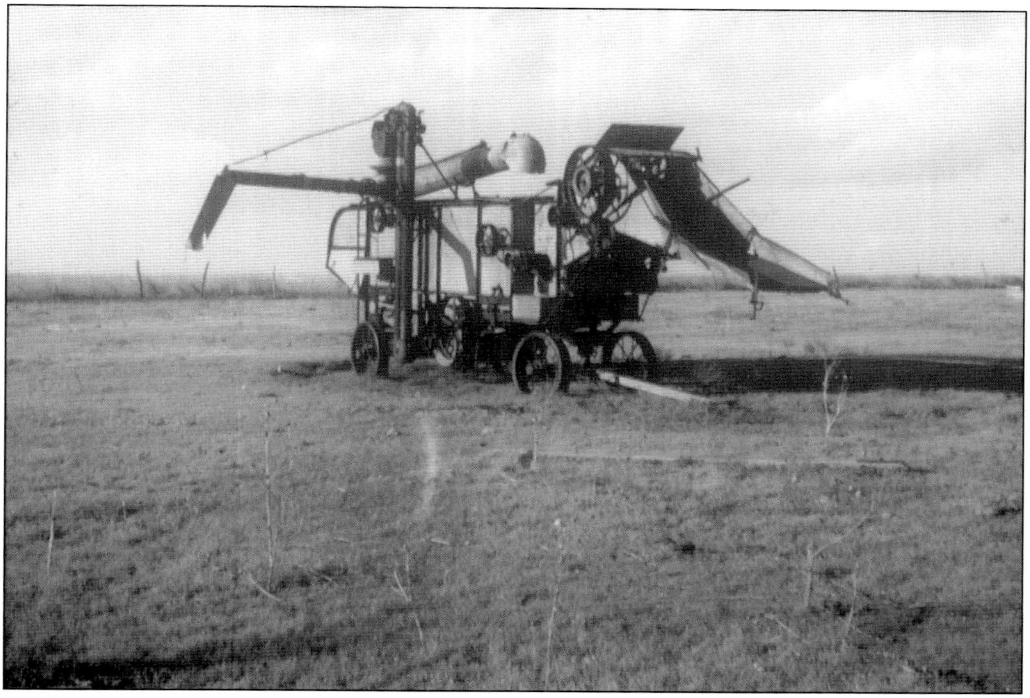

Mechanization came to the plains and improved the amount of grain harvested, but it also increased the number of acres plowed up and ready to blow away during the Dust Bowl of the 1930s. (HSK.)

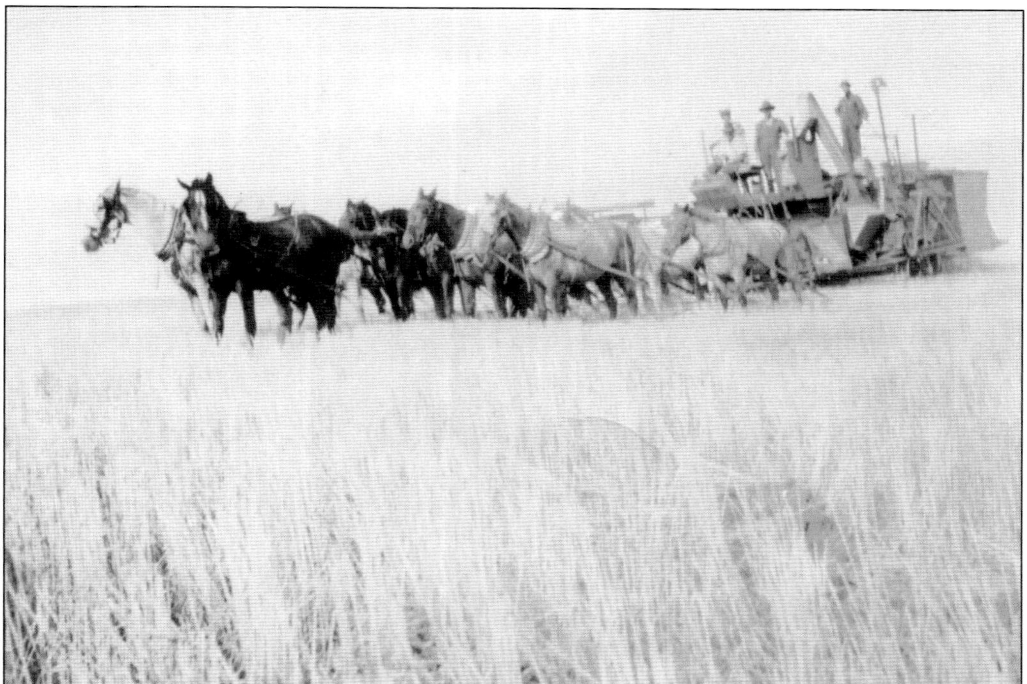

Combining harvesting with a horse and team was the "new" way to farm, at least for a while.

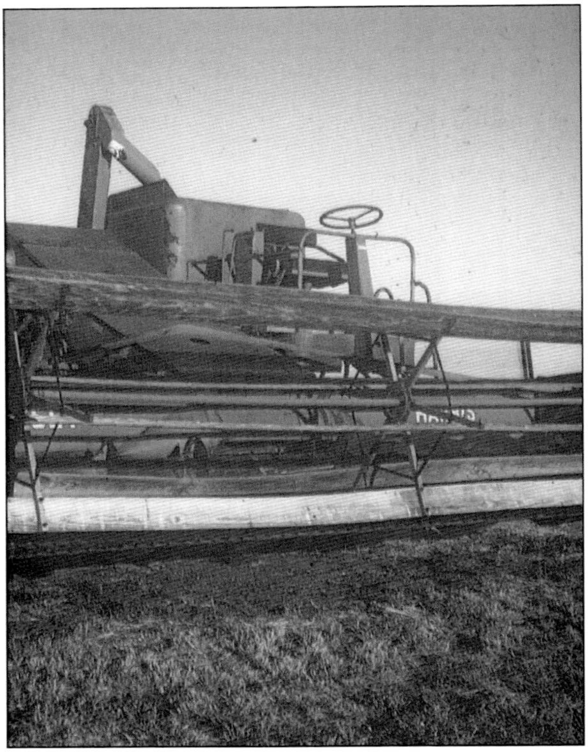

The self-propelled combine changed crop production and a way of life for farmers who had homesteaded in the early 1900s. Previously, they had farmed only a few acres; now they could farm hundreds of acres. (HSK.)

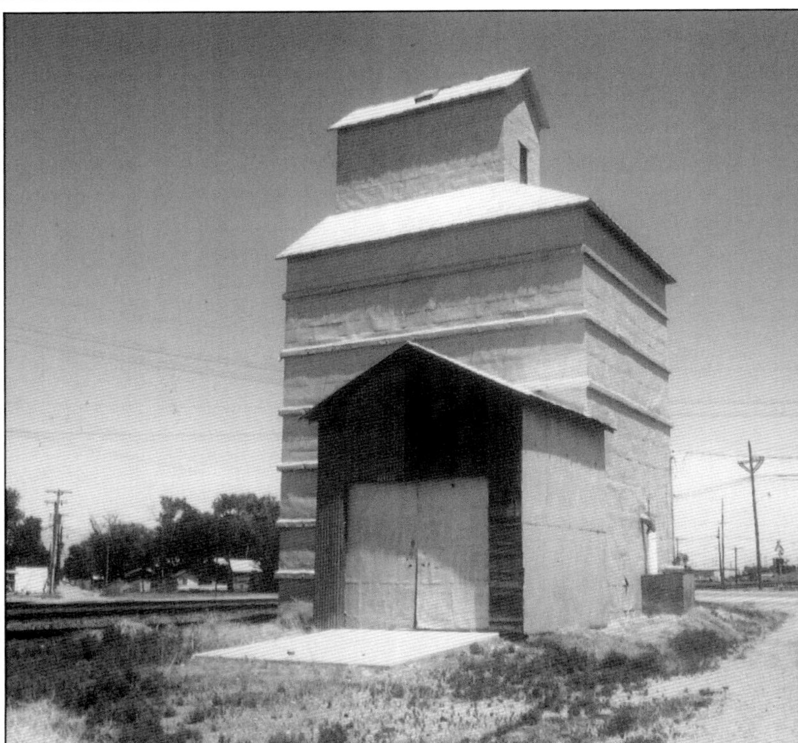

The Knowles elevator came with the new railroad in 1911 to store and ship the new crop of wheat that replaced broomcorn as the popular crop. (HSK.)

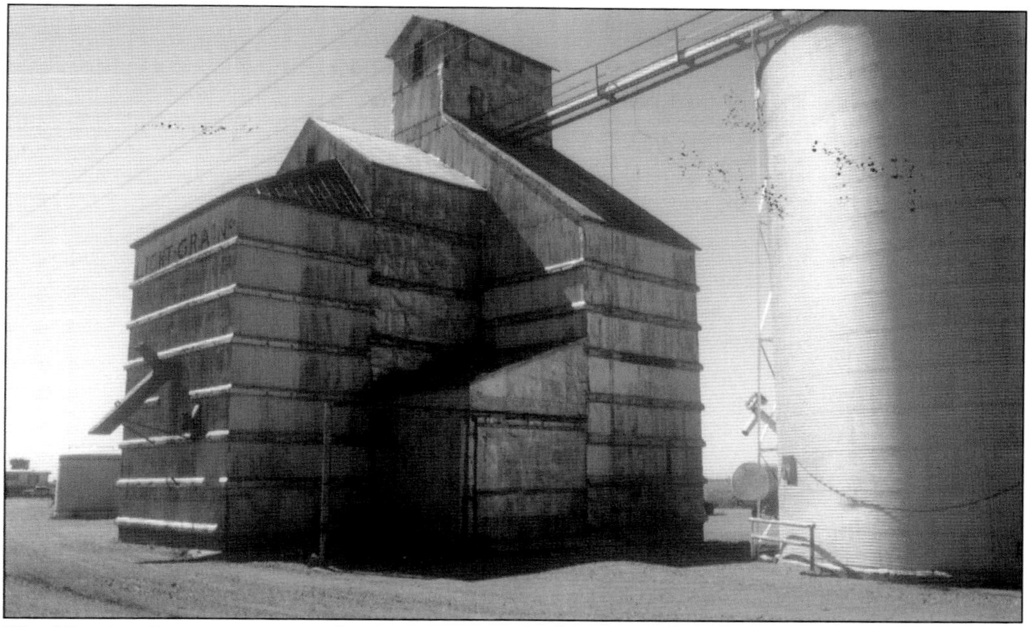

The Turpin elevator came to the new town with the new railroad in 1926, and local farmers no longer had to haul wheat to Liberal, Kansas, some 13 miles away, which was a long way in that time. (HSK.)

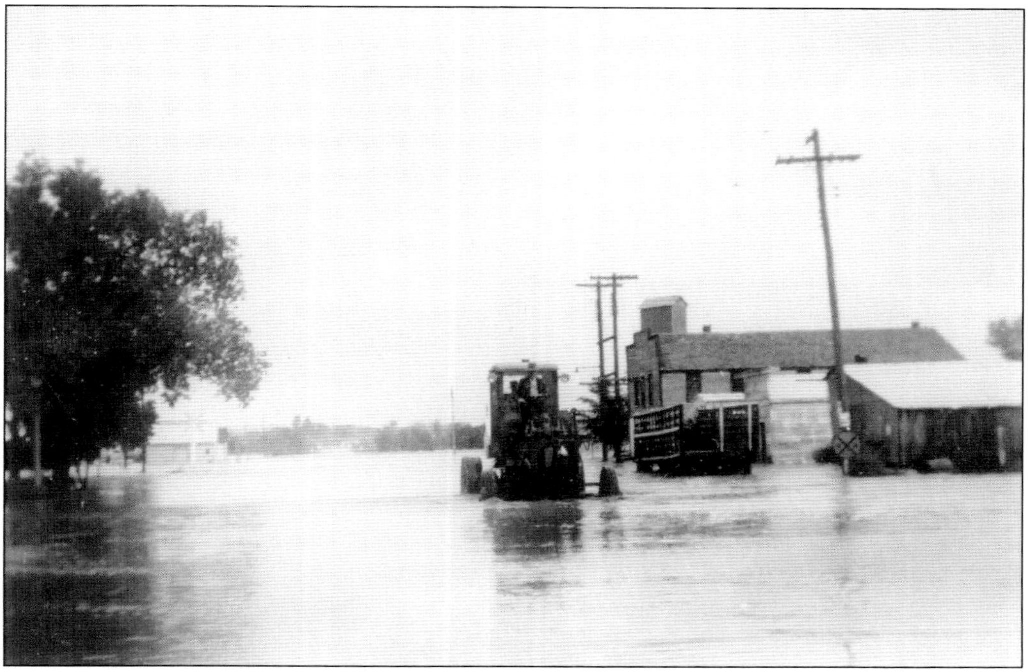

In this photograph, the Beaver River flooded the elevator area on Old Main Street in Beaver—not an uncommon occurrence until dams and other flood control measures were built in the last part of the 20th century.

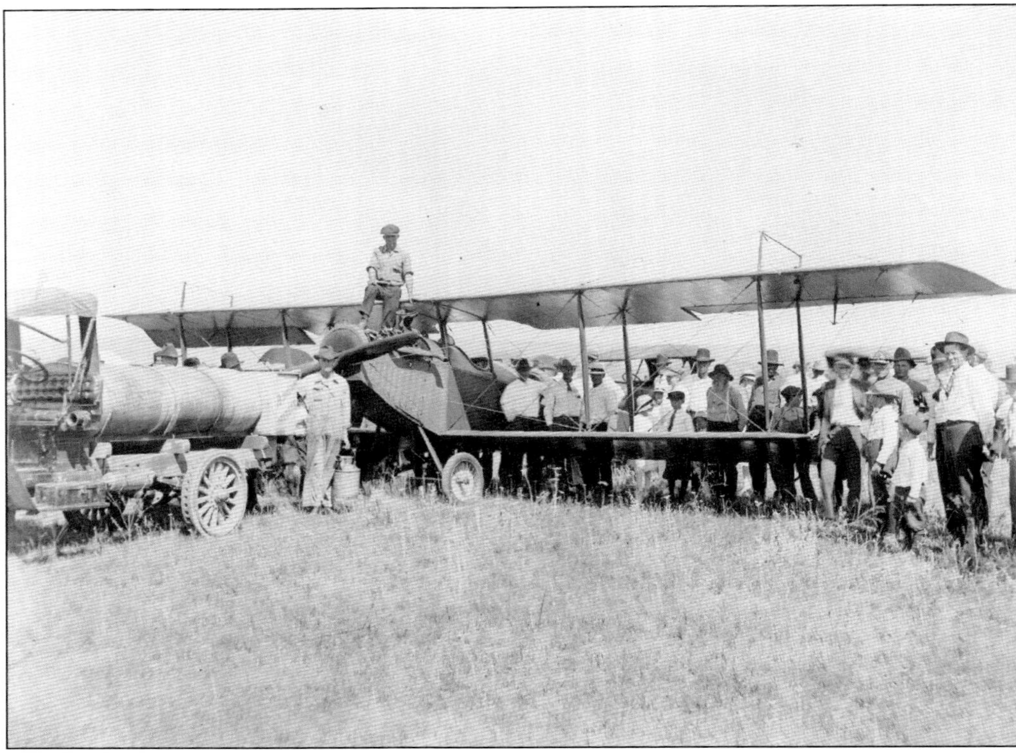

A barnstorming plane, in this 1919 photograph, was one of the popular recreations of the day. It was the first plane to land in the Oklahoma Panhandle.

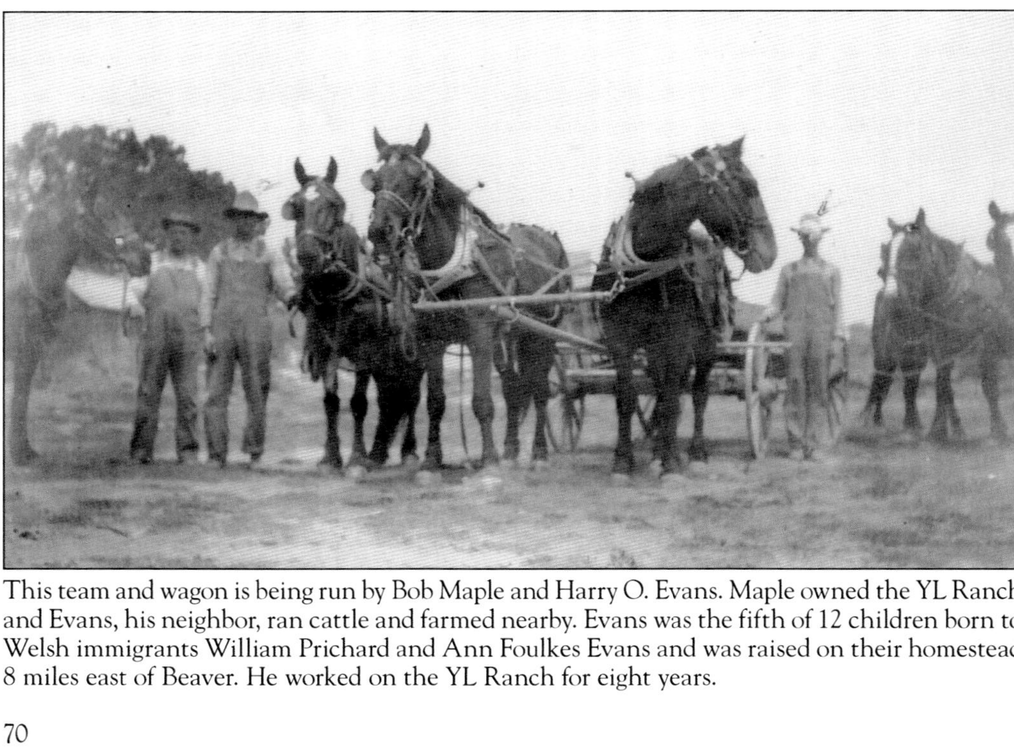

This team and wagon is being run by Bob Maple and Harry O. Evans. Maple owned the YL Ranch and Evans, his neighbor, ran cattle and farmed nearby. Evans was the fifth of 12 children born to Welsh immigrants William Prichard and Ann Foulkes Evans and was raised on their homestead 8 miles east of Beaver. He worked on the YL Ranch for eight years.

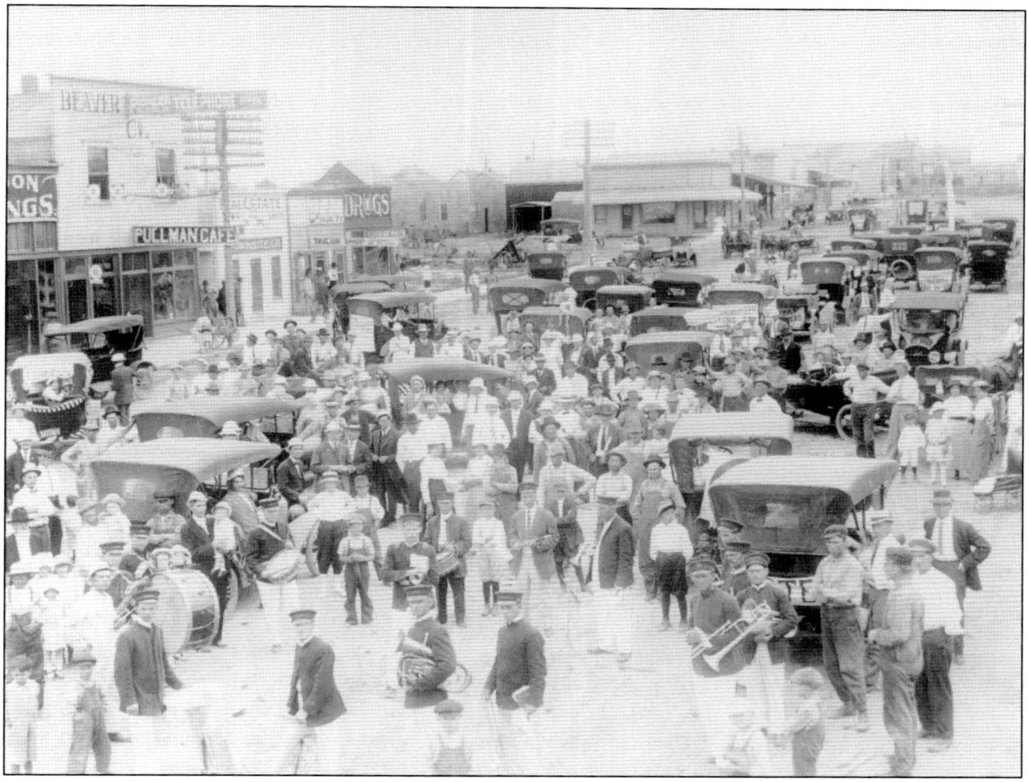

Forgan's market day demonstrates the quick growth of the new railroad town just 7 miles north of Beaver City. The railroad company was deliberately built north of Beaver to avoid building through the sand hills.

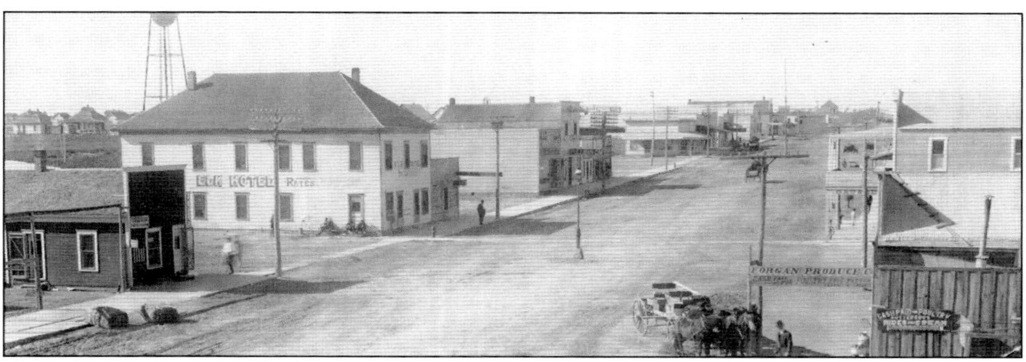

This Forgan street scene from 1915 shows the very first businesses in town. Only two of these buildings remain today, along with five of the houses in the background.

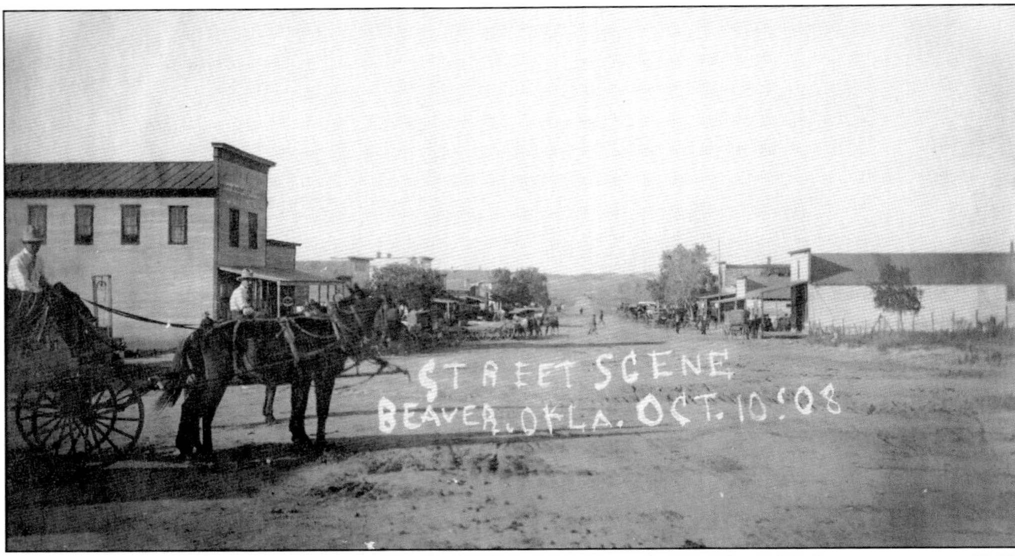

This Beaver street scene in 1908 shows how the town grew from its humble beginnings in 1879. The Homestead Act helped bring new people to the county and then to Beaver City to take care of business and buy essentials.

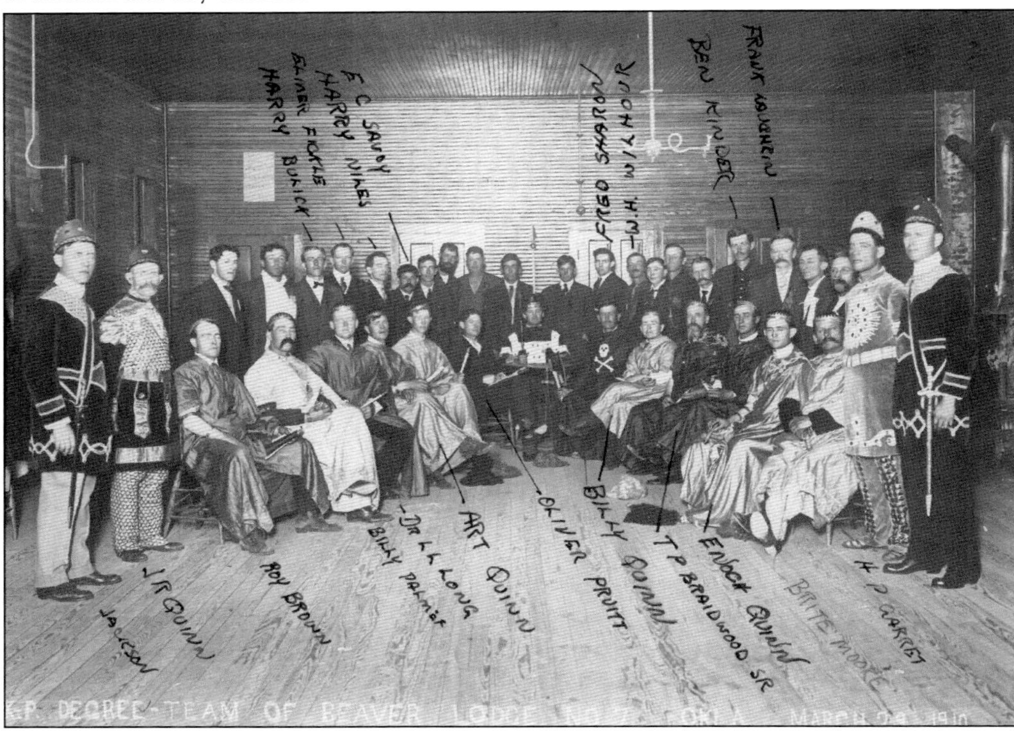

The Knights of Pythias, part of the Masonic Order, are at their March 29, 1910, meeting. Pictured among others are (first row) Mr. Jackson, J. R. Quinn, Roy Brown, Billy Palmer, Dr. L. L. Long, Art Quinn, Oliver Pruitt, Billy Quinn, T. P. Braidwood Sr., Enoch Quinn, Brite Moore, and H. P. Garret; (second row) Harry Bulick, Elmer Fickle, Harry Niles, F. C. Savoy, Fred Sharon, W. H. Wilhour, Ben Kinder, and Frank Laughlin.

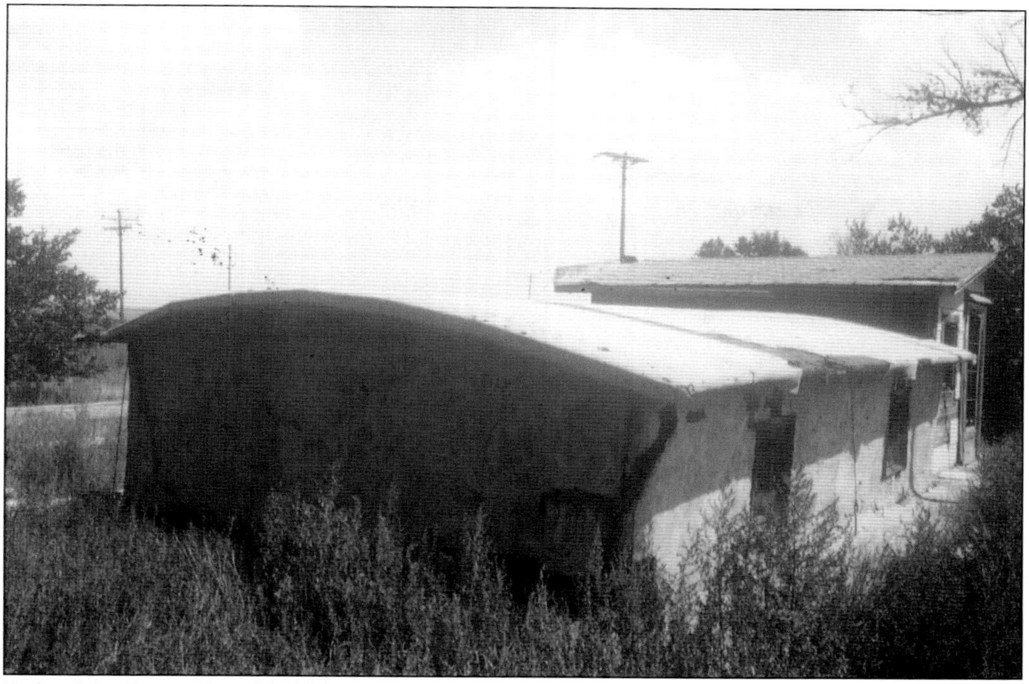

Esther Mae Reiswig's sod half-dugout was built from sod bricks and placed above the dugout cavity in the pastureland. Sod and dugouts were the two most popular building choices on the plains since there were no trees. (HSK.)

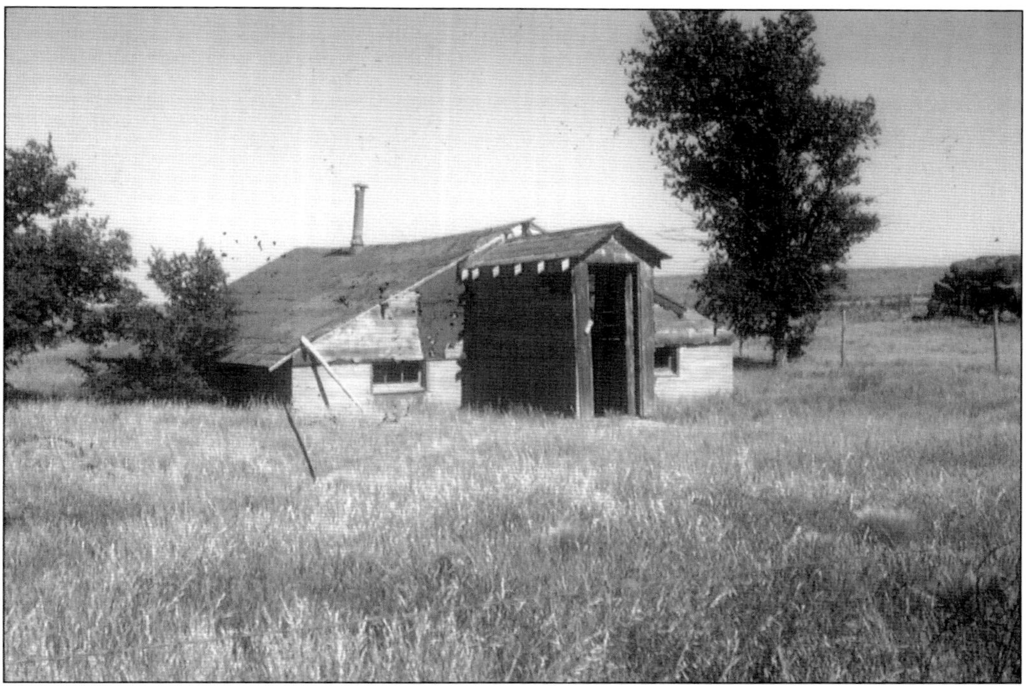

The Jackson family's half-dugout house was considered a finer dwelling for homesteaders since it incorporated both the dugout and aboveground-house concepts. (HSK.)

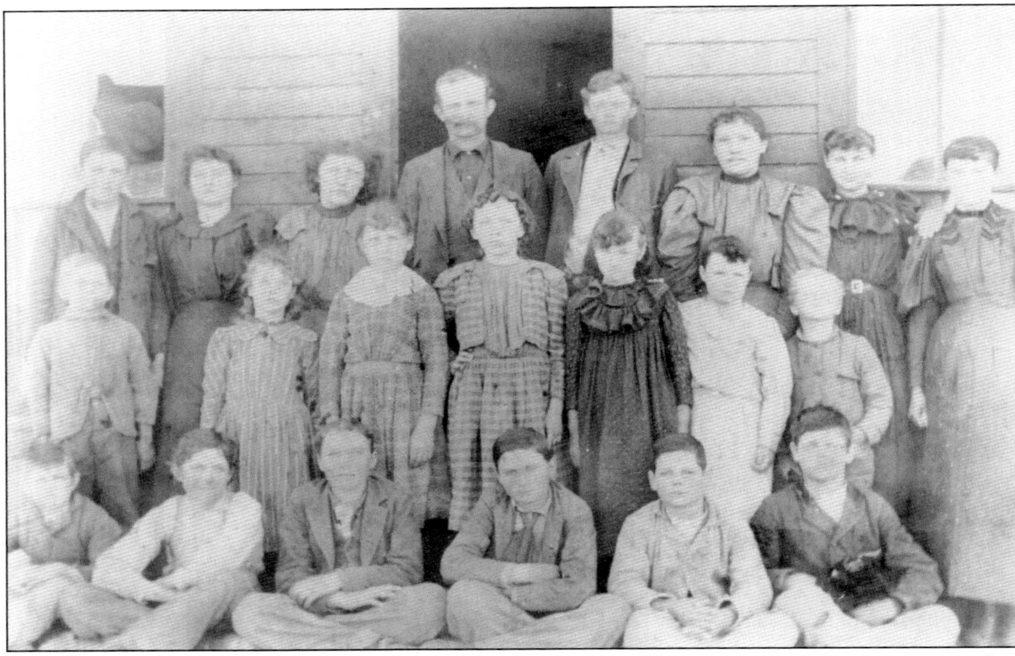

The Riverside Red Schoolhouse, 1897–1898, was typical of the one-room schools supported by nearby families. Classes were most often taught by young women who boarded with one of the families and followed strict rules for their behavior, such as not being allowed to marry or to "keep company" with men without a chaperone.

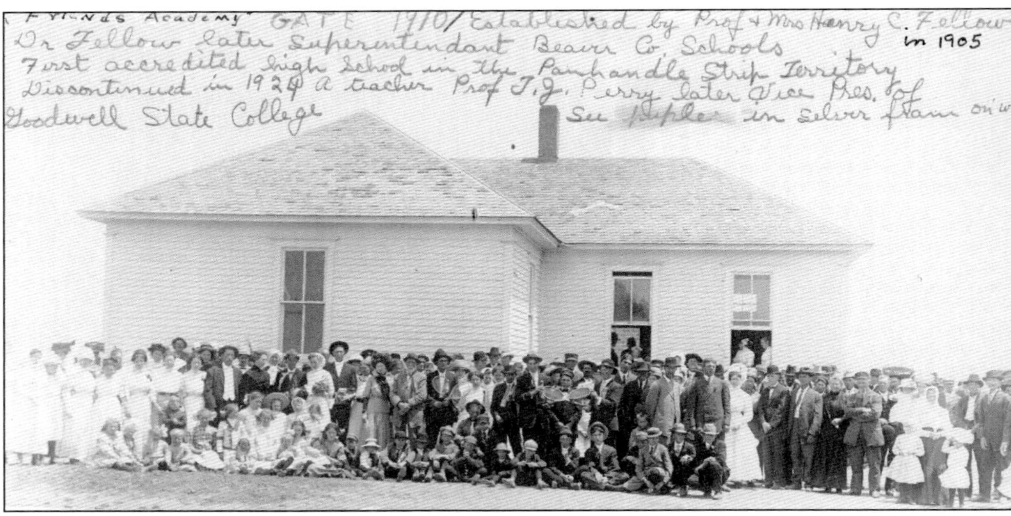

The Friends Academy at Gate City, seen here in 1910, was the first Accredited School in Seventh County, Oklahoma Territory (Beaver County). It was established by professor and Mrs. Henry C. Fellow in 1905 and operated until 1924. The Friends church is still active in Gate. Gate City was established in 1893 and was moved to its present location with the coming of the railroad in 1912. At one time, it had many businesses and a population of 958.

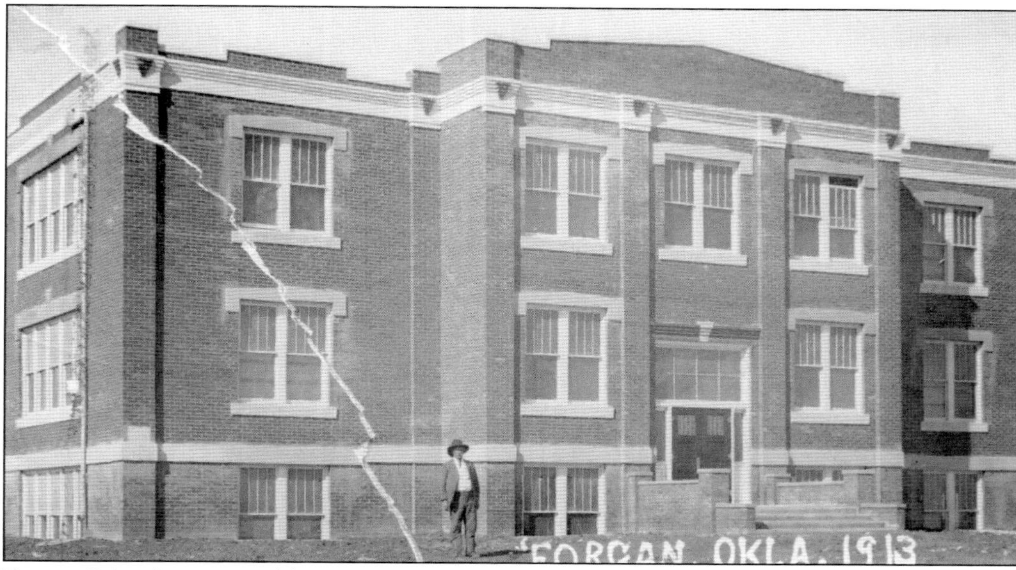

Forgan School is pictured here in 1913 during the first year of operation. The second story of the building was torn off in 1924 and the materials were used to build additions onto either end. During the 1930s, when there was little money for administration salaries, the superintendent and his family lived in the basement.

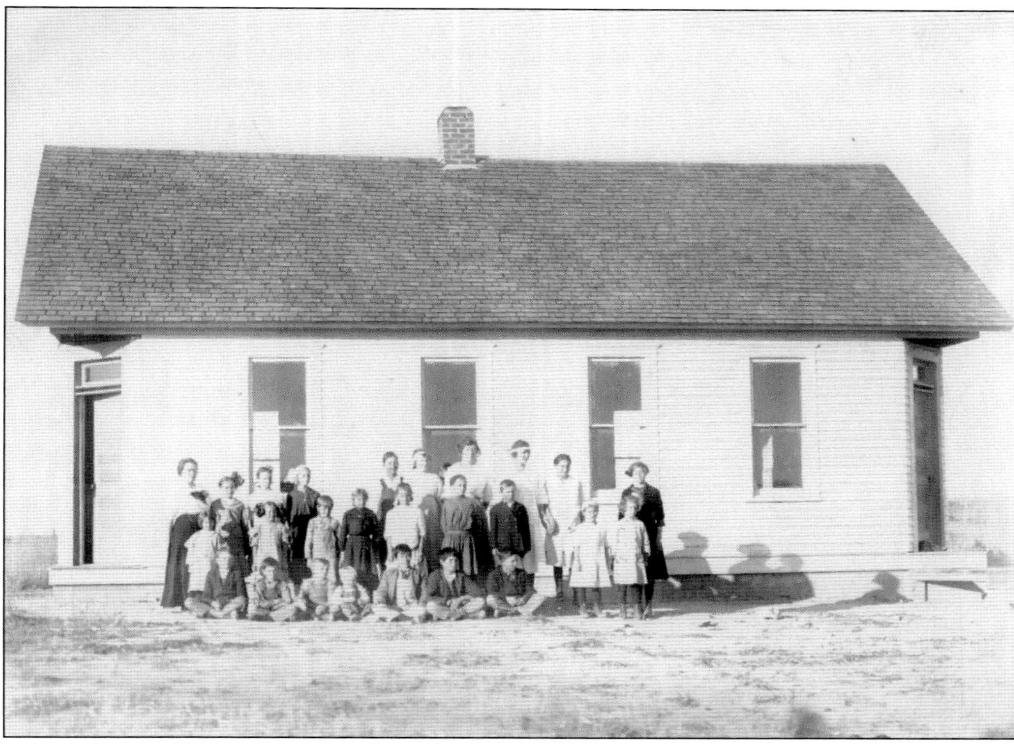

School District No. 21 was located 2 miles west and 3 miles north of the new town of Forgan, established in 1912. A number of similar small schools, including this one, were consolidated into the Forgan district during the 1940s.

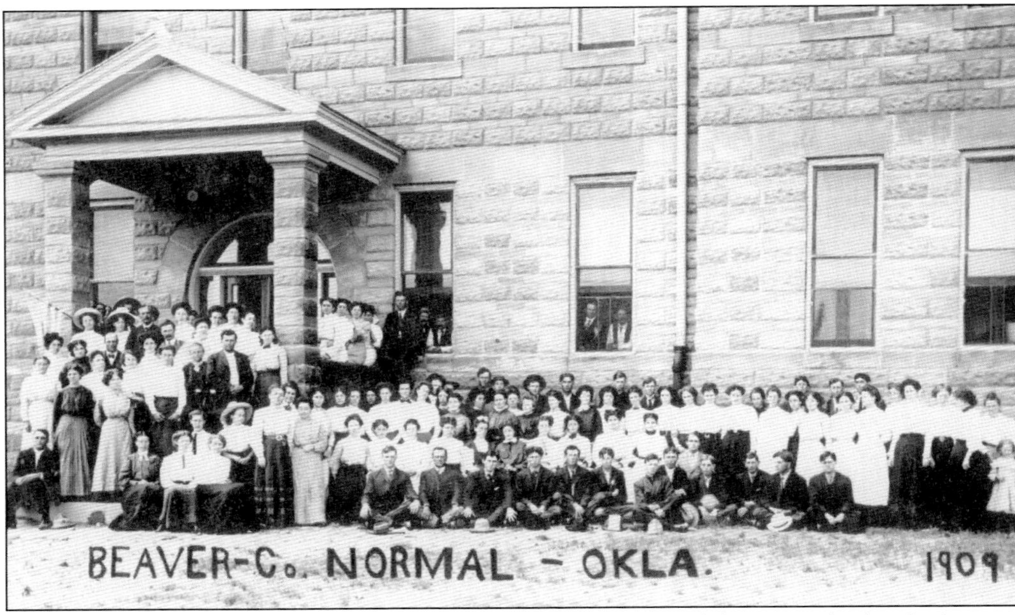

Beaver Normal School, photographed here in 1909, was one of the normal schools that was established to train teachers who were not required to have a college degree to teach public schools. These normal schools were essentially training schools.

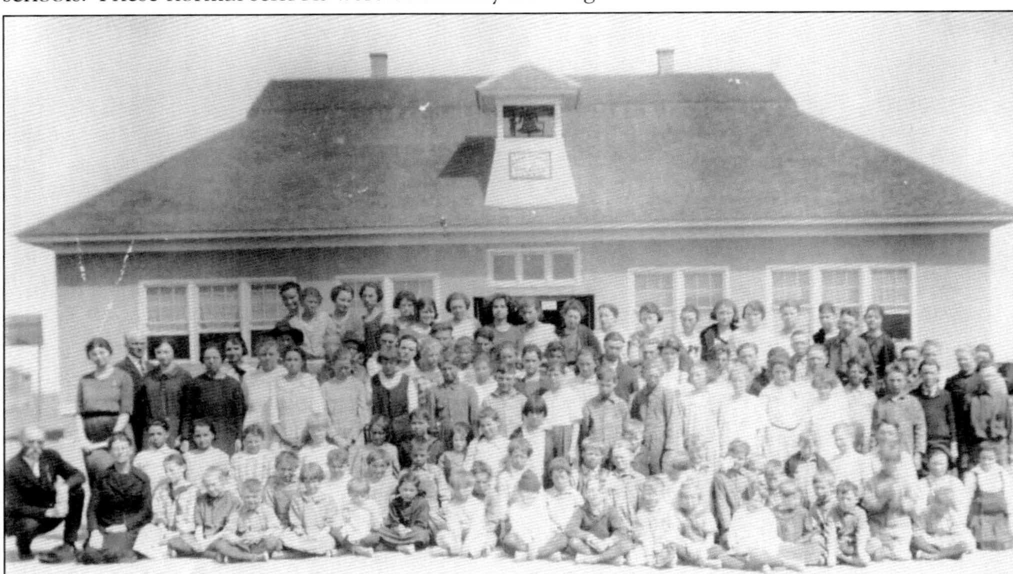
Blue Mound School is pictured here in 1912 or 1913. A. E. Pittman was a teacher in one of the one-room schools later consolidated into Balko Schools. The school was established in 1904 in a two-story, four-room home owned by Mrs. Milo Munger. In 1905, a building with adobe walls and a shingle roof was built from lumber hauled from Higgins, Texas. In 1915, the school was moved to a white frame building, and in 1925 a teacherage was built. It became a fully accredited 12-year school in 1926, but by 1936 only 20 students were in high school. They were transferred to Balko, but the elementary school remained until 1942 when students were transferred to Perryton. The entire district dissolved in 1947.

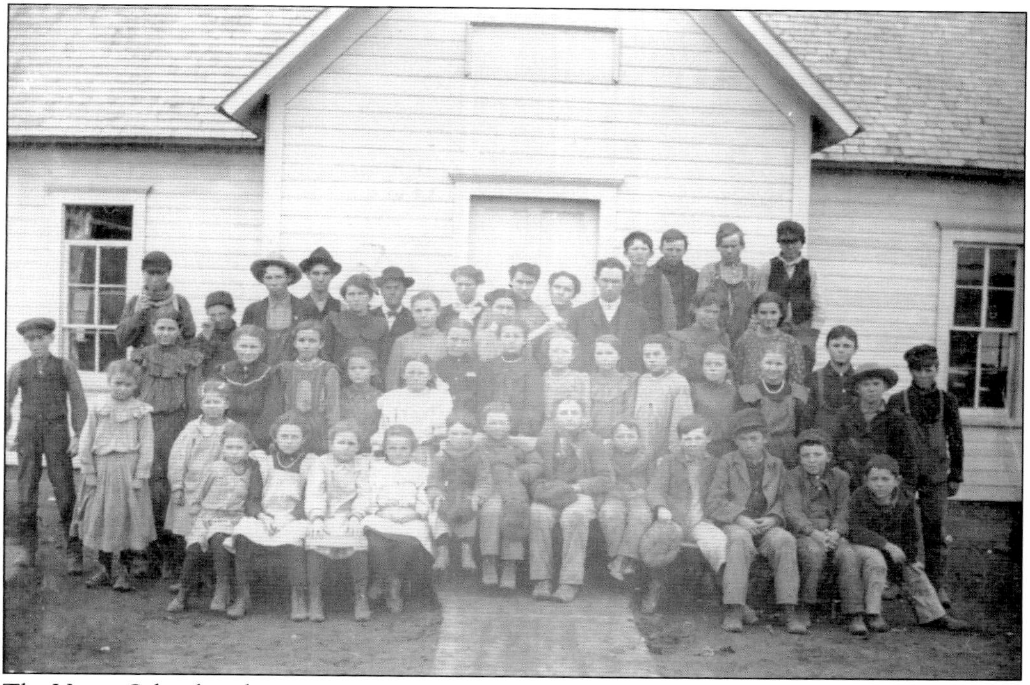

The Union School in this picture remains a mystery since there were five Union School Districts in Beaver County at one time. They were Union No. 4 located 2 miles north and 1 mile east of Gate in 1908; Union No. 8, also called the Braidwood School, located 11 miles southwest of Beaver in 1909; Union No. 46 located 3 miles south of the Kansas line and east of Turpin a few miles in 1927; Union No. 68 located near Bethany and Gray in 1919; and Union No. 125 located 3 miles east of Hibbs in 1906.

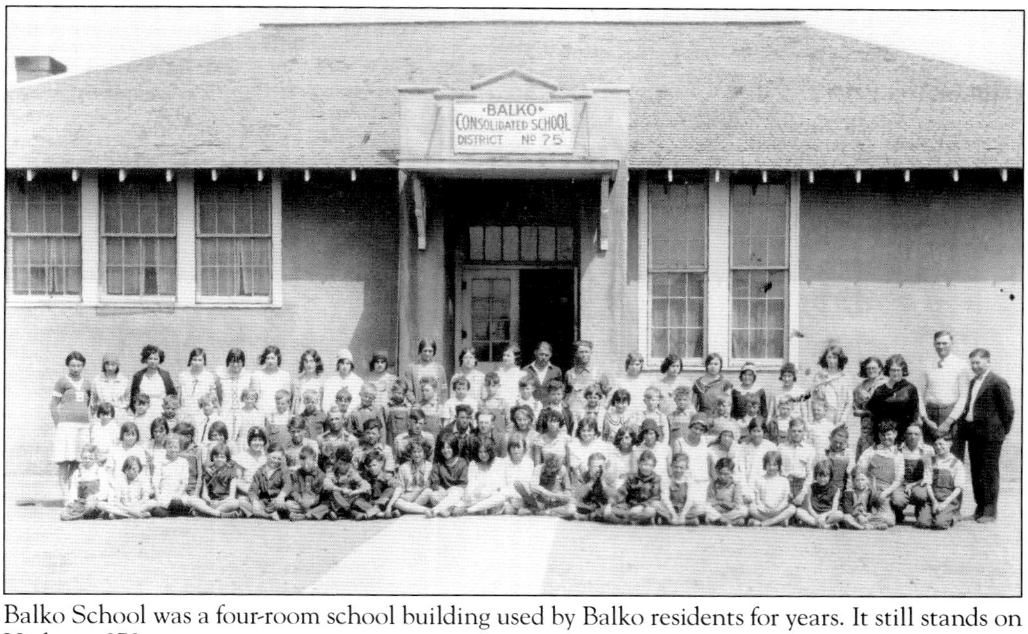

Balko School was a four-room school building used by Balko residents for years. It still stands on Highway 270.

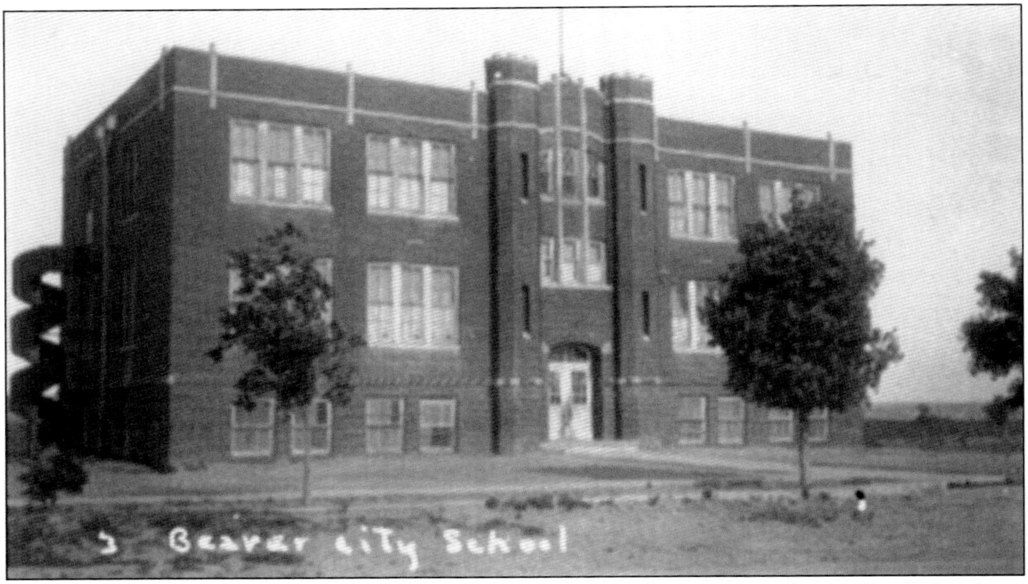

Beaver Elementary School as shown in this picture was an effort to meet the needs of school-age children in the fast-growing town. The district school was formed in 1893 in a rented building of two rooms located on what is now Douglas Avenue. The first eighth grade commencement was in 1896. Maude O. Thomas was one of those graduates. In 1906, bonds were voted for a new building with two stories and four rooms. In 1917, a brick building with eight rooms and a basement was built three blocks west of Douglas Avenue on what is now called G Street. In the early 1950s, the current building was built on South G Street.

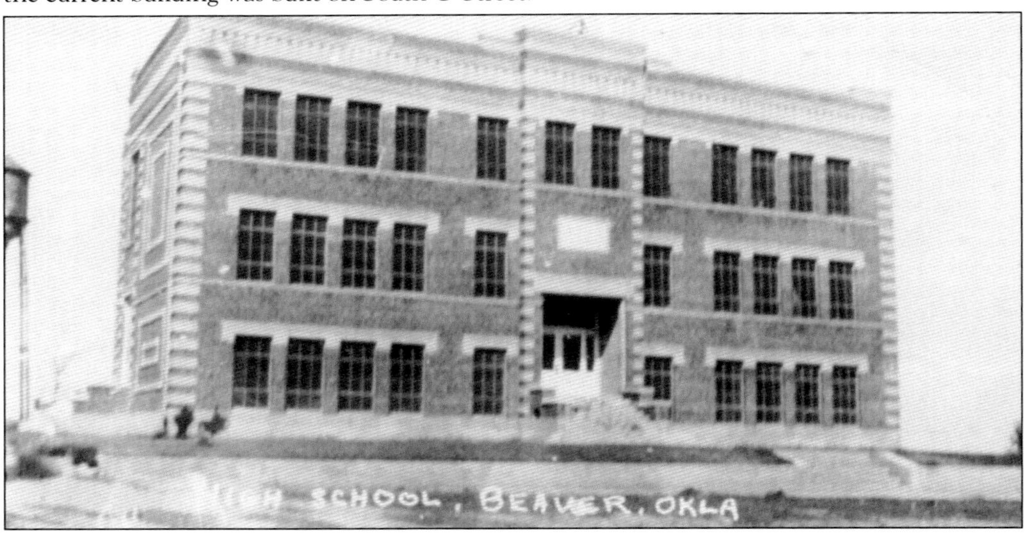

Beaver High School began in a two-story building in 1911. It burned in 1923 and was rebuilt of brick. In 1958, when the idea of junior high schools became popular, Beaver Junior High School was built adjacent to the elementary school on G Avenue. In the mid-1940s, a small fire in the high school caused students to attend classes in church buildings until repairs could be made. In 1962, the present building was erected, and in the early 1980s a state-of-the-art gymnasium was built across the street from the elementary school, as well as a primary building to the north of the gymnasium.

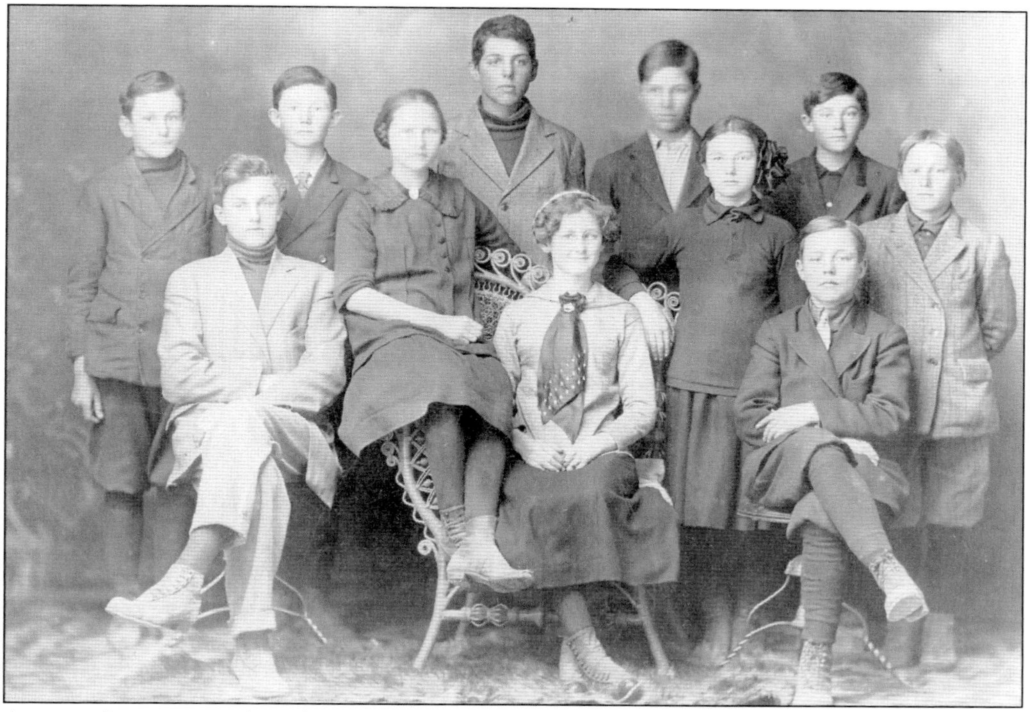

Among those pictured in this 1911 Beaver Elementary School eighth-grade graduation class photograph are Esther Taylor, Lois Quinn, Clarence Tackett, Basil Peckham, Bill Meese, and Zeke Rush.

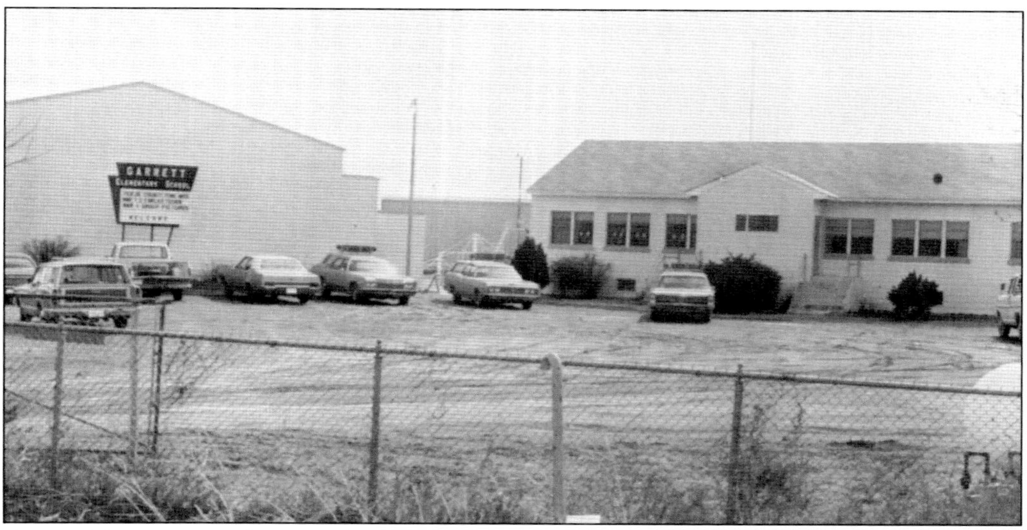

Garrett Elementary School was located on Highway 3 east of Elmwood. The first Garrett school was in a dugout and began in 1907. In 1935, it became an accredited school, but from 1938 to 1945 children went to Beaver schools since there were not enough students to hold a school at Garrett. In 1945, the school reopened, then in 1953 a new building was erected. The school finally closed in 2001.

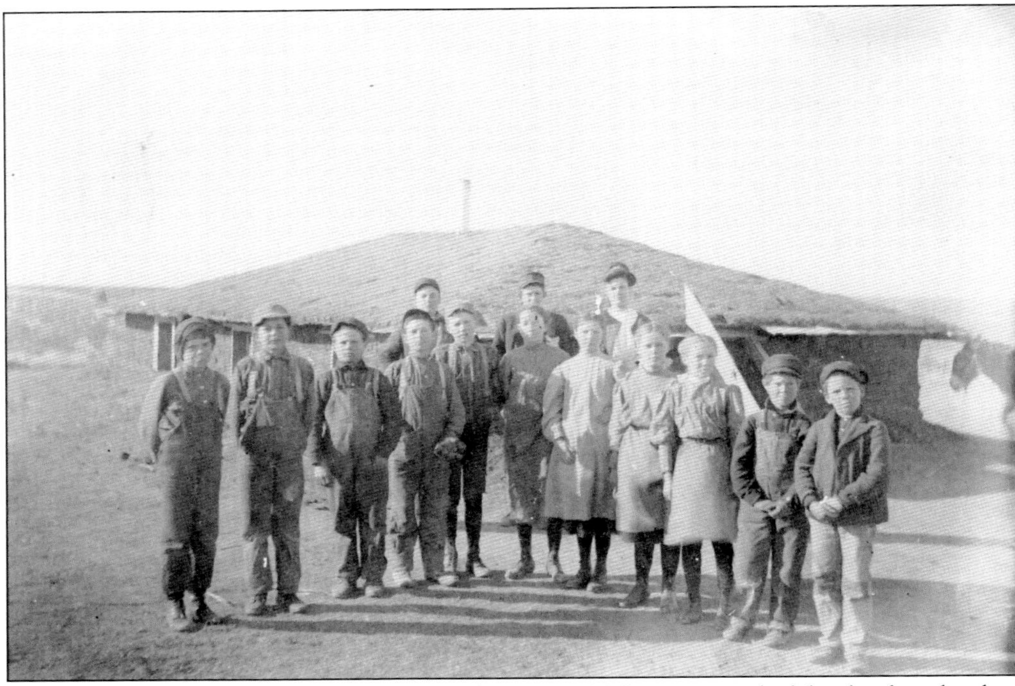

Sod School on John Ridgeway Farm is seen here in 1906. It was typical of the day for schools to be built on land donated by area farmers or ranchers.

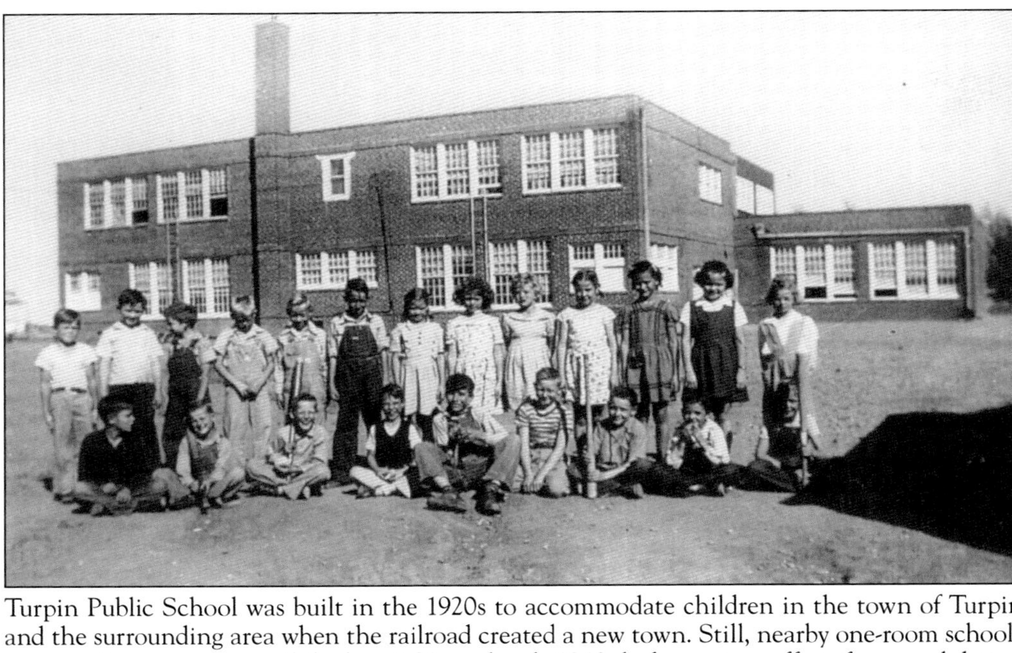

Turpin Public School was built in the 1920s to accommodate children in the town of Turpin and the surrounding area when the railroad created a new town. Still, nearby one-room schools remained in operation until the late 1930s and early 1940s before serious efforts for consolidation were made by the state.

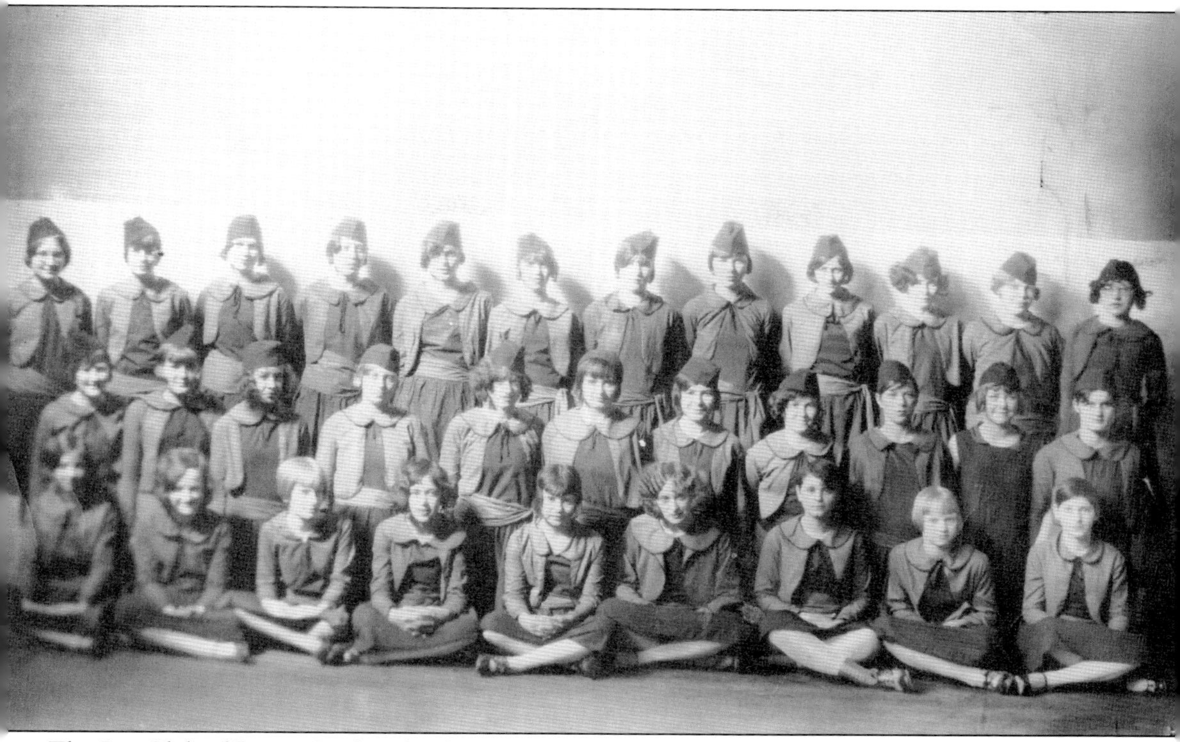

The Pep Club of Beaver High School, pictured here from left to right in the 1926–1927 school year, was made up of the following young women: (first row) Lillie Ottinger, LaVera Pierson, Esther Cowan, Grace Potter, Georgia Ottinger, Pauline Woolery, Mildred William, Robbie Rizley, and Nellie Phelps; (second row) Zoa Quinn, Myrna Russell, Nellon Humphrey, Iris Bridgewater, Myra Henson, Bertha McArthur, Verela Jones, Merle McCall, Eleen Kile, Virgie Pierson, and Jo Saunders; (third row) Doreen Fickle, Mildred Boren, Laura Petty, Fay Myers, Evelyn Barnes, Pallie Williams, Ruth McCall, Lula Stedman, Thelma Reeves, Dymple Shockley, Oma Shock, and Alice Lawson.

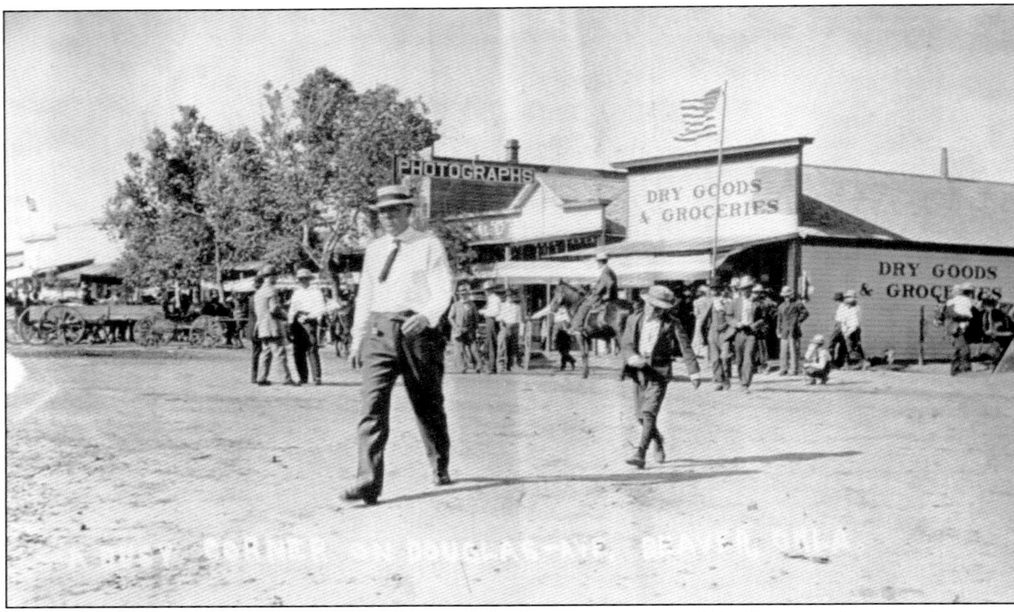

This busy corner on Douglas Avenue proved that times were good for Beaver City merchants, as well as for surrounding homesteaders and ranchers.

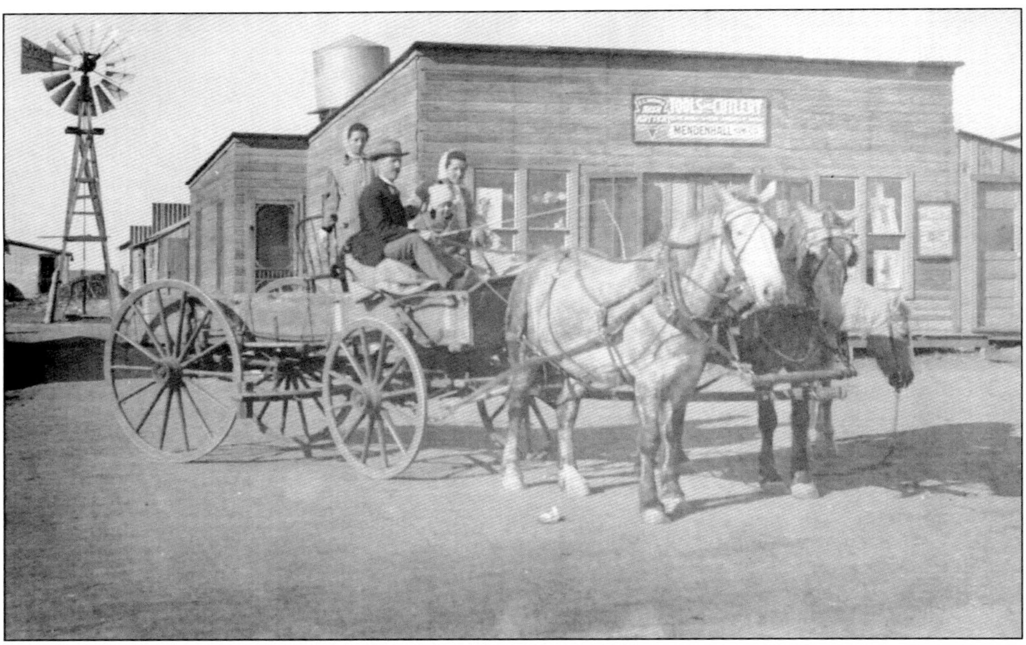

Mendenhall Tools and Cutlery Store provided much-needed equipment for farmers and ranchers, as well as for people to cultivate gardens or cook family meals. The windmill and storage tower held water for those businesses in the photograph. This store operated in Clearlake until 1918.

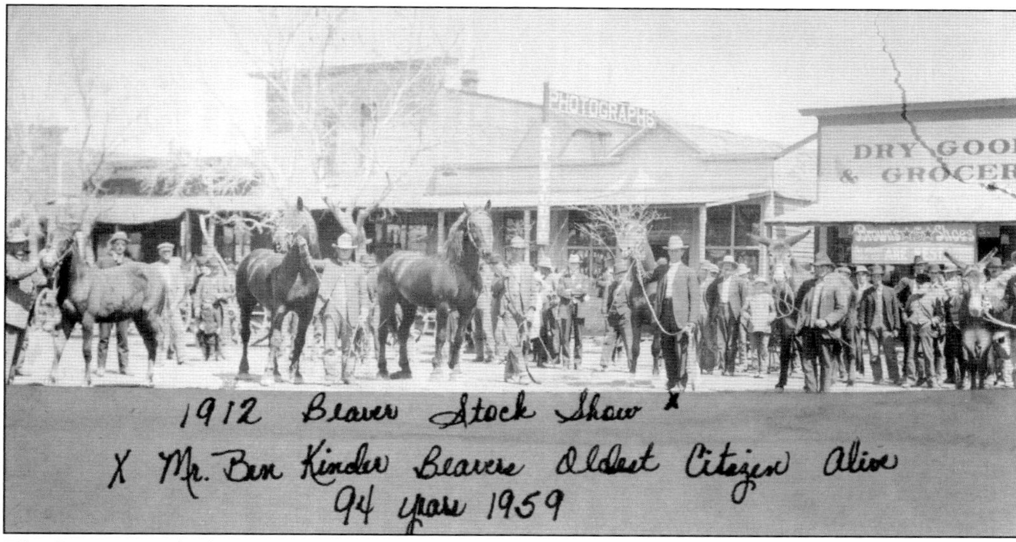

The Beaver stock show in 1912 was a venue for cattle ranchers but also served as a point of sale for show animals and for training young people who showed their stock. Ben Kinder, shown above the "X" at the front of the photograph, was honored later in 1959 as the oldest Beaver County citizen alive at that year.

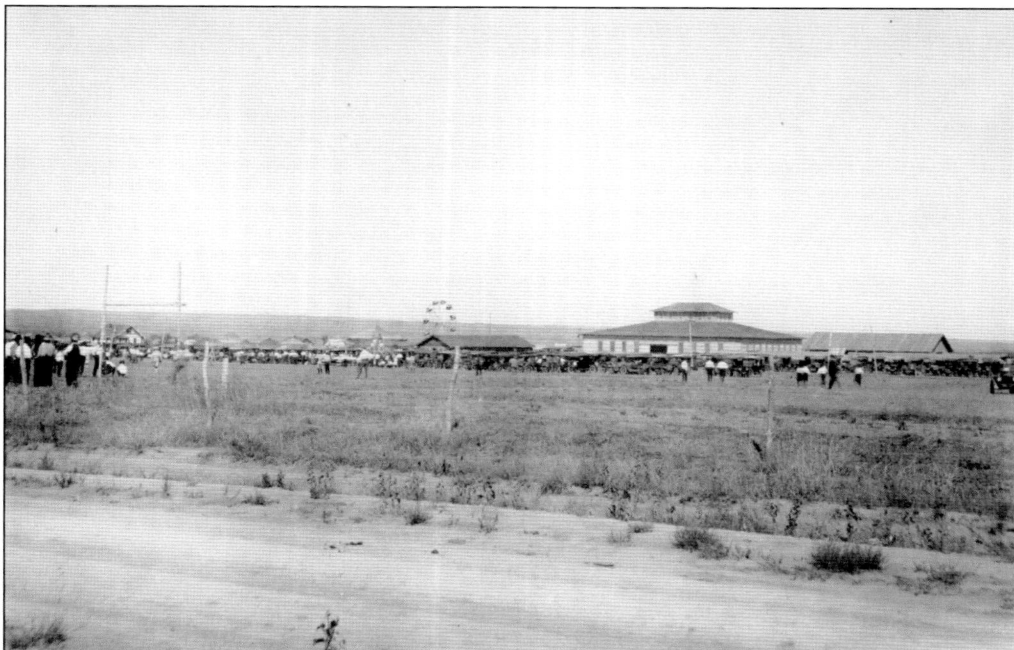

The 1920 county fair provided an outlet for demonstrating crops and food for residents of the county, as well as entertainment. The fair pavilion was later moved to the Barby Ranch, and a new building was erected in 1960. The influence of Frank Lloyd Wright as an architect was prevalent all over the country in the 1950s and 1960s and is evident in the buildings' designs. The county fair is still a September event in Beaver County. Other buildings now provide space for more animals and other exhibits each year.

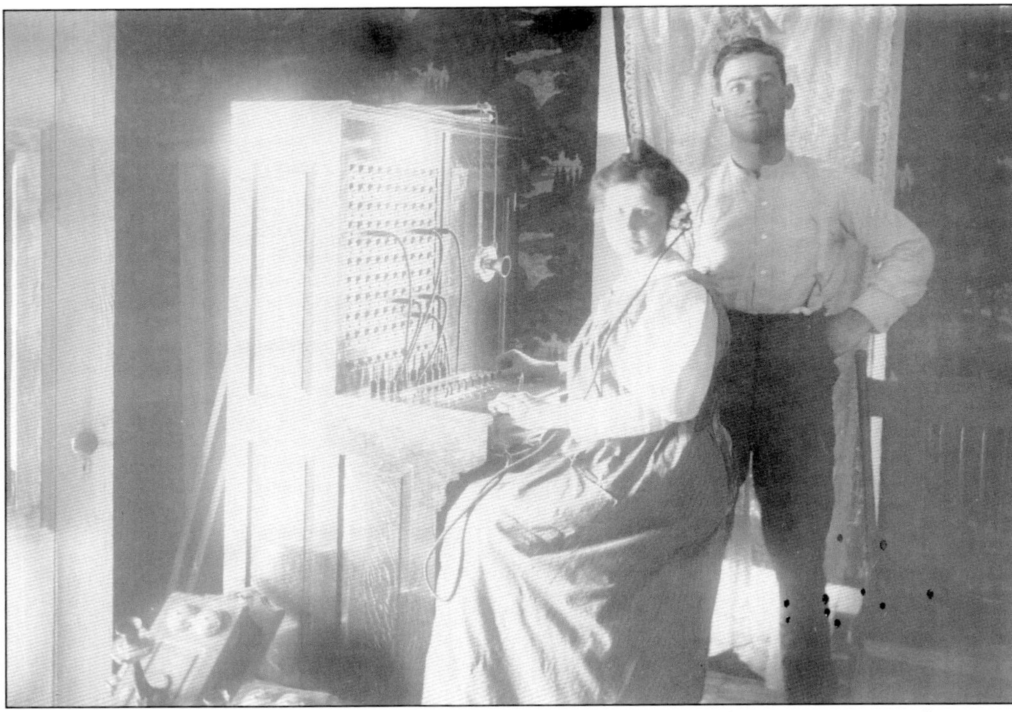

Beaver Telephone Company is pictured here with operators Edna and Henry Garrett. There were not many subscribers and most were on a party line, but the system served a serious function for isolated farms and ranches, as well as for those in town. Notice the size of the switchboard.

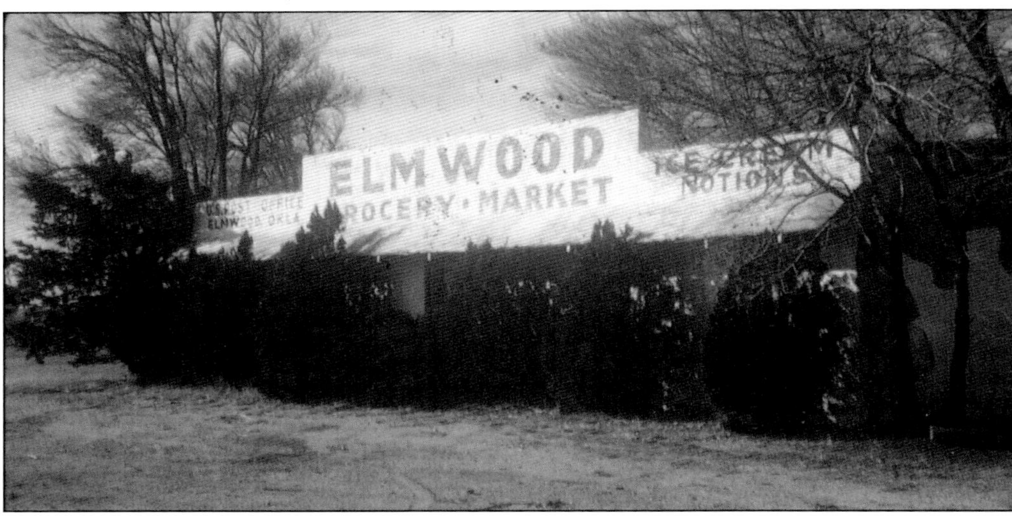

The Elmwood Grocery and Market was once located on the corner of what is now Highway 3 and Highway 270. Elmwood began as a post office in 1888 located 12 miles south and 1 mile east of Beaver. In 1893, it was reestablished on land 12 miles south and 2 miles east, then established once again in the 1920s, 12 miles south and 3 miles east on Lin Baggerly's land. Finally, with the construction of Highway 3, it was moved to the intersection of Highways 3 and 270. The grocery served farmers and ranchers well, so they did not have to ride or drive to Beaver City or Booker, Texas, to obtain groceries and other staples. (HSK.)

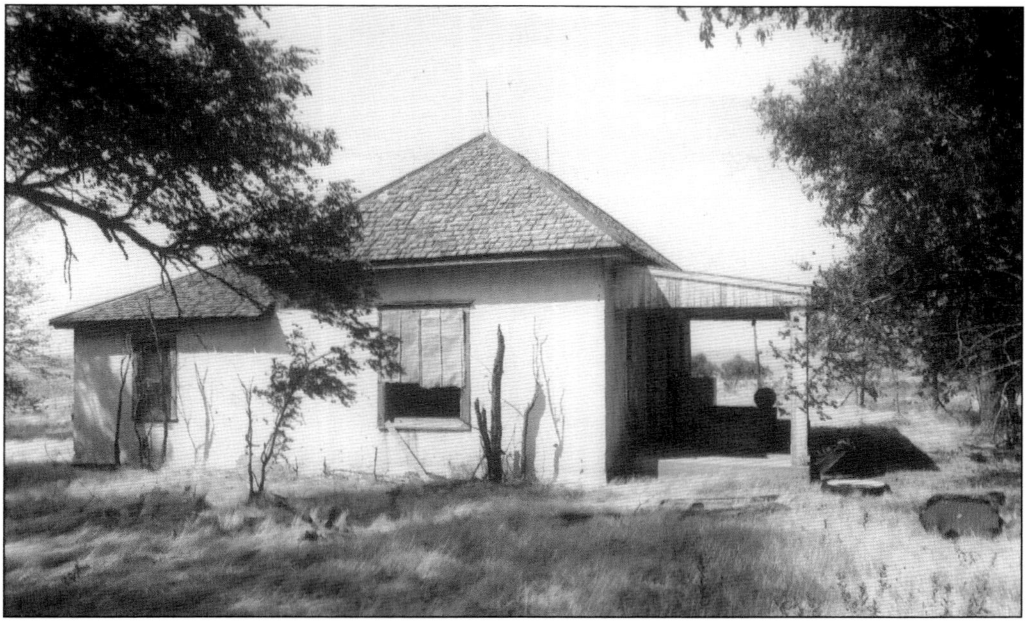

The Cecil Drum homestead, pictured here, was typical of the houses of the time in that it was of wood construction with a porch on the front of the house. Trees were planted near the house since there were no native trees for shade. (HSK.)

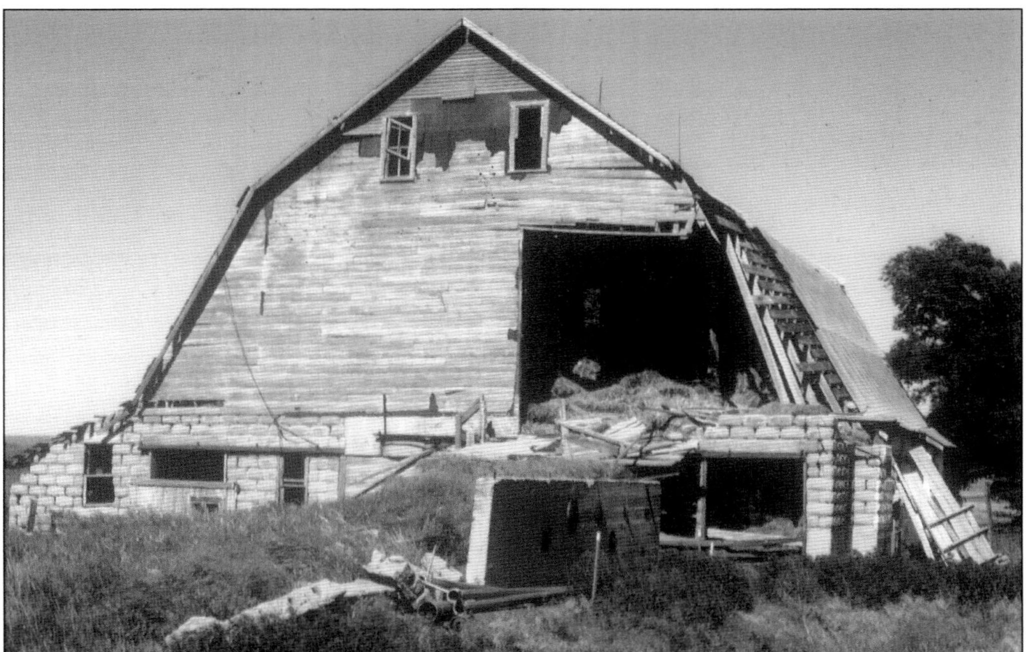

The ramp at Albert Seal's barn was a most unusual feature in barn building in early days, but it made loading feed and animals much faster and easier. (HSK.)

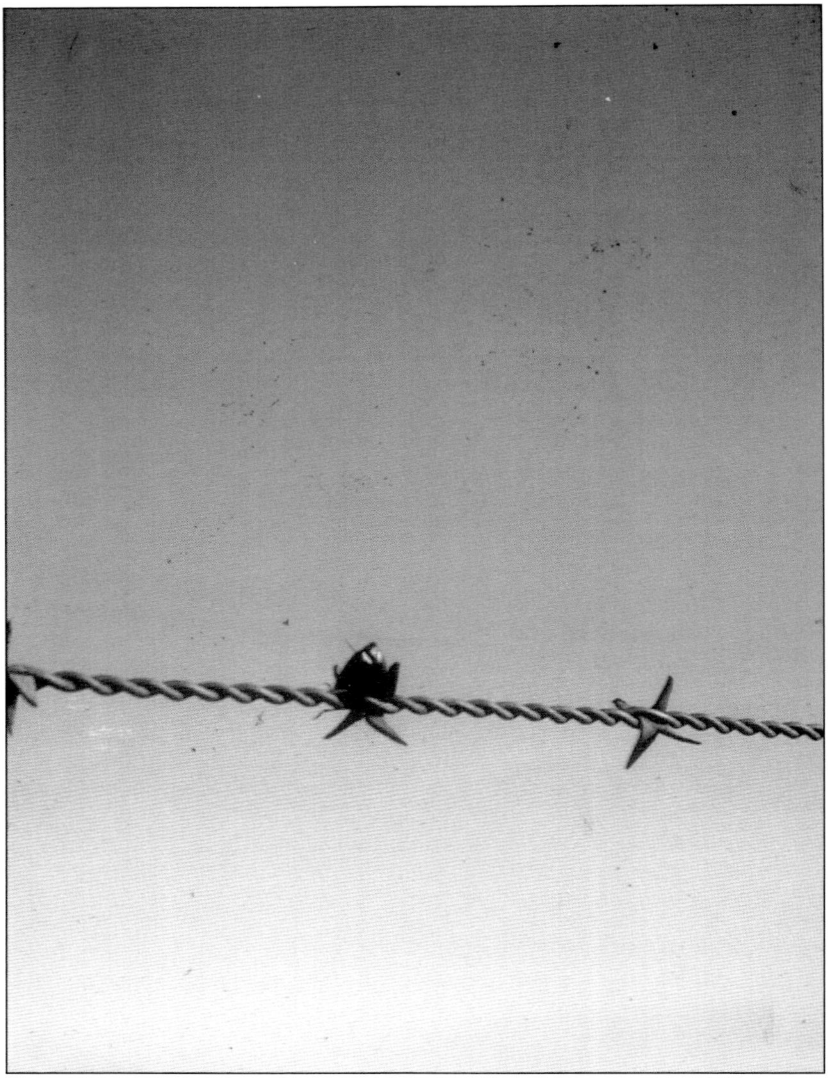

A loggerhead shrike, a species of bird, has left an extra meal on a barbed wire fence. Barbed wire changed the west far more than the six-gun did. (HSK.)

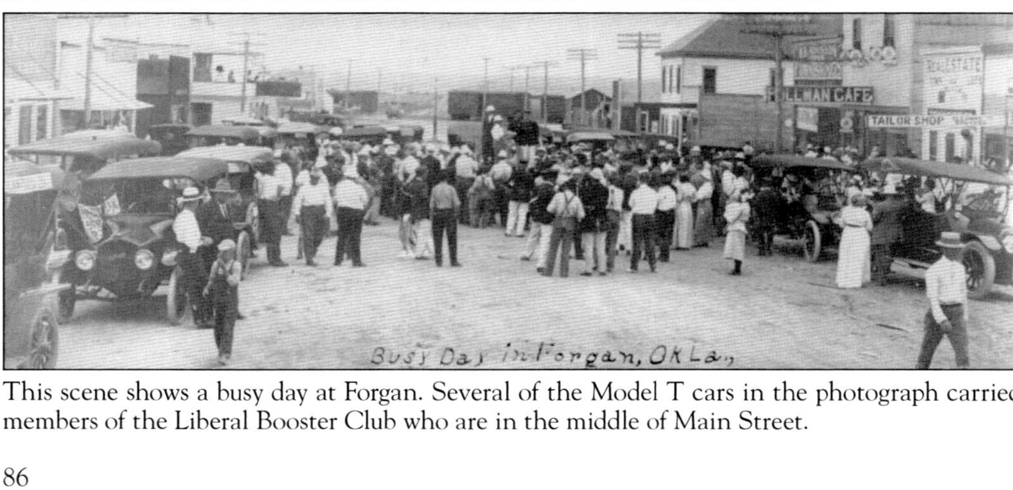

This scene shows a busy day at Forgan. Several of the Model T cars in the photograph carried members of the Liberal Booster Club who are in the middle of Main Street.

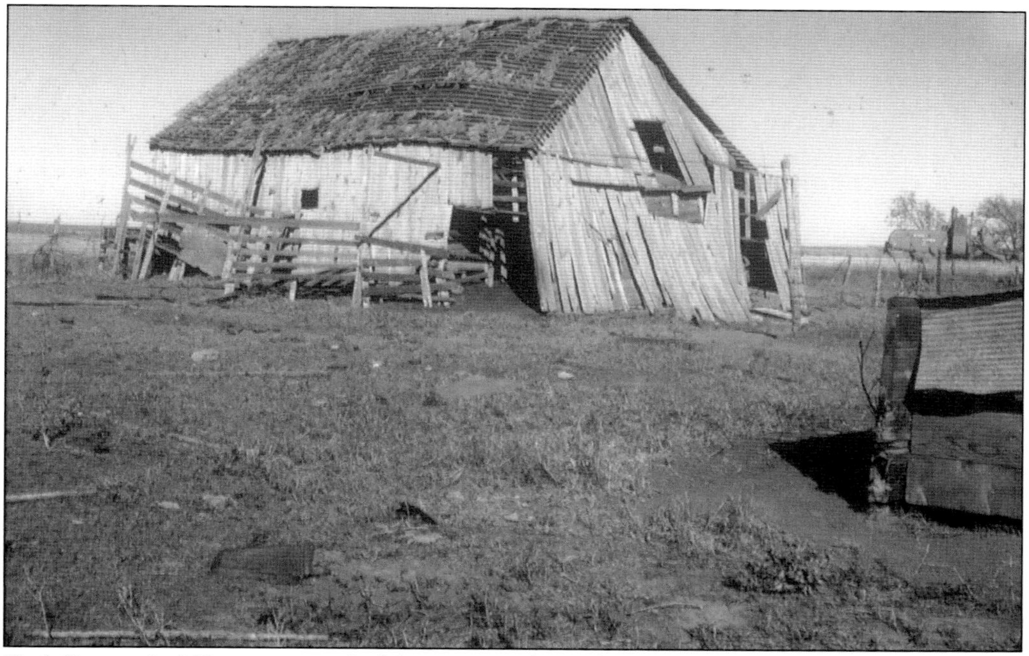

Herb Sprague's old barn is typical of the times in the early 1900s. Most of these barns were left to deteriorate and fall down, even though almost every farm had one on the property. A common practice of the German settlement where this barn was located was to build the barn first, then the house. (HSK.)

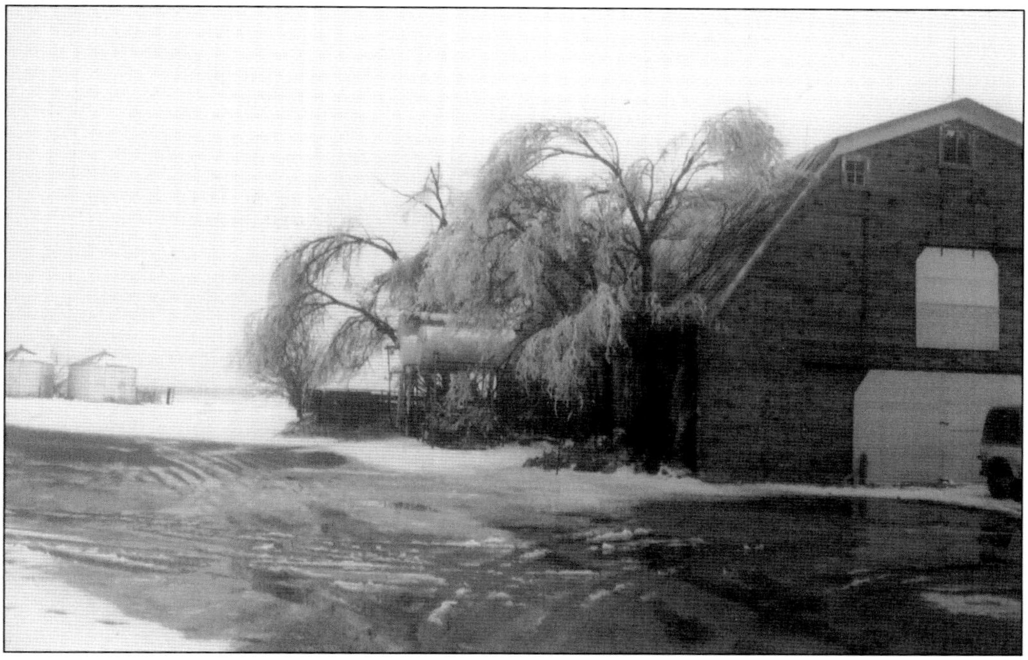

Harold Kachel's barn, built in 1915, has been featured in articles and productions as representative of that era. At the present time, this barn is being refurbished for its historical significance. (HSK.)

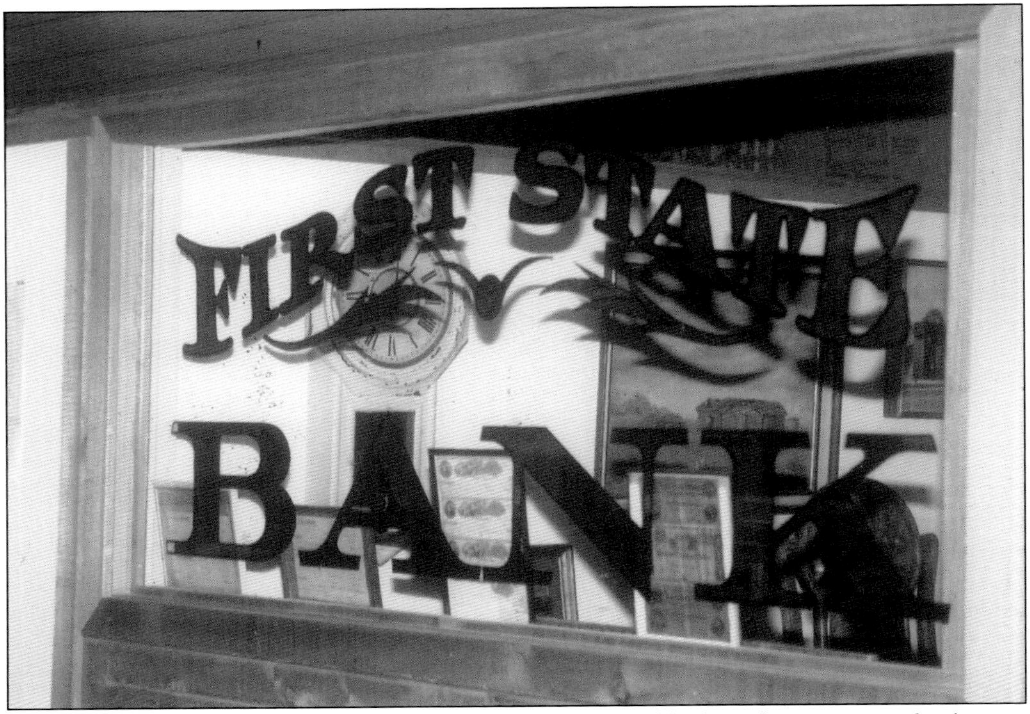

First State Bank in Forgan is pictured here in 1915. The gold leaf window was one of only nine in the United States. In 1984, Charles Kuralt did a special television feature about it when it was replaced. It is on display at the Jones and Plummer Trail Museum. In 1913, O. H. Cafky had moved to the new town of Forgan and he, R. A., Maple, and W. E. Hocker bought the bank that Cafky had operated until his death. His son John then managed it the rest of his life. (JWL.)

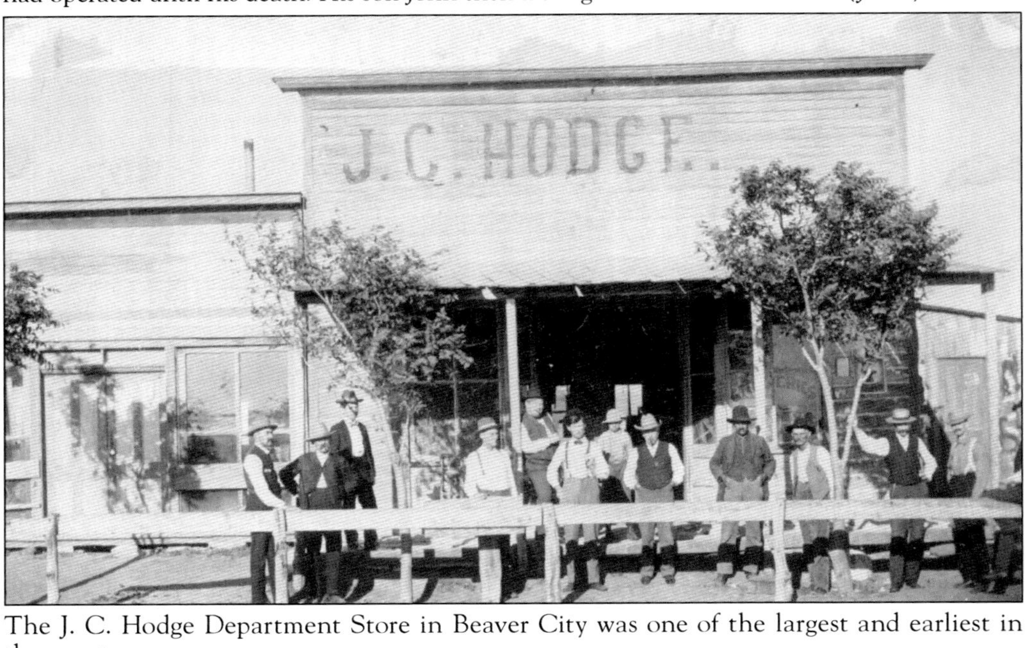

The J. C. Hodge Department Store in Beaver City was one of the largest and earliest in the county.

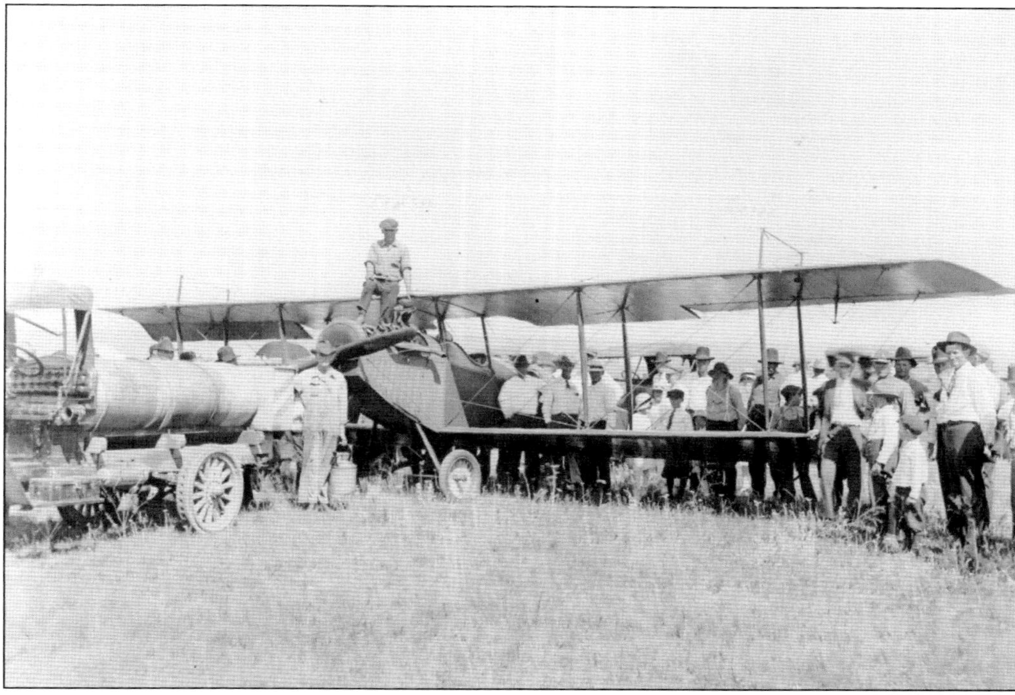

The Beaver Booster Plane used new technology to promote Beaver and bring folks to town for "show and tell."

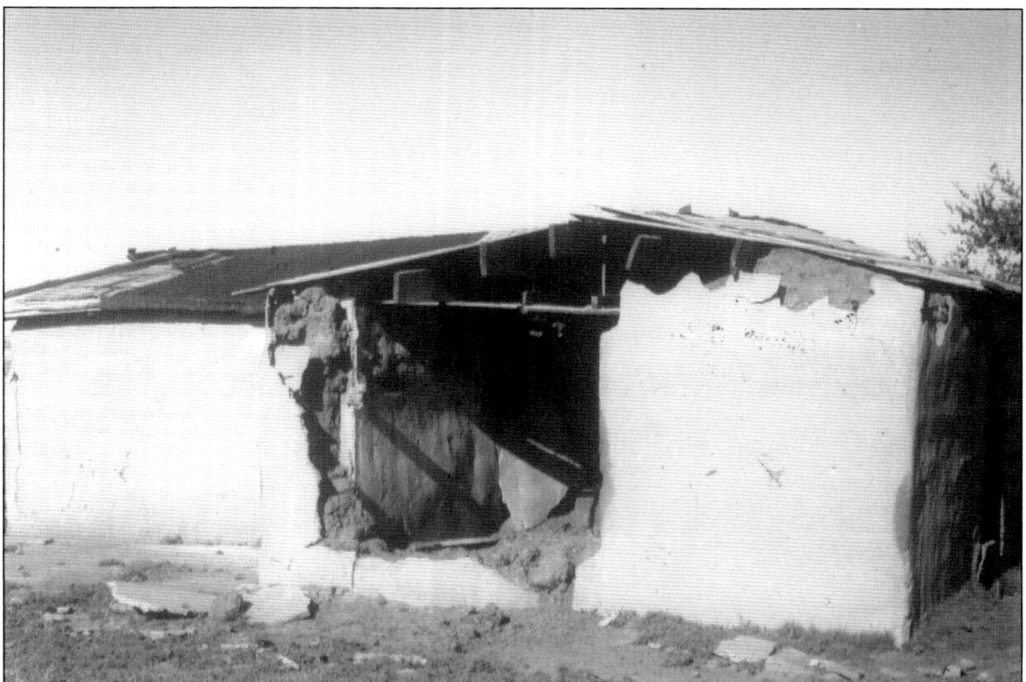

Caldwell's sod house is another example of how people made do with what they had: no trees, no lumber, but lots of unbroken land. (HSK.)

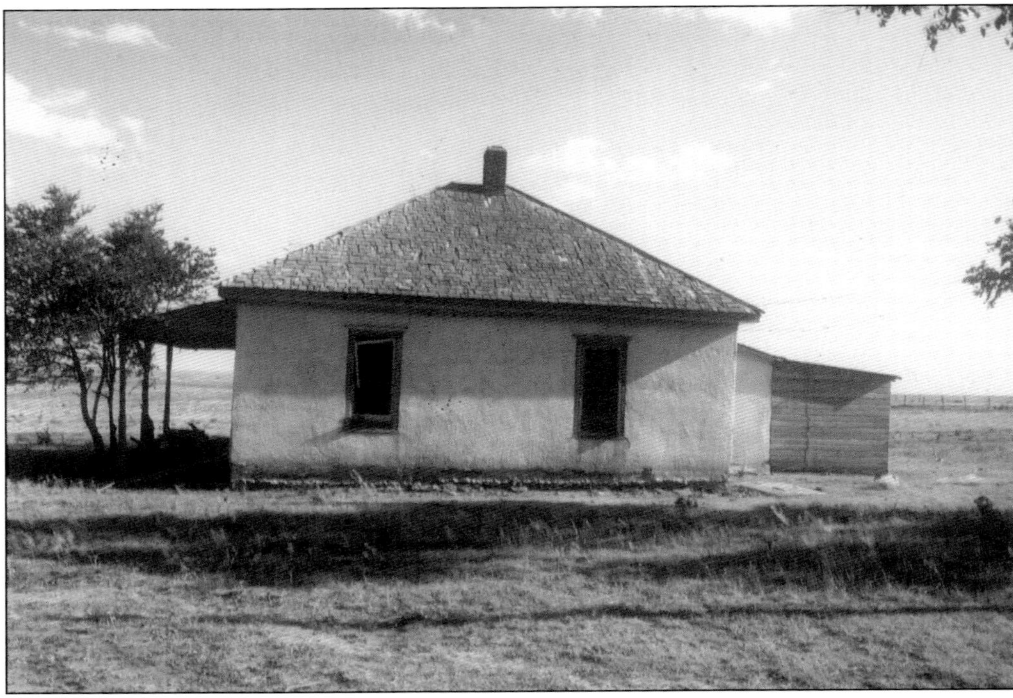

Harrison House was considered to be of one of the finer houses of early homesteaders. The Harrisons raised and released some of the first ring-necked and golden pheasants in the area. (HSK.)

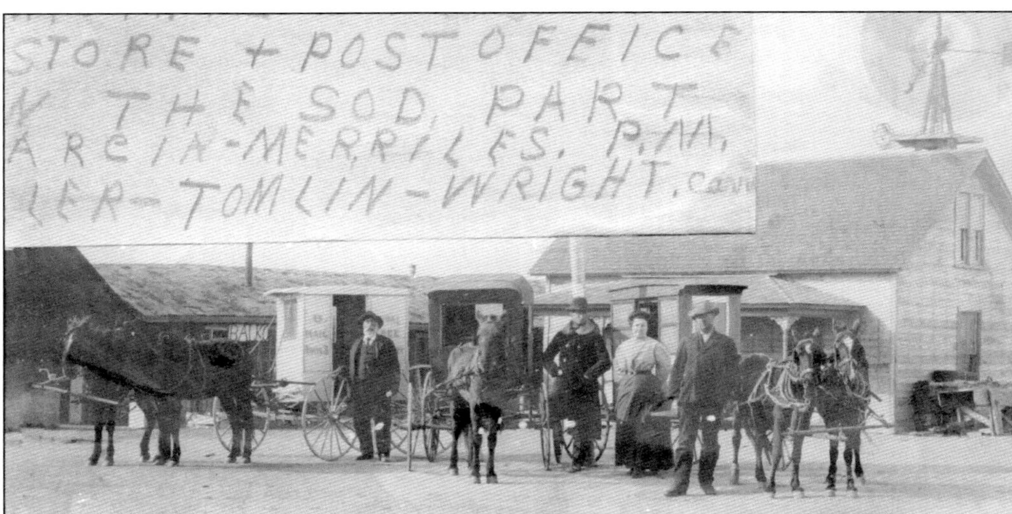

The original Balko Store and post office was located in a sod house belonging to P. M. Keller and Thompson Wright.

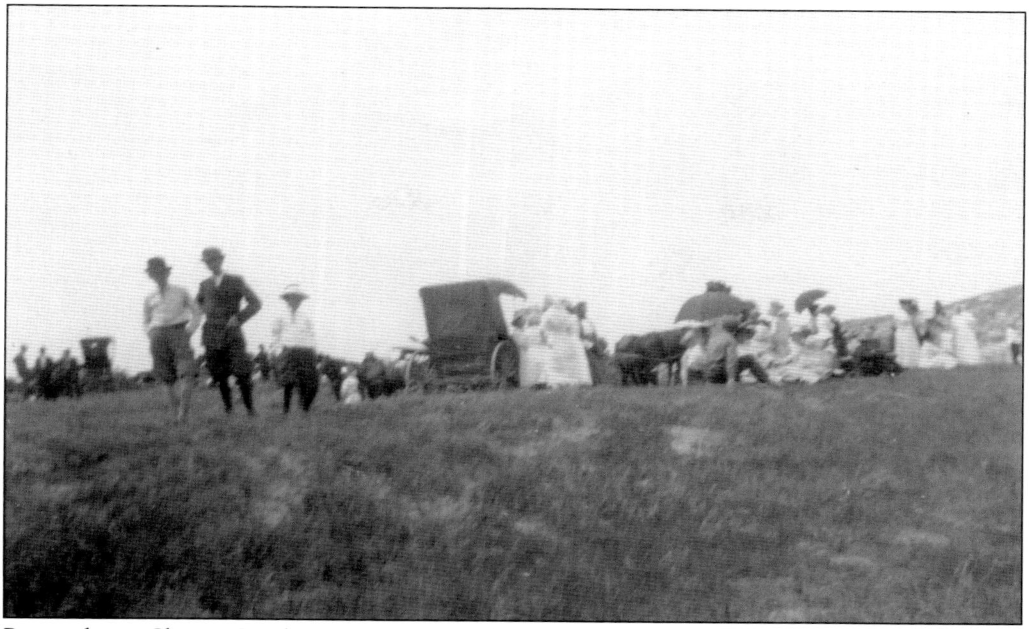

Picnic day at Sharps Creek was a favorite gathering place, even in the days of getting there in Model Ts. There was a school located here between 1904 and 1928.

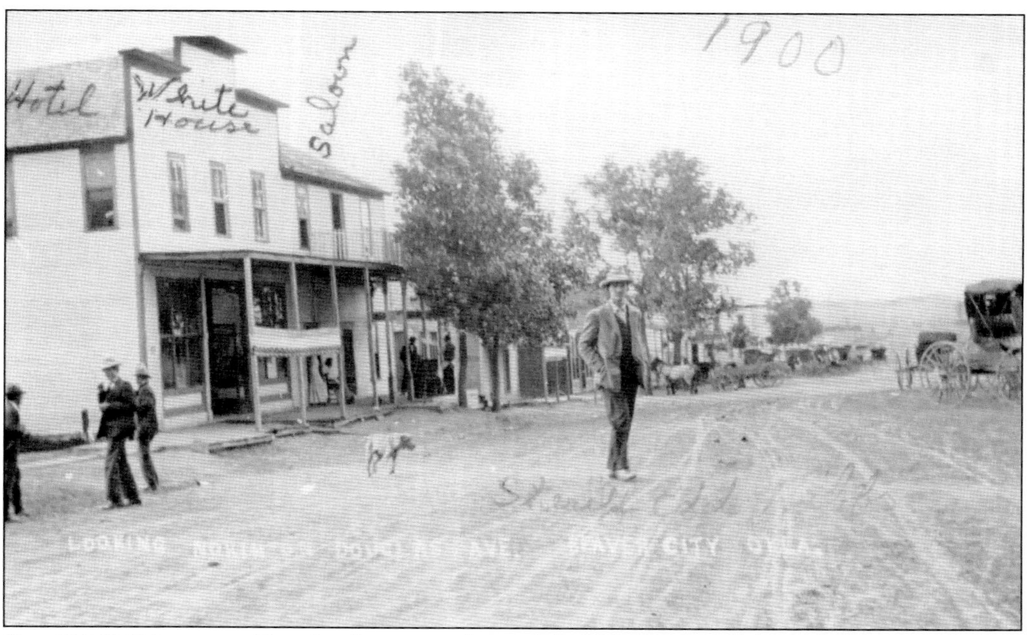

Sheriff Ed Hibbs crosses Douglas Avenue in front of the White House Saloon, with the Thompson Hotel down the street on the corner and the sand hills in the far distance.

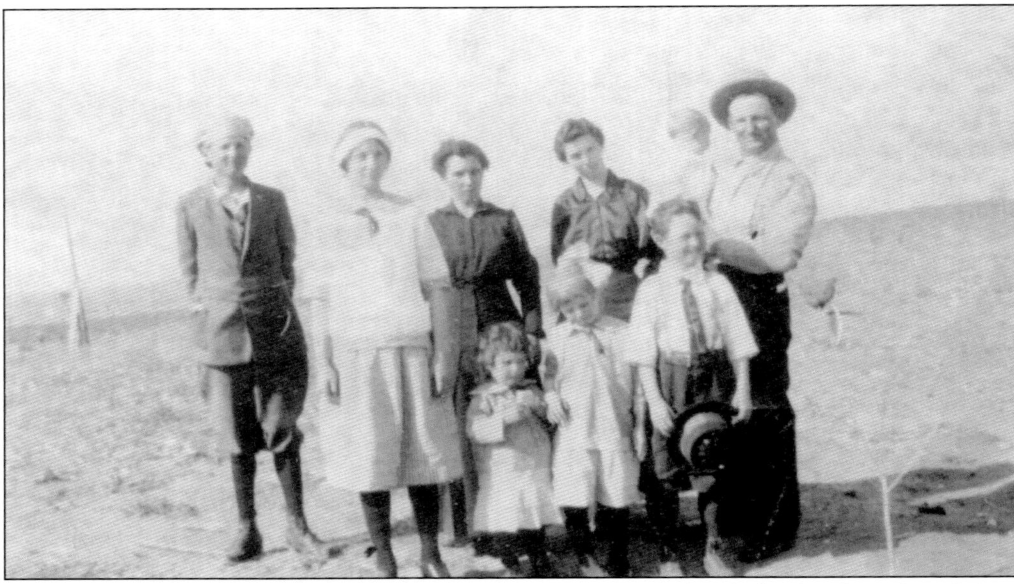

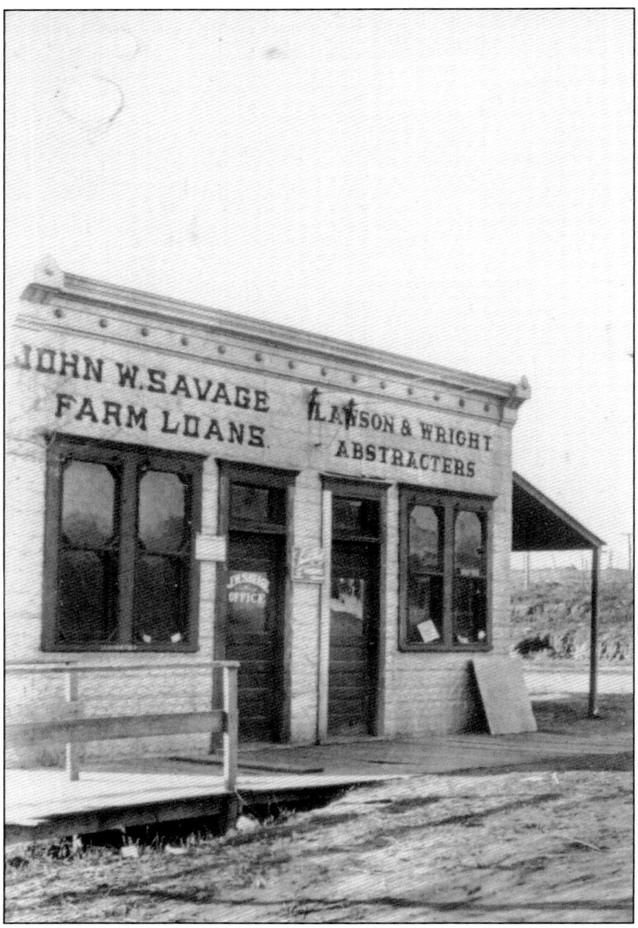

The Phelps family is, from left to right, (first row) John Phelps, Louise Phelps, Nellie Phelps, Merlee Phelps, and Donald Phelps; (second row) Nell Phelps (mother), Mabel Phelps, Robert Phelps (baby), and I. N. Phelps (father). (I. N. Phelps family.)

John W. Savage Farm Loans and Lawson and Wright Abstracters served the homesteaders and other folks moving to the county. (JS.)

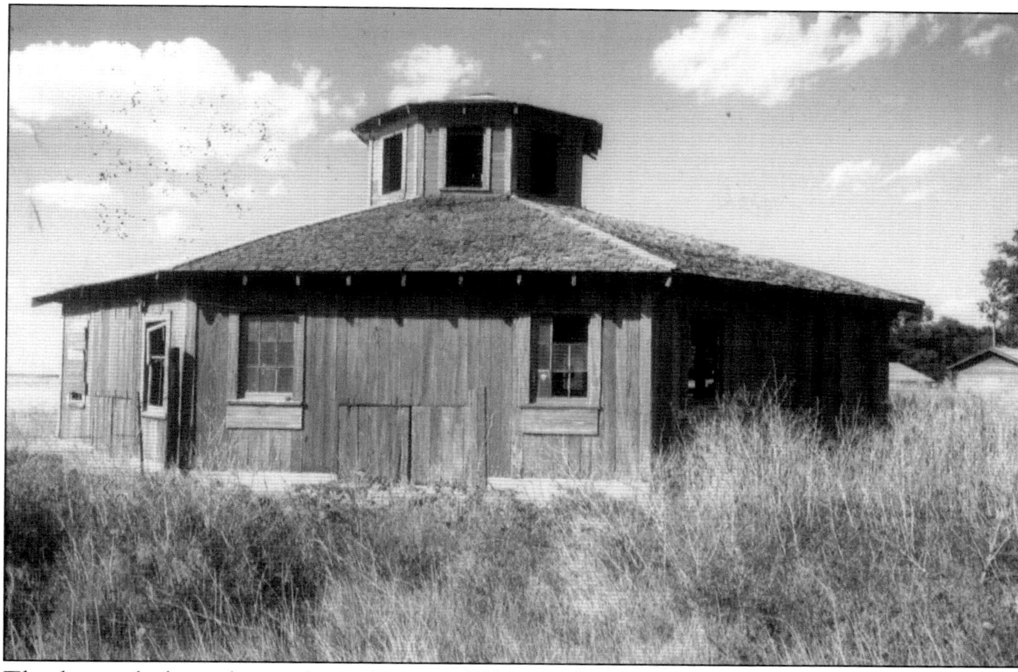

The hog sale barn located northwest of Elmwood was one of first sale barns in Beaver County. (HSK.)

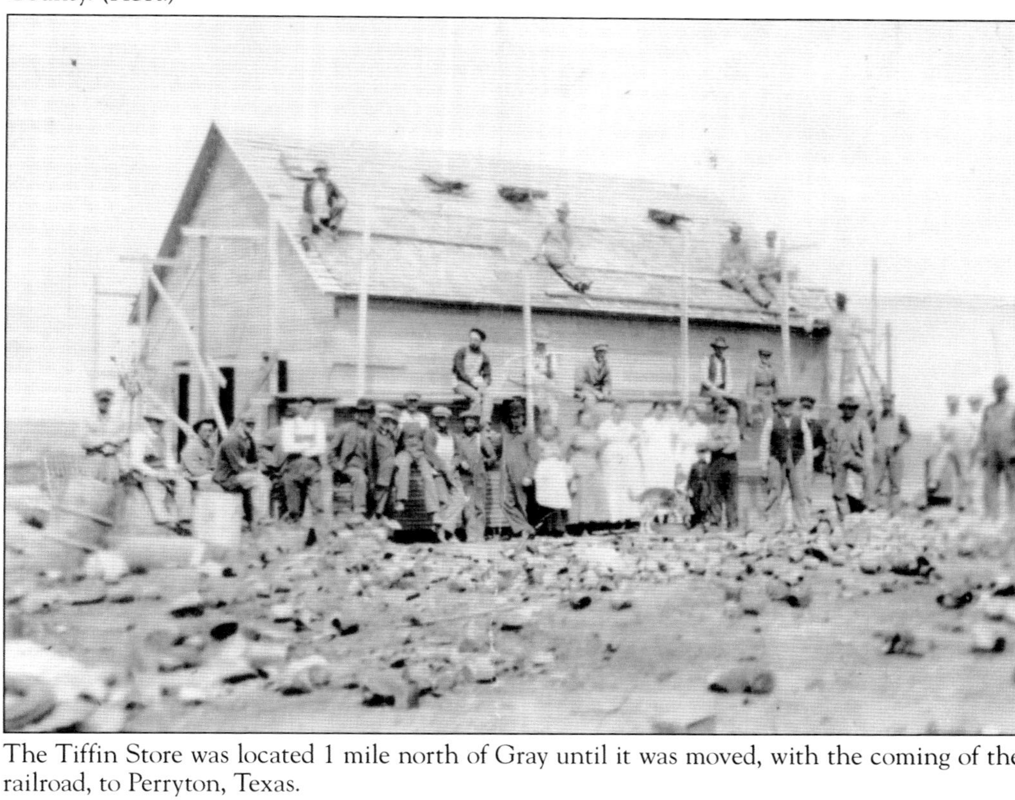

The Tiffin Store was located 1 mile north of Gray until it was moved, with the coming of the railroad, to Perryton, Texas.

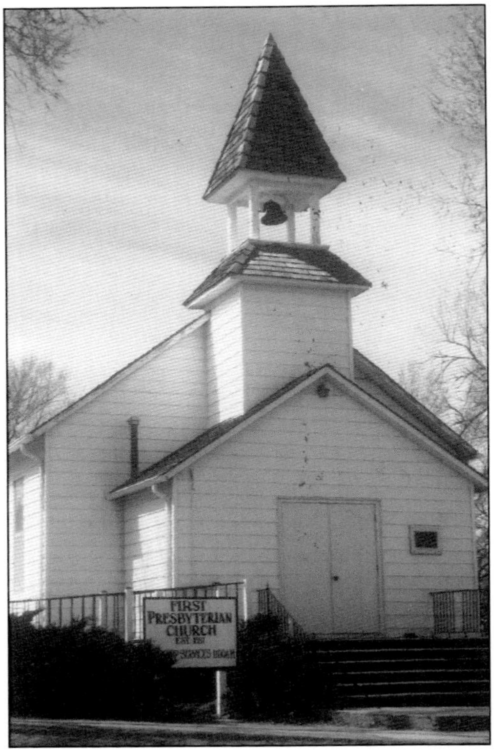

First Presbyterian Church is the oldest church building in what was the Oklahoma Territory. It was established on June 12, 1887, at a cost of $1,000. Rev. R. M. Overstreet was the first minister. It still serves its congregation today with regular services and special projects and dinners in its fellowship hall next door.

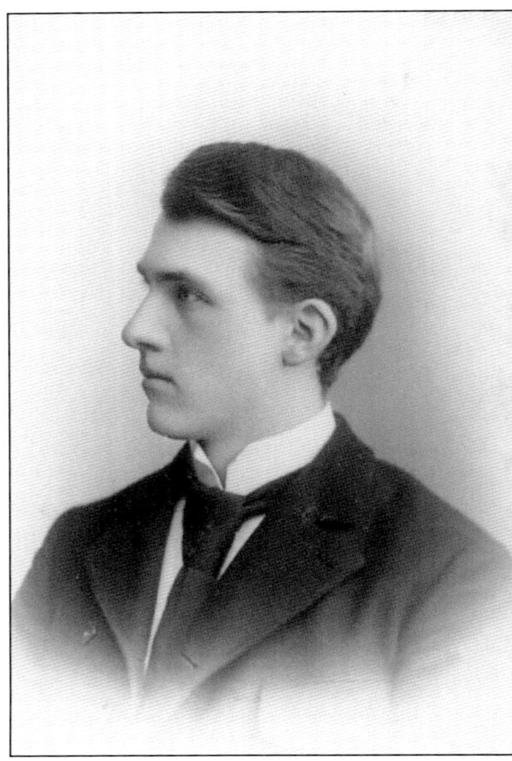

Rev. William Barr Leonard was the pastor of the First Presbyterian Church from 1905 to 1910 and again from 1915 until his death in 1924. His wife, Mary Elizabeth Rich Leonard, was the Sunday school superintendent for many years. (WLL.)

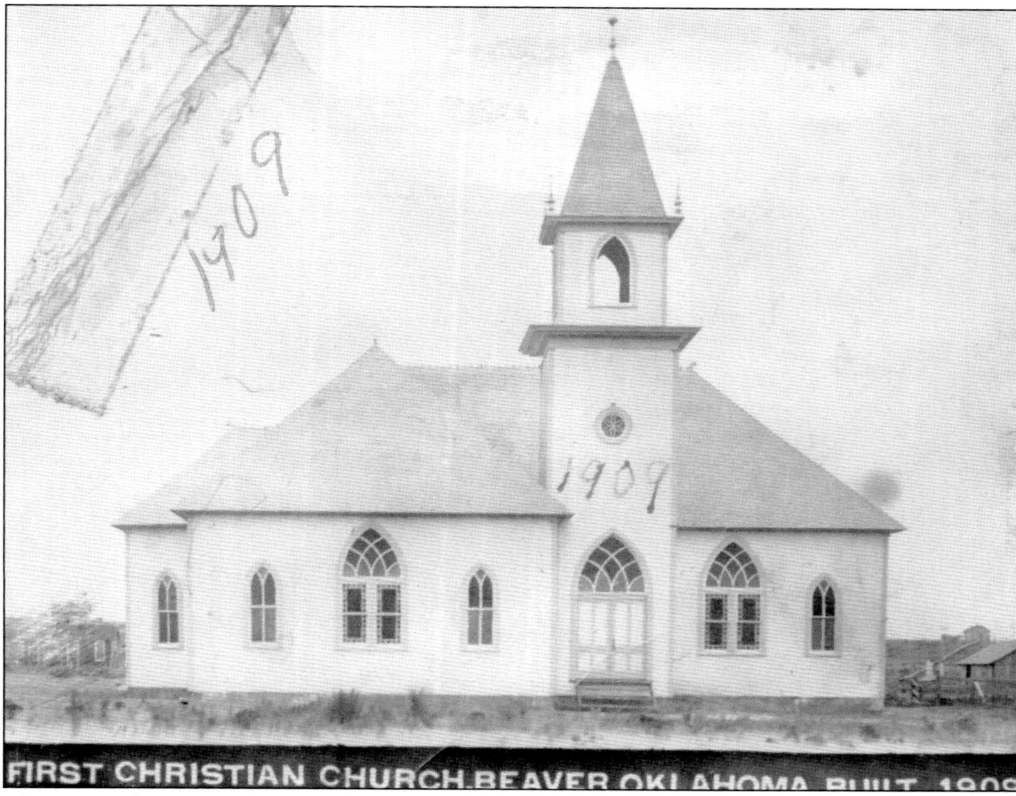

The First Christian Church in Beaver was built in 1909 with construction by the members themselves.

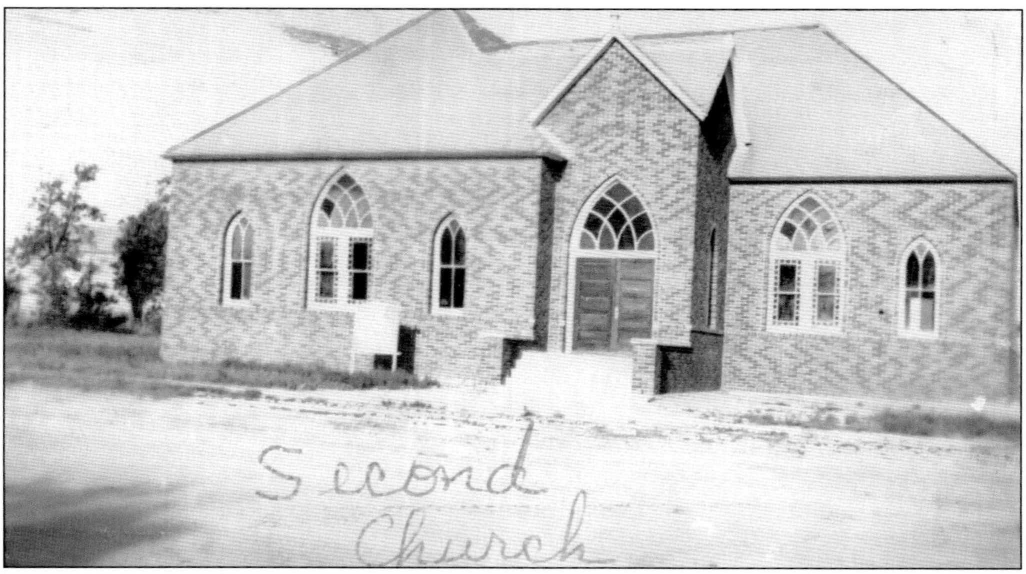

This is the second building of the First Christian Church in Beaver. The church has been remodeled, built anew, and added onto many times since 1909. It is still one of the most active churches in Beaver.

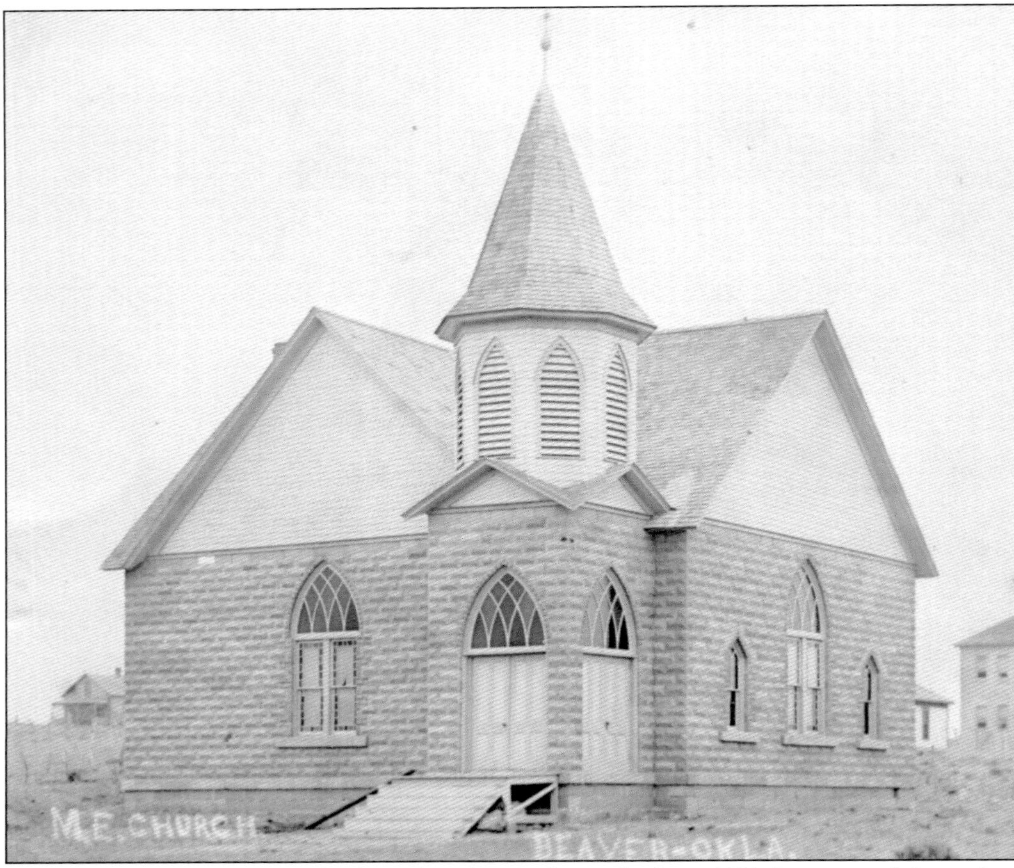

This view is of the First Methodist Church, which was built in 1901. It is one of the earliest churches in Beaver City.

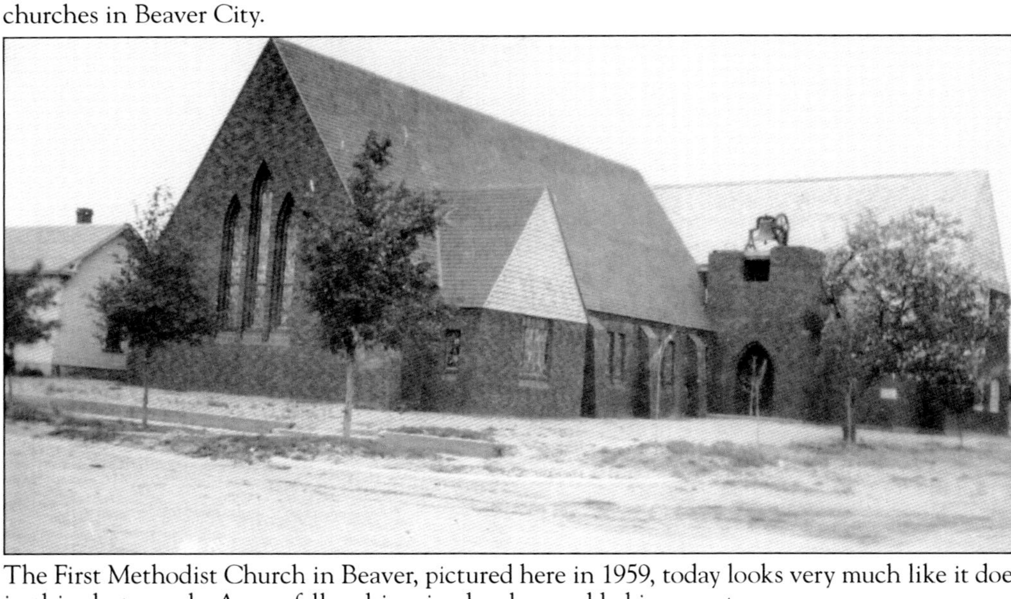
The First Methodist Church in Beaver, pictured here in 1959, today looks very much like it does in this photograph. A new fellowship wing has been added in recent years.

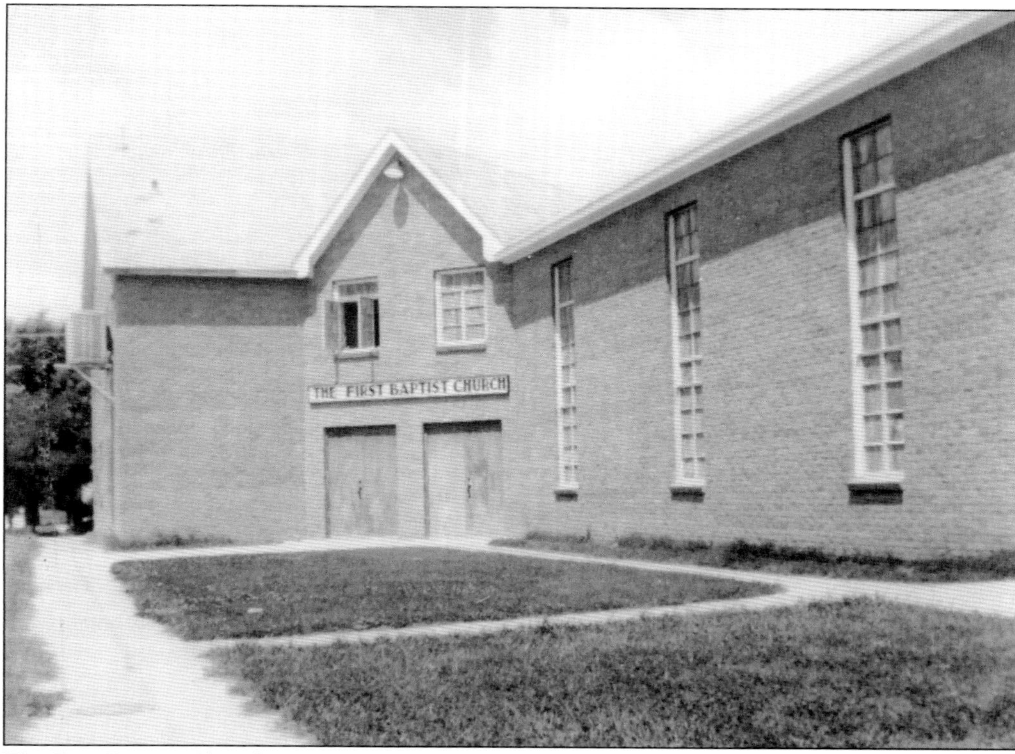

The First Baptist Church is one of the largest and most active churches in Beaver. The Nazarene church next door to the west was recently purchased when it disbanded and the annexed building now serves as the *iglesia bautista*, or Baptist church, for the Hispanic community.

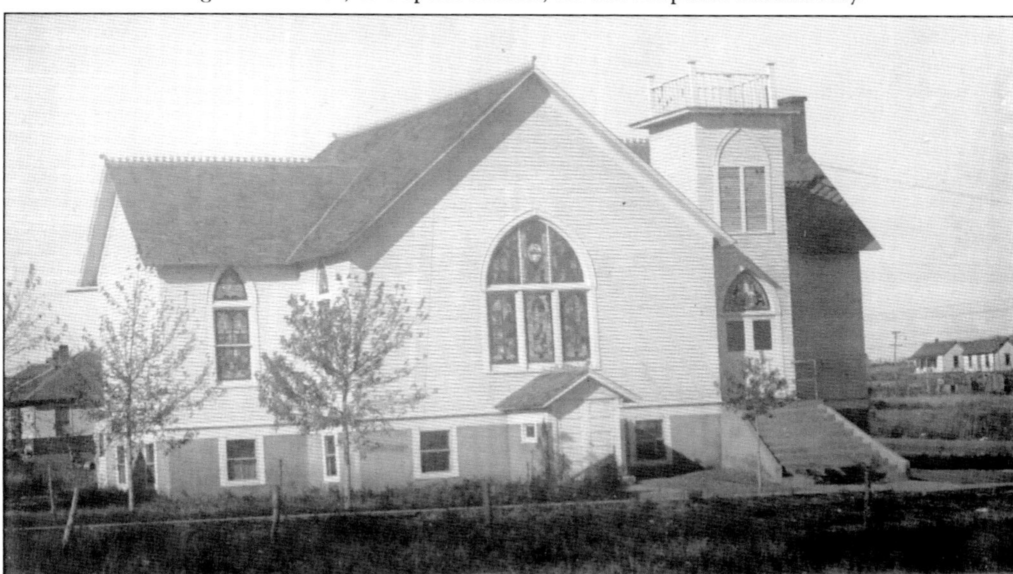
The First Methodist Church in the town of Forgan was first built in the North Flats and then moved into Forgan when the railroad created the town. This building served the community until the early 1970s when the present building was erected just west of the original church.

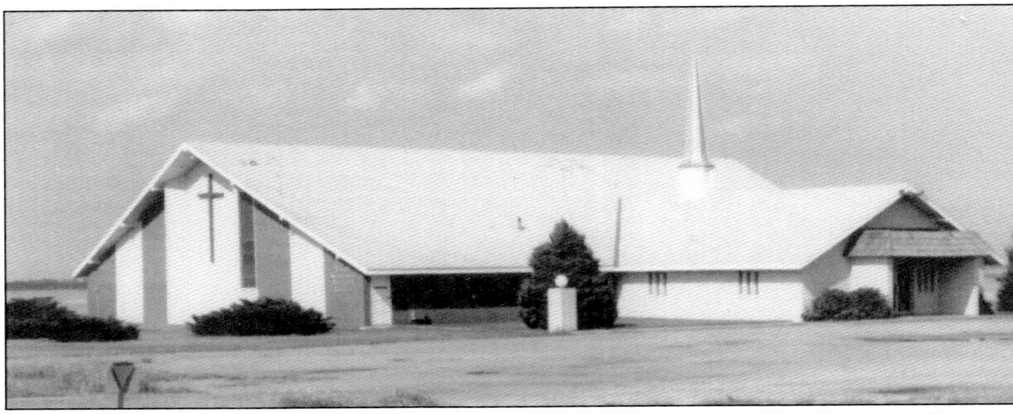

In June 2010, a tornado ripped off the front of the Fourth Mennonite Church, just as the script for this book was being written. However, church members quickly went to work restoring their church, as pioneers have always done in a crisis. (ABE.)

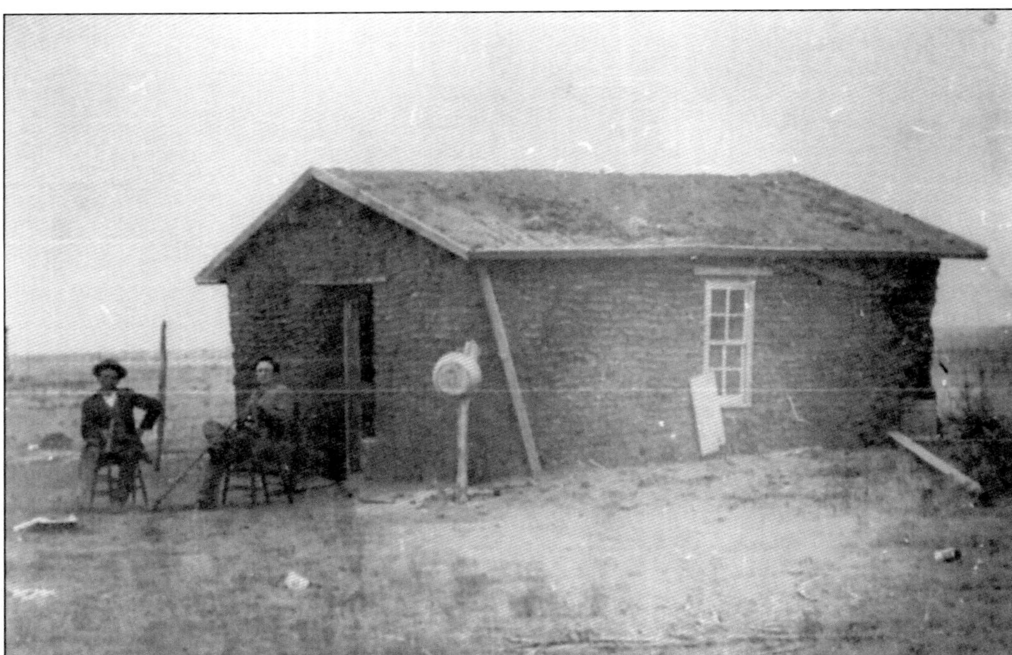

The Fourth Mennonite Church, near Bryan's Corner, was built in 1970. It still serves the descendants of those early Mennonites who met in Kliewer's (one of the members) sod house, shown above, in 1906. The first Mennonite church was known as the Bethel Mennonite Brethren. In 1969, the name was changed to Balko Mennonite Church and now is known also as the Crossroads Bible Fellowship. (ABE.)

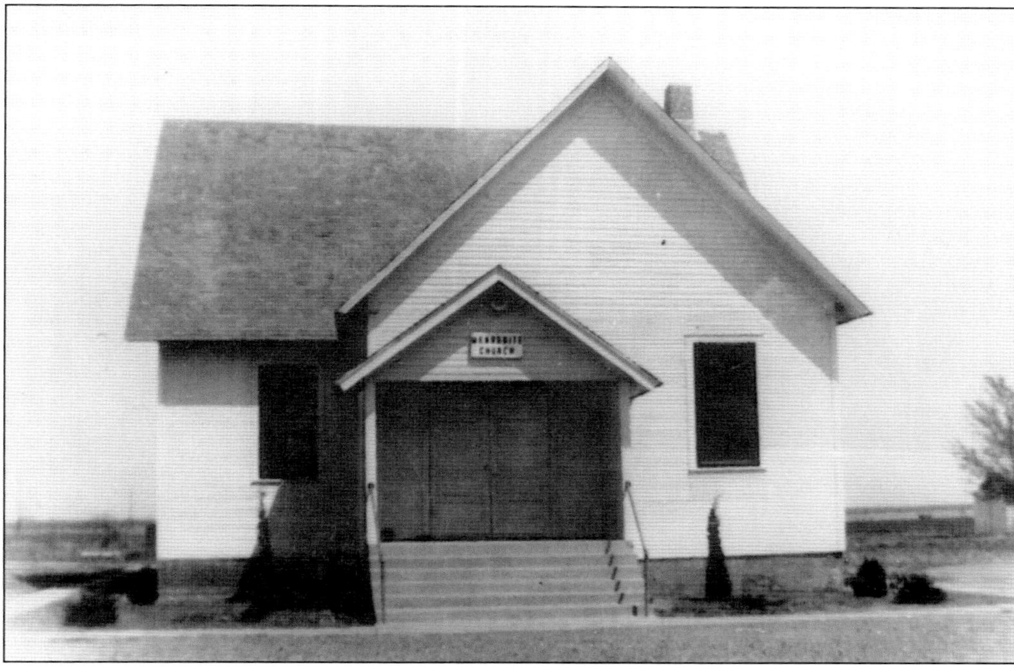

It was 1903 when the first Mennonite families settled near where the present church building stands and a church was organized in 1907, originally called the Friedensfeld Church. The first building to house the church was on land donated by Brother and Sister G. H. Epp. The second building was an abandoned church in the Greenough community that was moved to the current church site on land donated by John Dirks and completed for worship in 1940. In 1966, a new church was built near the old structure and is used today. (SDK.)

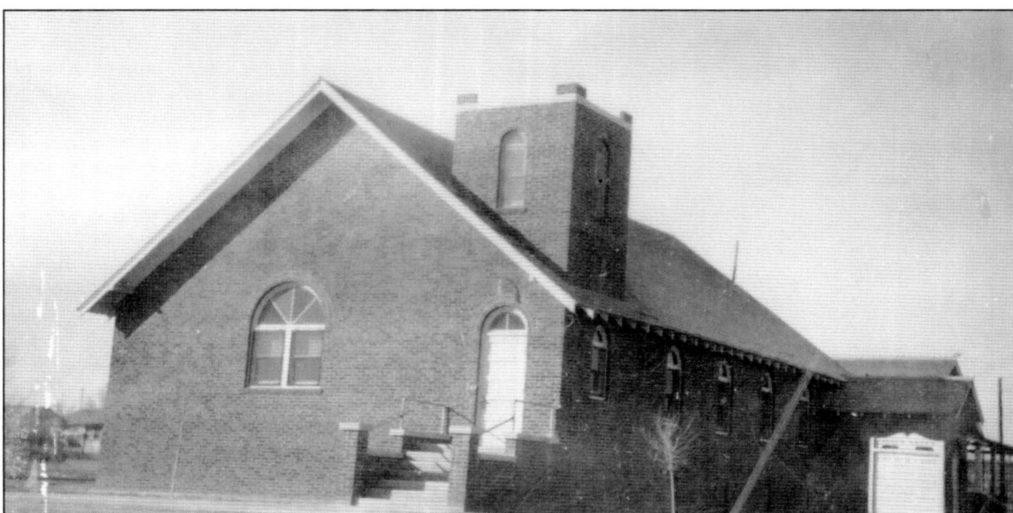

The Church of God in Beaver was established in 1909 and was once was a very active church. One of the early leaders in the church was Lennie Mae Thomas, wife of "Top" Thomas, a prominent barber in Beaver. However, as the years went by and the congregation got older, membership declined. When church membership consisted of nine elderly women in the early 1990s, the congregation was disbanded and the building was sold as a private residence.

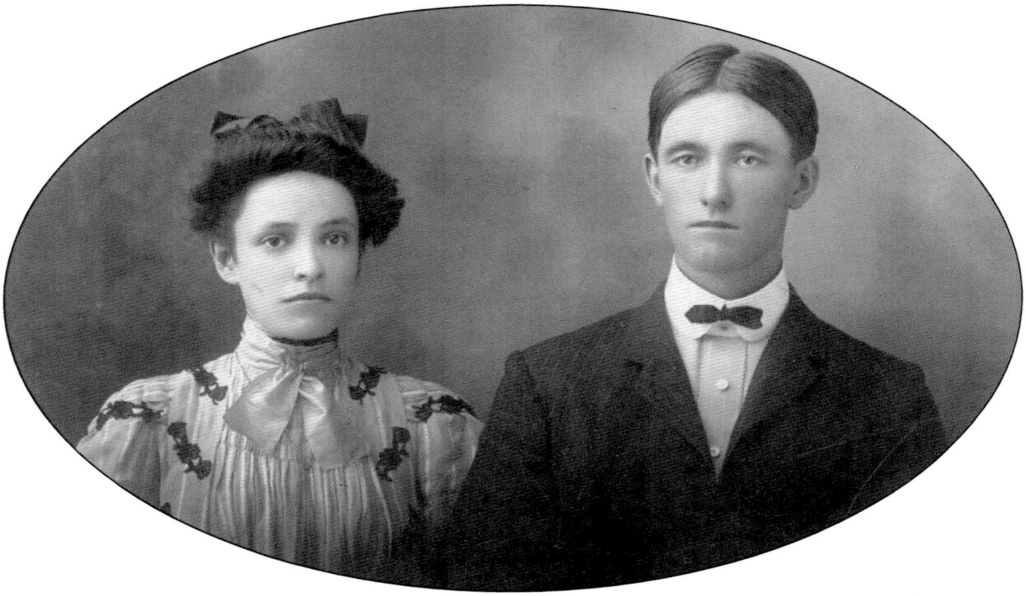

R. B. and Margaret Roberta Harrington were homesteaders north of Forgan and were the parents of Faye Day, Irene Canfield, and Floyd Harrington. Faye lived most of her life near Forgan on the homestead. Floyd served as superintendent of the Forgan schools, was elected to the Oklahoma Legislature in 1936 and 1938, and later worked for the Oklahoma Department of Health. Irene lived her adult life in Colorado. (IHL.)

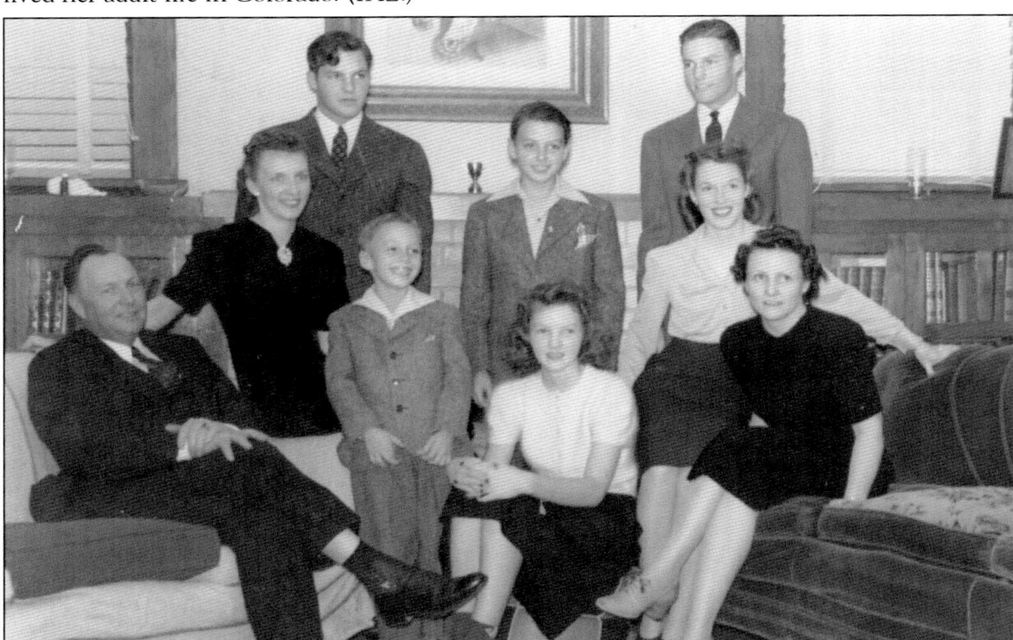

Ross Rizley served the area as a state senator, a three-term U.S. congressman, judge of the U.S. district court for western Oklahoma, and many other offices. Pictured are Ross and Ruby Rizley with their children. From left to right are (first row) Rizley, Quentin, Hortense, and Edith; (second row) Ruby, Max, and LaMoyne; (third row) Robert and Jerry.

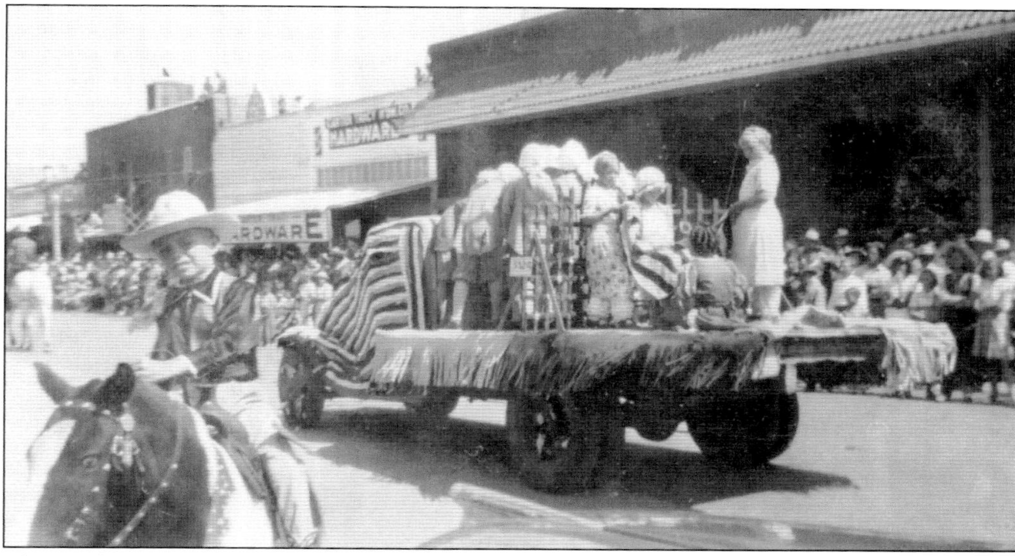

The Anthony School float moved down Douglas Avenue during the Beaver County Fair in 1940. On the float but not identified in the picture are Betty Davis and Lester Janzen, who later married and taught school in Forgan and Garrett. Lester also served as principal at both schools.

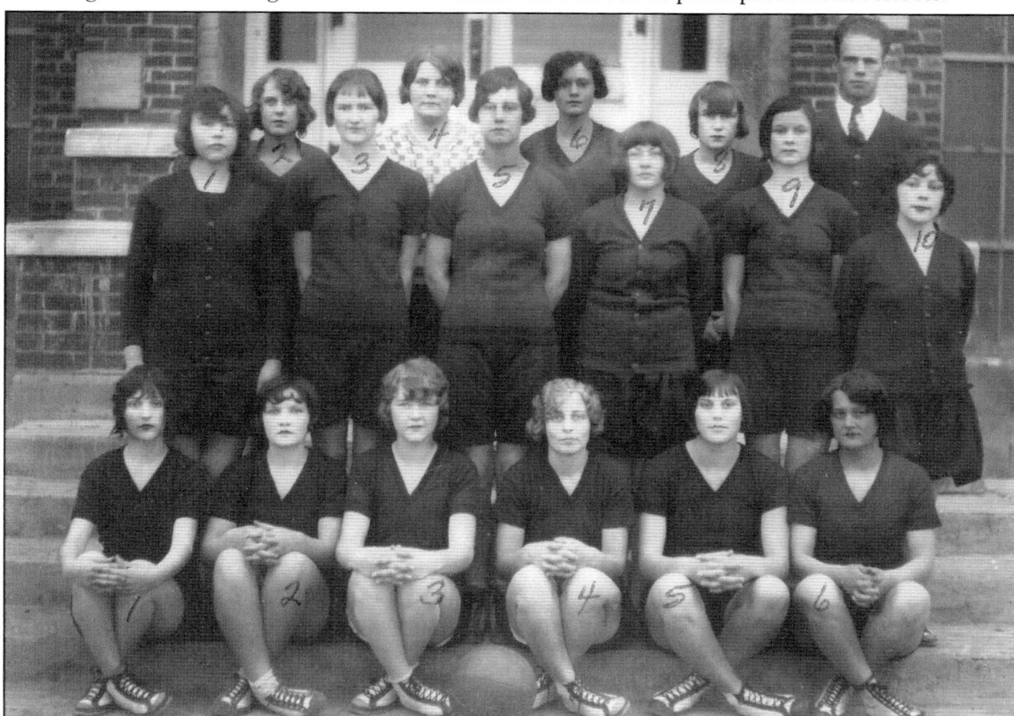

Pictured here is the 1929–1930 Beaver High School basketball team. Picture from left to right are (first row) Nellie Phelps Sharp, Gertrude Cates, Virgie Pierson Altman, Iris Bridgewater Malone, Alyce Stevens Jones, and unidentified; (second row) Delpha Davis, Louella Henson, Maurie Robertson, Evelyn Vandeburgh, Alberta Pruitt Getz, Marie Floyd, Ellen Frazee Gregory, Marcella Crossley Potter, Jewell Hewatt Hodges, and Florence Burditt. The coach was Marshall Ross.

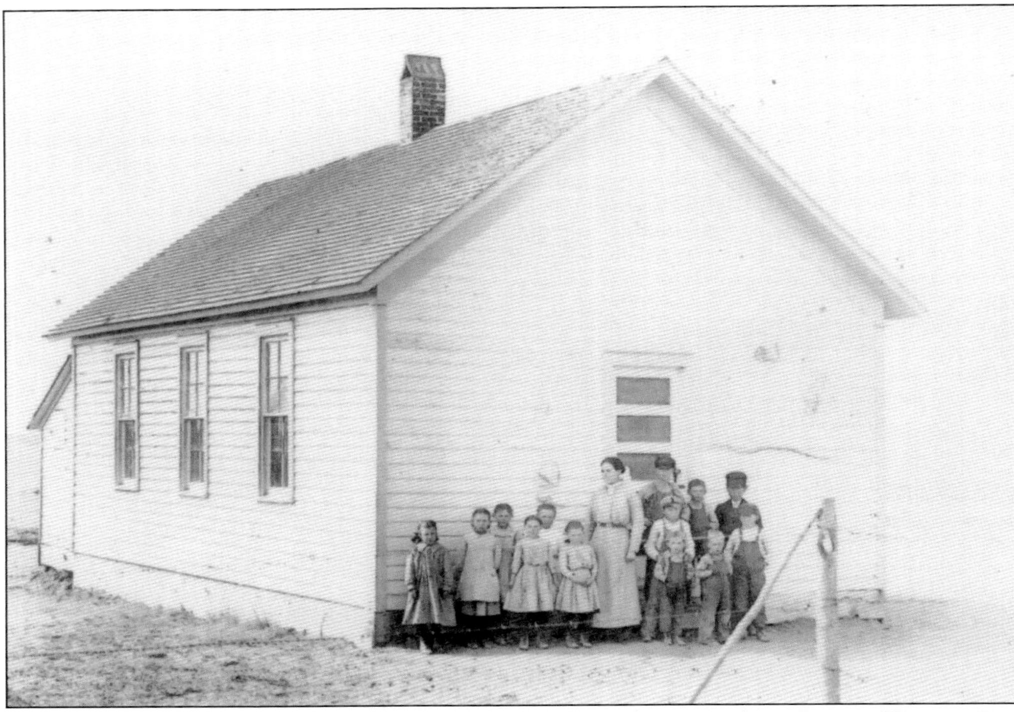

Goetzinger School was located near the John Goetzinger homestead southeast of Beaver City. Ann Evans was the teacher.

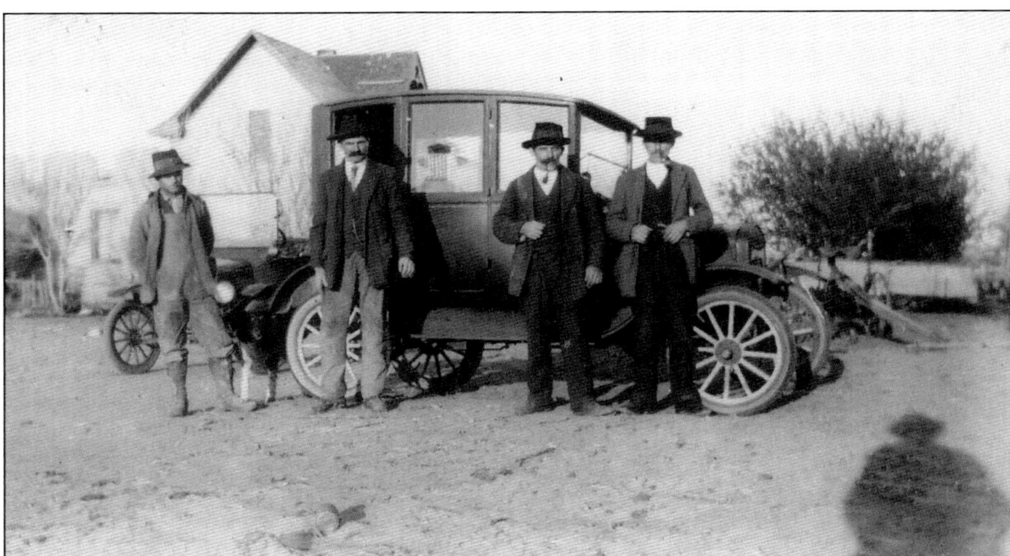

The Matt Posl farmhouse was located near Greenough School. Pictured are, from left to right, Joseph Niebaus, Matt Posl, John Pfeiffer, and Jack Pfeiffer. The Greenough School was established 9 miles west and 3 miles north of the town of Forgan in 1922 upon the promise of a railroad coming through from Forgan to Liberal. Even though the railroad never materialized, the high school remained until 1948 and the elementary school until 1958 when the district was annexed to Turpin and Forgan.

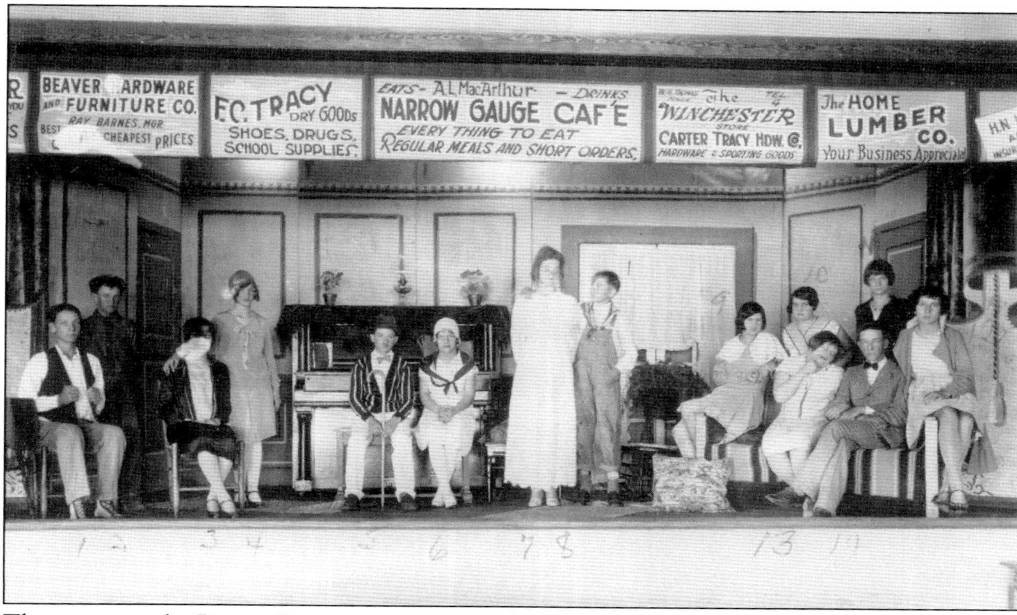

The actors on the Beaver Stage are, as numbered, Leo Bishop, Samuel Wright, Ruby Kuykendall, Edith Lewis, Edwin Lewis, Lucille Couch, Maurie Robinson, Burton Wills, Marie Niles, Hazel Floyd, Eva Hubbard, Marie Sanders, Louise Goetzinger, and Boyd Dinger. This was a community event. (BJ.)

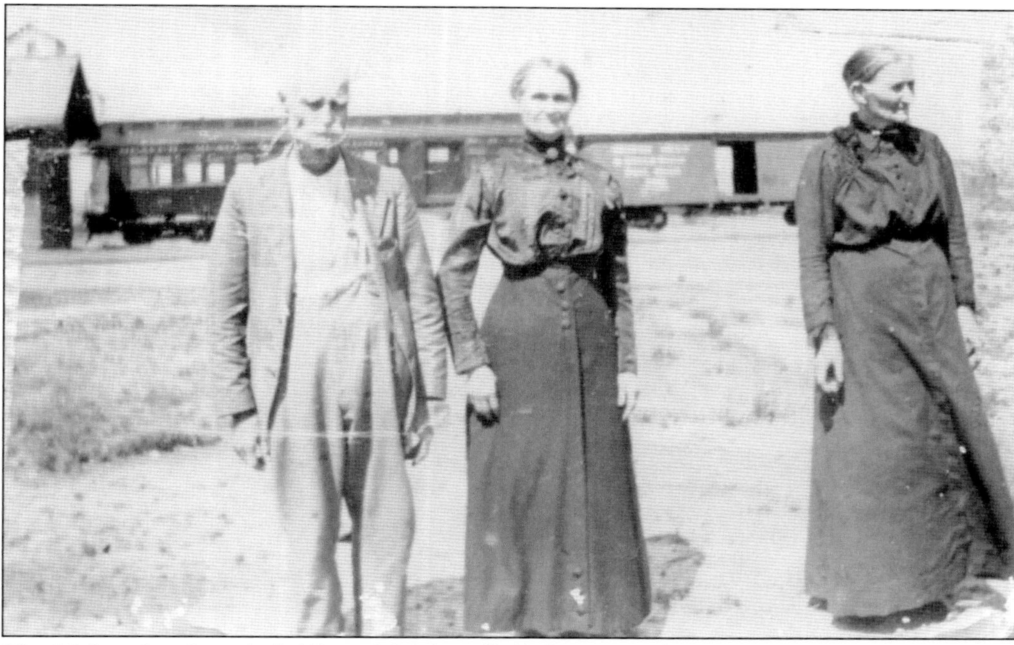

The Mulvey family included Patrick Mulvey (left), born in Ireland in 1833 in County Cork; his wife, Margaret (center); and his daughter, Mary Mulvey Lee (right). Patrick was the grandfather of Willis and Merle Lansden, who grew up in Forgan and later became a newspaper publisher and a lawyer, respectively.

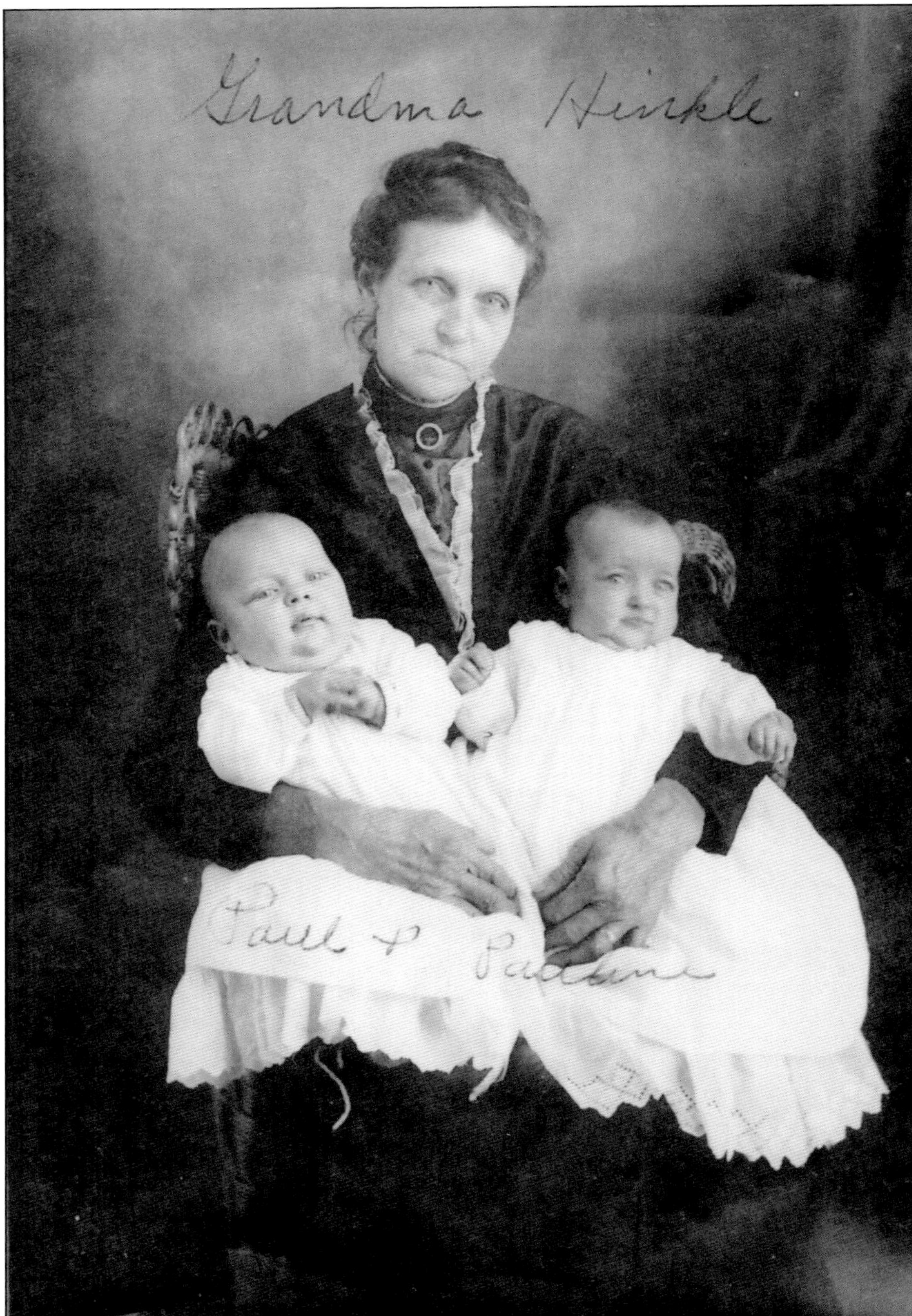

Sarah "Grandma" (Crabtree) Hinkle was photographed here with twins Paul and Pauline (who married Harry Evans). Sarah Hinkle and her husband, John, had raised most of their children when they decided to move from El Dorado, Kansas, to Beaver. One of their sons, Charlie, moved with them. They were lifelong ranchers, and John was also a blacksmith. The children in the picture are the children of Charlie Hinkle. (JO'R.)

Six

The Coming of the Railroads

Farming in Beaver County or the rest of the Oklahoma Panhandle would never have succeeded had it not been for the coming of the railroads. This event changed the kind of people who settled the area. It changed the kinds of crops that could be grown in order to make a living. It provided new jobs for many people. It changed the kinds of businesses that would grow and prosper. It also created six new towns in the county, as well as caused the disappearance of three.

The newly created, or newly moved and re-created, towns were Gate City, Knowles, (formerly Sands City), Mocane, Forgan, Floris, and Turpin. Gate, Sands City, and Floris simply moved their stores and residences to the new rail stations. Mocane, Forgan, and Turpin were established to meet the needs of the railroads by providing water tanks roughly every 10 miles so trains could fill up with steam to run their engines.

Since the early 1960s when railroad companies deemed the railroad no longer profitable for the area, these small rail towns have all but died out. Only Beaver remains of any size and with stores and other services other than gas stations. That is probably because it is the county seat and had established businesses long before the coming of railroads, even though it, too, has lost population over the years. All in all, it was the coming of the railroads that caused new towns to come into being; it was also the railroads that caused them to no longer exist, or if they did, to have only a store or two or a small school.

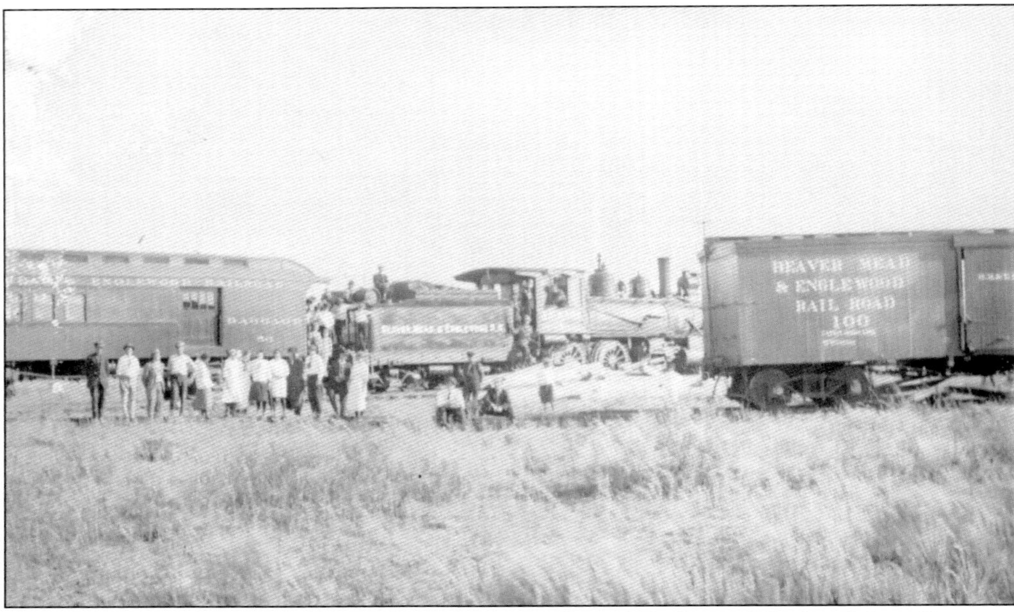

This picture shows the building of the Beaver, Meade and Englewood Railroad from Beaver to Forgan. This spur was not built until 1916 when money was raised by F. C. Tracy and others from Beaver City. It joined the Missouri–Kansas–Texas Railroad at Forgan since that company did not want to build through the sand hills.

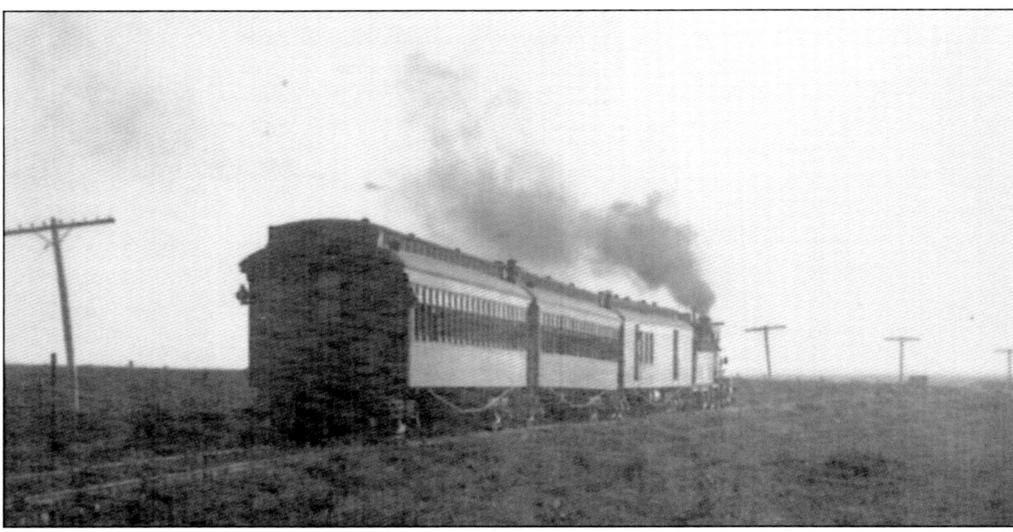

A Beaver, Meade and Englewood Railroad train is caught in a flood at Beaver, which was not an unusual occurrence in early days until upstream flood control contained much of the water that often covered the lower north end of town.

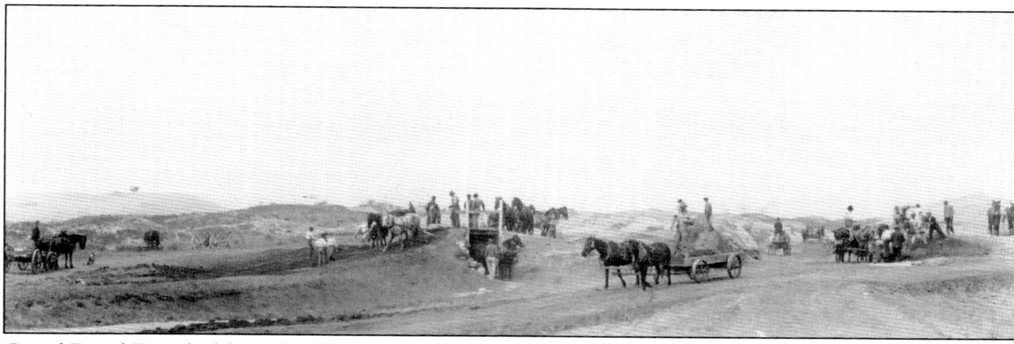

Good Road Day, held south of Forgan, celebrated the coming of the railroad from Woodward to Forgan and then to Beaver City.

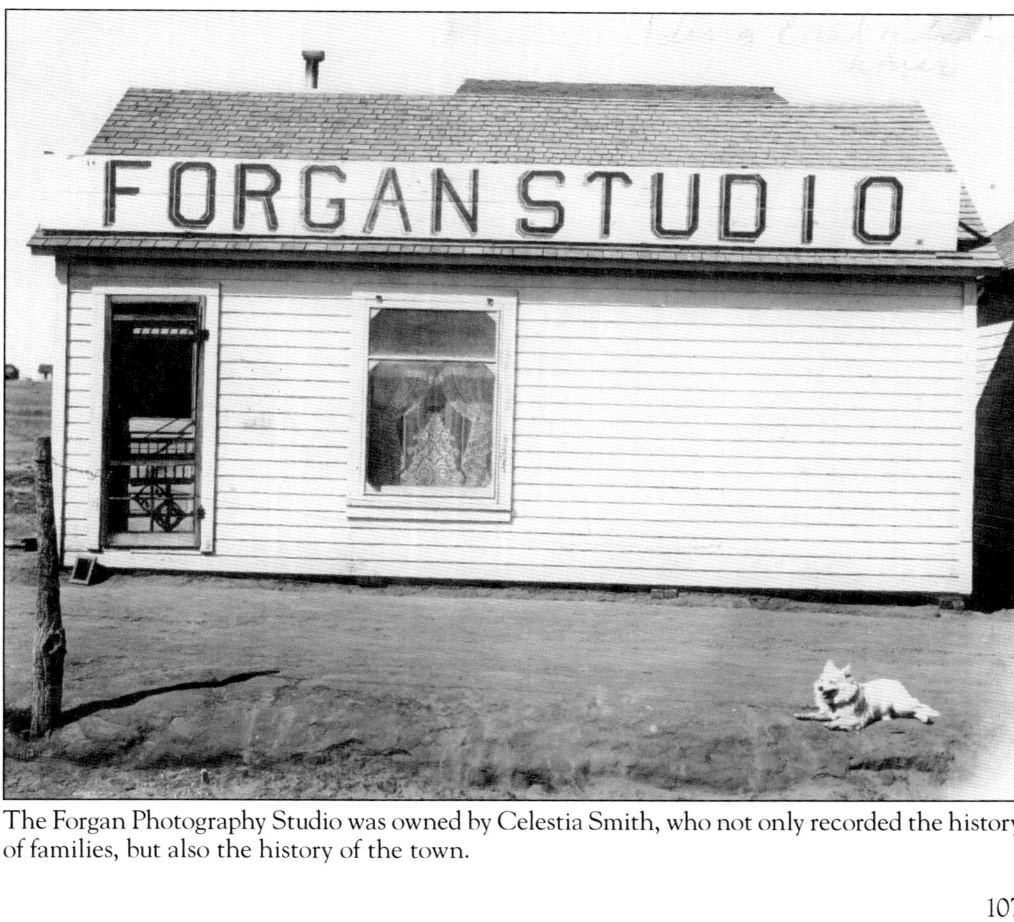

The Forgan Photography Studio was owned by Celestia Smith, who not only recorded the history of families, but also the history of the town.

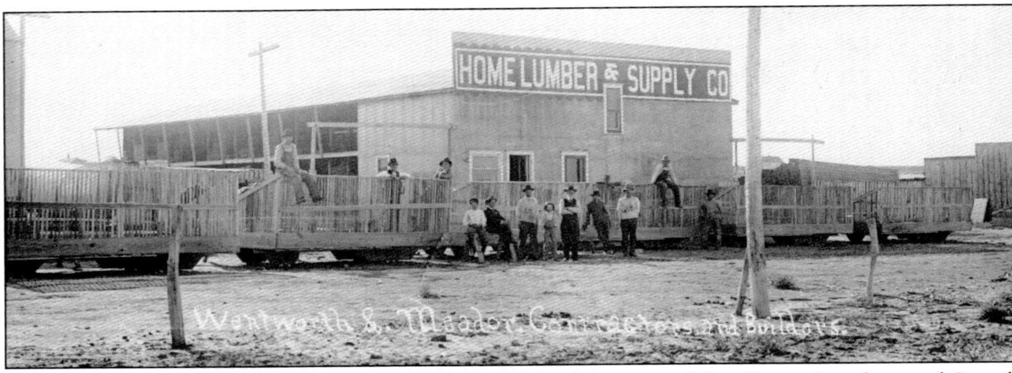

A. W. Wentworth and Walt Meador, contractors and owners of the Home Lumber and Supply Company at Forgan, provided the materials to construct new buildings for surrounding farms and ranches.

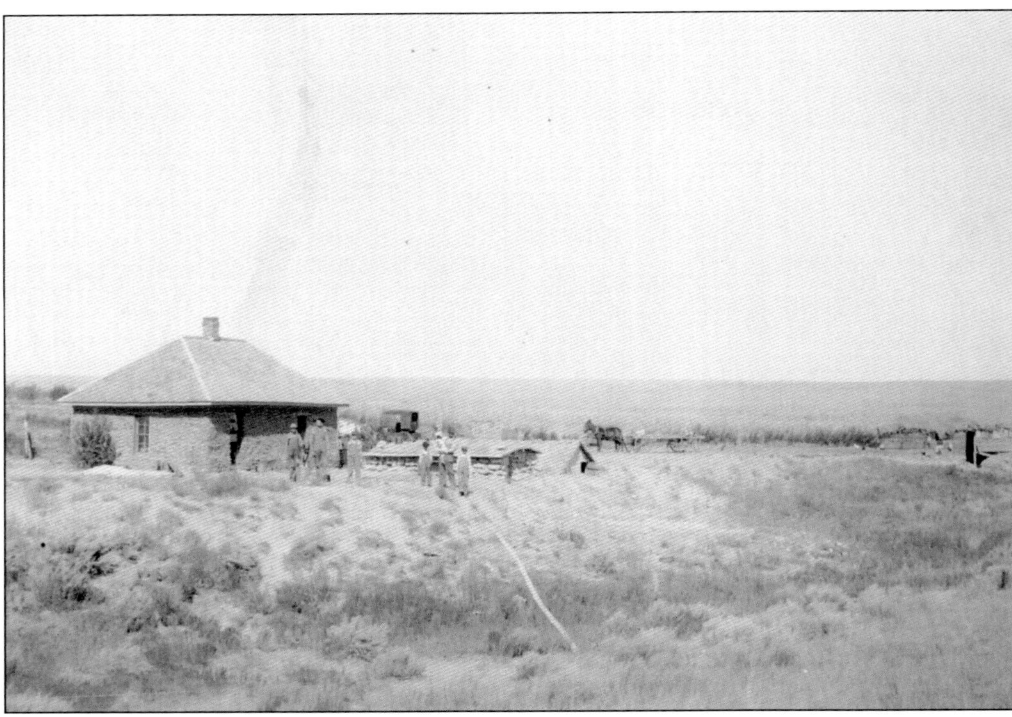

The James and Bertha Lebo homestead, seen here in the early 1900s, was originally located south of the town of Elmwood. The Lebos later moved north of Forgan with the coming of the railroads. One of their sons, Murry, owned a car dealership and garage in Forgan in the 1940s and early 1950s.

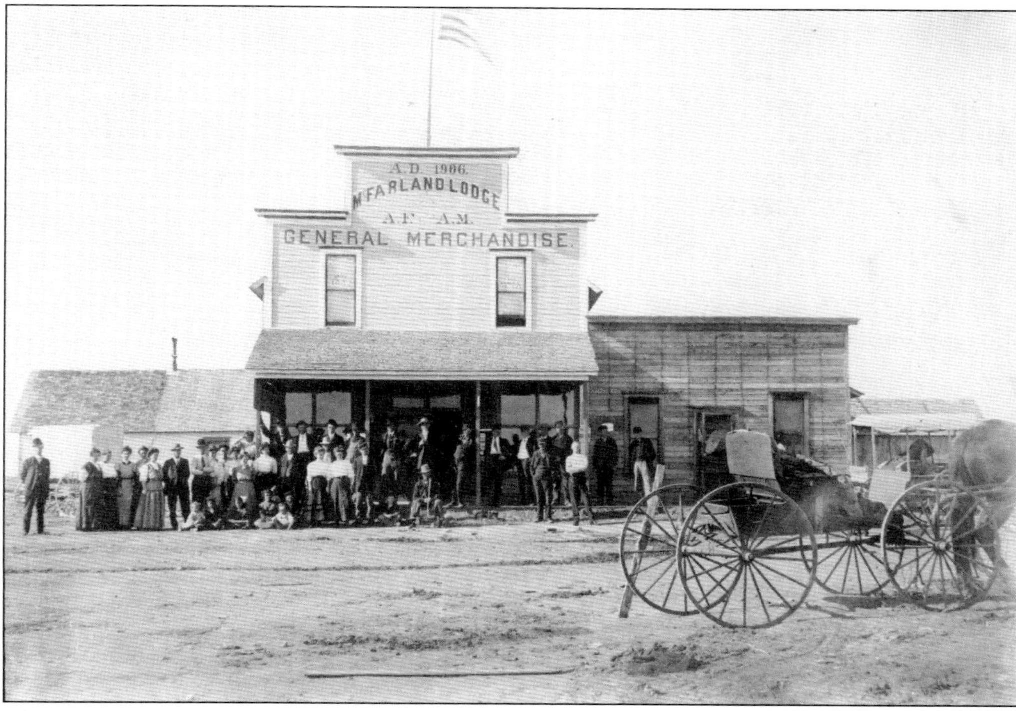

The Floris McFarland Masonic Lodge building housed a grocery store on the ground floor. The original town of Floris was founded in 1903, about 10 miles west of the present town of Forgan on what is today Highway 64. The lodge is seen here in its original location in 1906. In 1924, the town was moved 3 miles south to the new railroad. When the town of Floris disbanded in the 1960s, this building was moved to Forgan where the lower story still stands beside the post office. The original town was named for Floris Derthick, daughter of Byron Derthick, whose other daughter, Hazel, became one of the Munchkins in *The Wizard of Oz*.

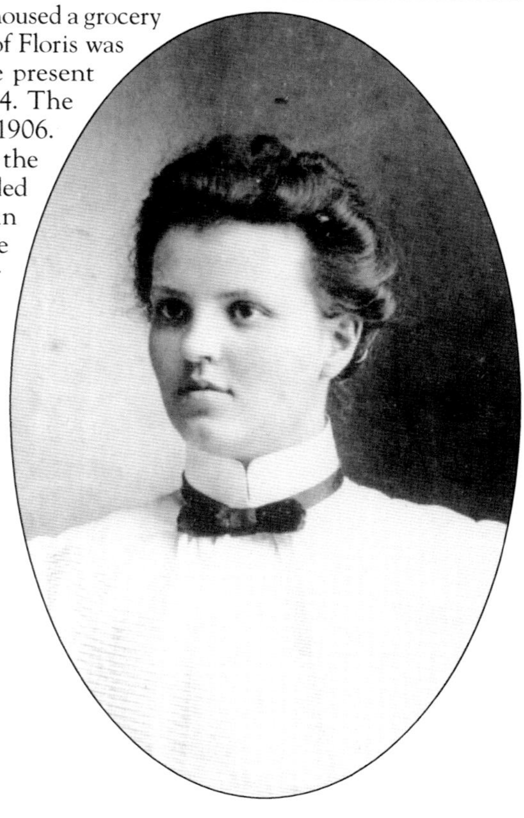

Lorena Stone was the first postmaster of Lorena, Oklahoma. This photograph was taken in 1904, the year the town and post office were founded. The town later moved to form Turpin when the railroad came in 1924.

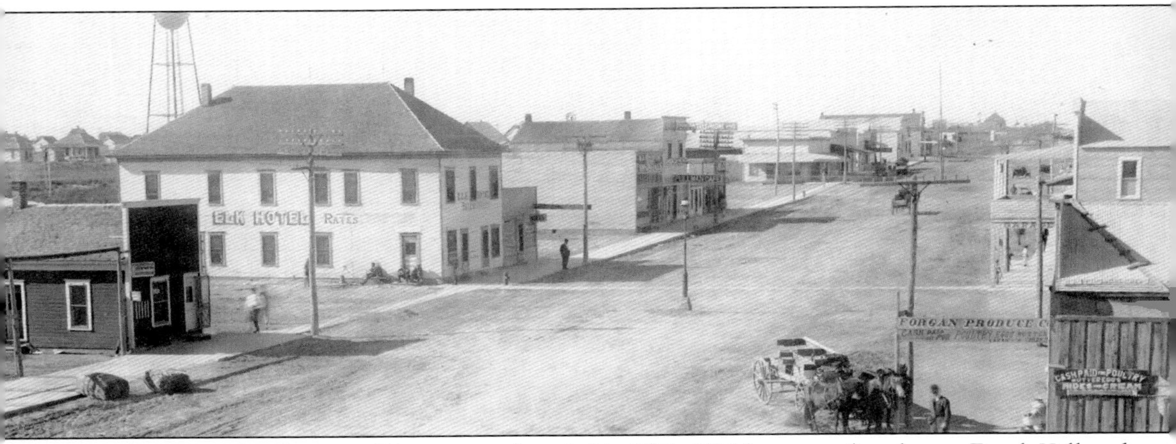

The new railroad town of Forgan was founded in 1911–1912 by two railroad men, Frank Kell and J. N. Cook. On February 12, 1912, W. L. Beardsley, a company representative for the Wichita Falls and Northwestern Railroad, sold the first town lots for Kell and Cook, who had purchased the land from D. B. Hutson, L. L. Long, W. A. Coldwater, David A. Marlow, and W. C. Hodges. By 1921, the town had two banks, two hardware stores, three grocery stores, three drug stores, a theater, and three hotels, with a total of 53 businesses and nearly 1,900 people.

Seven

The Dust Bowl Destroys Farms

The coming of the era known as the Dust Bowl in the Great Plains was the worst climate disaster in recorded history. Those ranchers and homesteaders who had come to No Man's Land, and later to the Seventh County, Oklahoma Territory, with such high hopes for a bright future living off the land were met with conditions they could not control and did not understand. Most had come from the Midwest where they lived with rain, streams, and creeks.

Land speculators enticed these folk to come to the Great Plains area with erroneous advertising stating things such as "the rain will follow the plow" and "free land." To those farmers living in the Midwest—such as Missouri, Illinois, Iowa, eastern Nebraska—it sounded like a real opportunity to get ahead financially. They came with the best intentions of having a better life for their families and themselves. They did not realize that the promised 640 acres or 160 acres was not the mecca it seemed to be. They did not understand conservation practices or how to deal with seven years of drought.

Those who had come to the area between 1903 and 1908 were able to survive because they had "proved up" their land—meaning they had built homes and farmed through the provisions of the Homestead Act—and owned it outright. However, many who came in the years between 1908 and 1929 had borrowed money to purchase their land. They did remarkably well, especially from 1915 to 1929 when crop prices were high, the rains came, and crops were plentiful. They thought it would last forever and that they could pay off the mortgages in the next 10 years or so.

But beginning in 1931, the rains dried up, the land blew away, no crops grew, and wheat—if any could be raised—sold for as little as 29¢ per bushel. This caused many families to lose their farms to the banks. It was a good seven years before the rains came again and the land began to recover. By that time, nearly 20,000 folks had left the Oklahoma Panhandle area and the population of Beaver County had dropped by about 10,000 people. Those who stayed were those who had come to the area at the turn of the century or those who could get jobs with the Works Progress Administration (WPA) or other government programs and survived even though their farms were gone. One can drive through Forgan and Beaver and see the buildings that were built with WPA money or can drive on the paved highways through the county and remember that, prior to WPA projects, these were gravel roads. The WPA did a lot to help the folks who had lost everything to the drought.

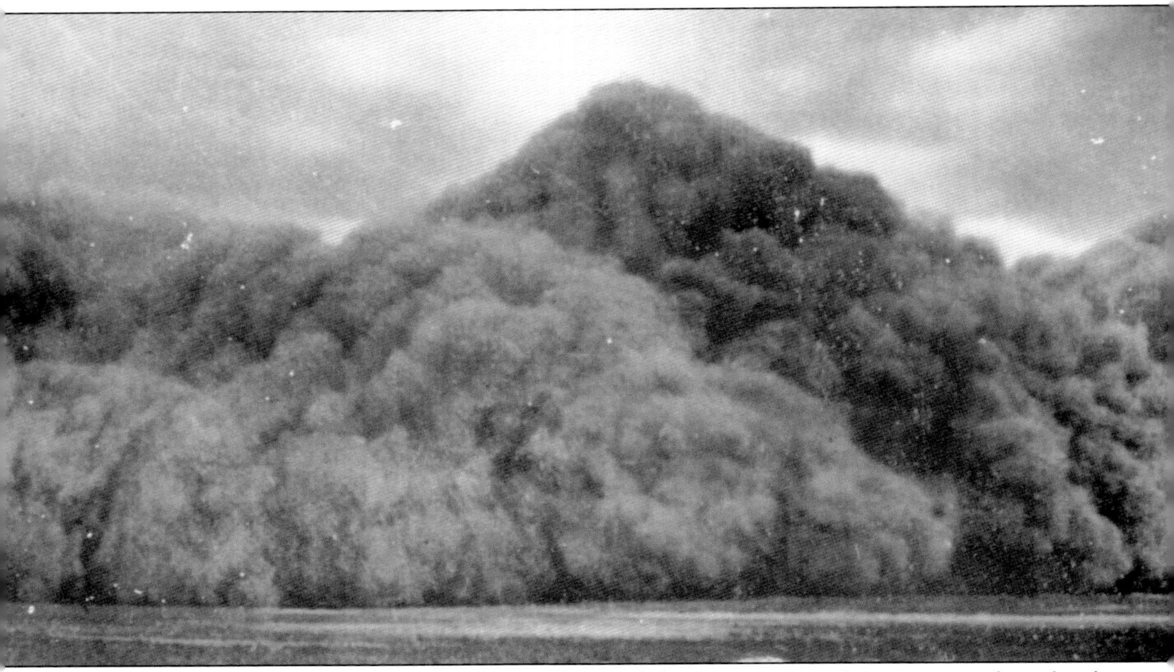

The dust cloud of 1935 was indicative of one of the worst years of a nine-year drought that devastated six states. The Oklahoma Panhandle was one of the areas hardest hit.

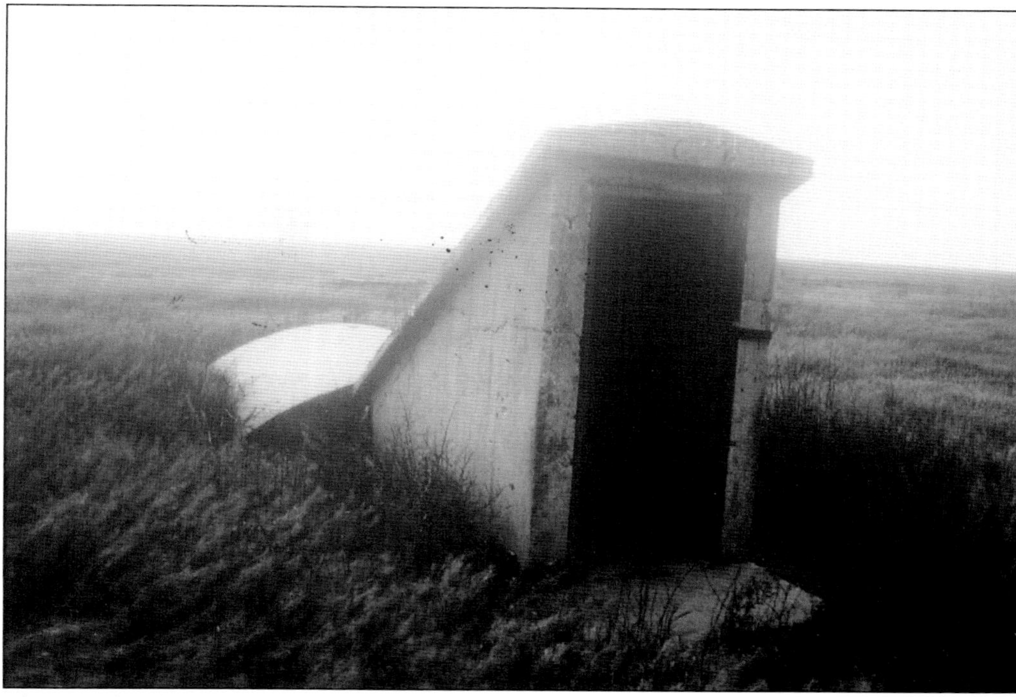

The Tice family storm cellar was often a hiding place when dust threatened to blow the family away, along with crops and fields. (HSK.)

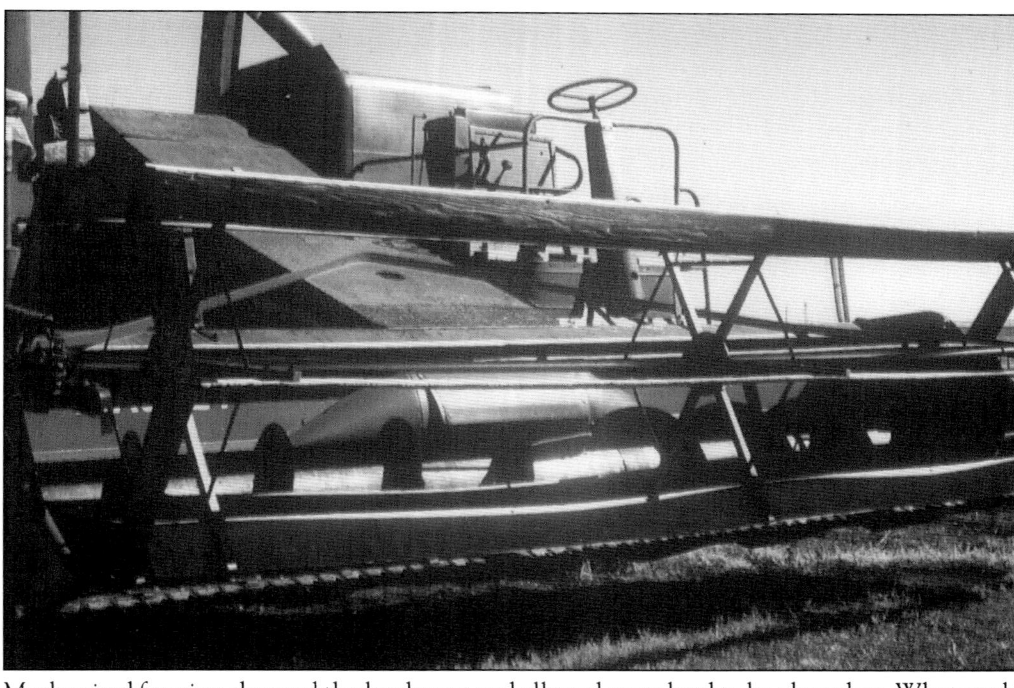

Mechanized farming changed the landscape and allowed more land to be plowed up. What could be harvested in a day with mechanization equaled that of multiple days in earlier times. (HSK.)

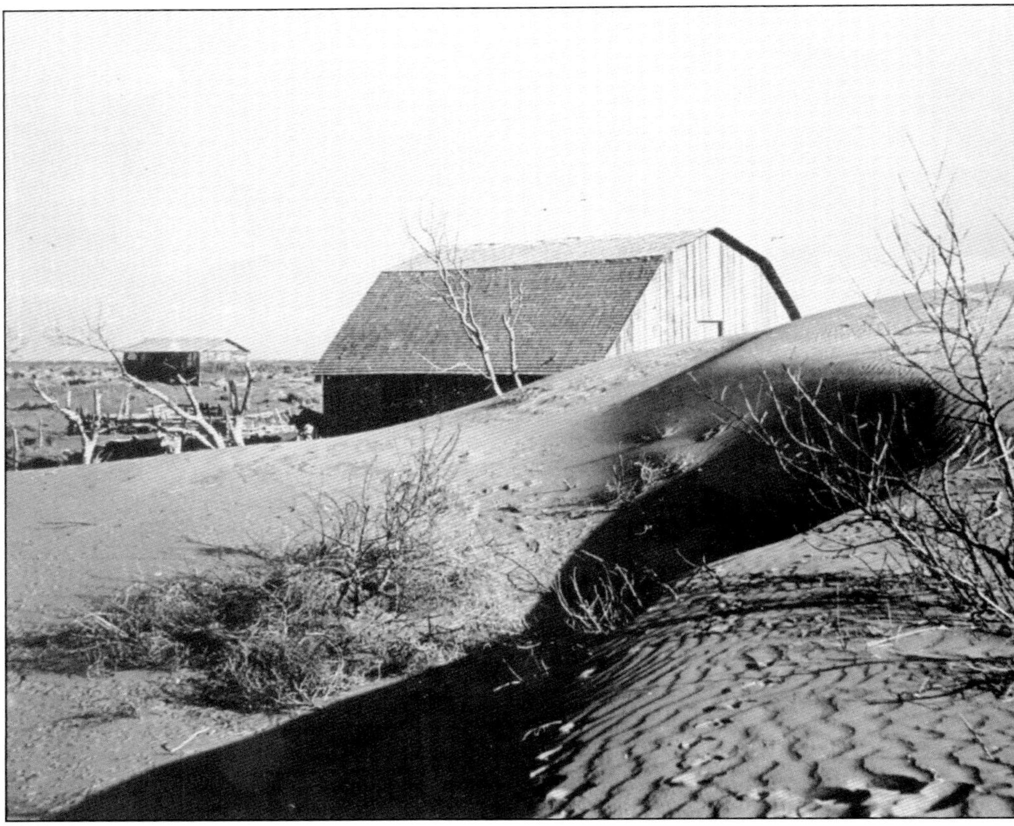

This barn, covered by blow dirt, was an all-too-common site throughout the area affected by the Dust Bowl. The area west of Forgan to the Texas county line was especially hard hit as the land had been plowed up and is very flat.

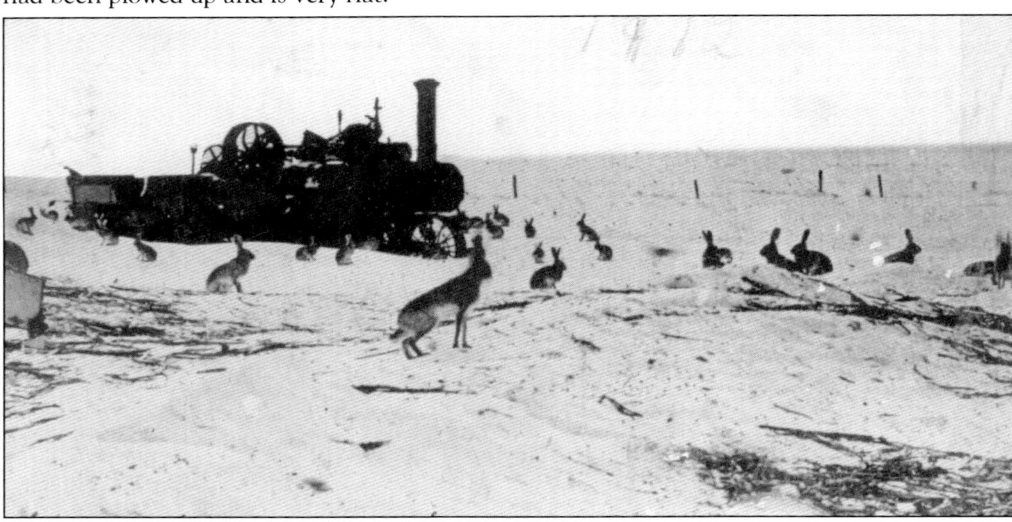

Surrounding an old steam engine in this photograph, jackrabbits were considered a plague upon the land in 1936. The Dust Bowl is when the rabbit drives started. Hides, carcasses, and feet were sold. The meat was purchased by mink farmers and the feet were used for key chains.

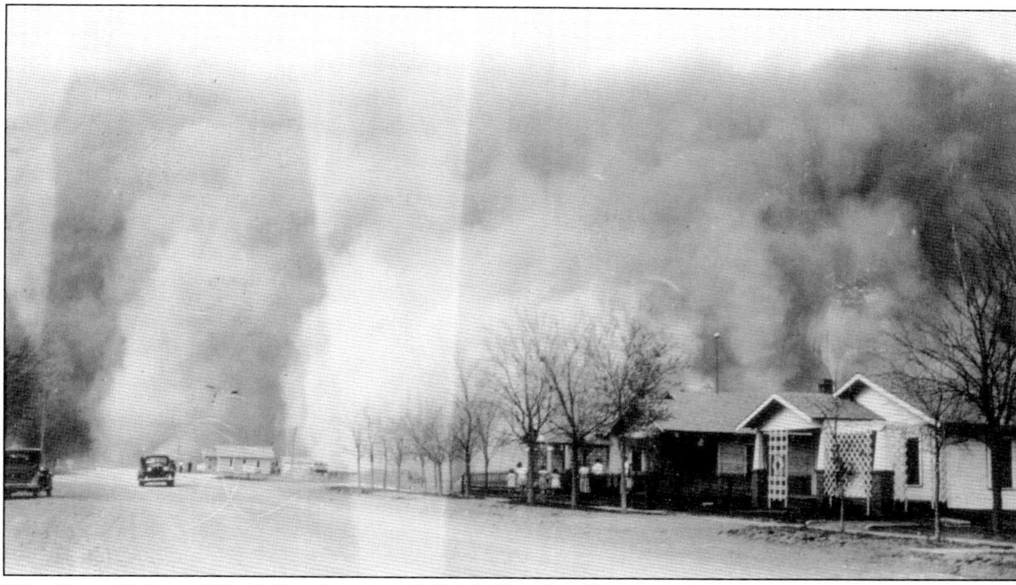

The dirt rolls in on Black Sunday, April 14, 1935, a day that went down in history as the worst day of the "Dirty Thirties." The sky was as black as night all over the area in the Oklahoma Panhandle, as well as in Colorado, Mexico, Kansas, the Texas Panhandle, and southern Nebraska. (IL.)

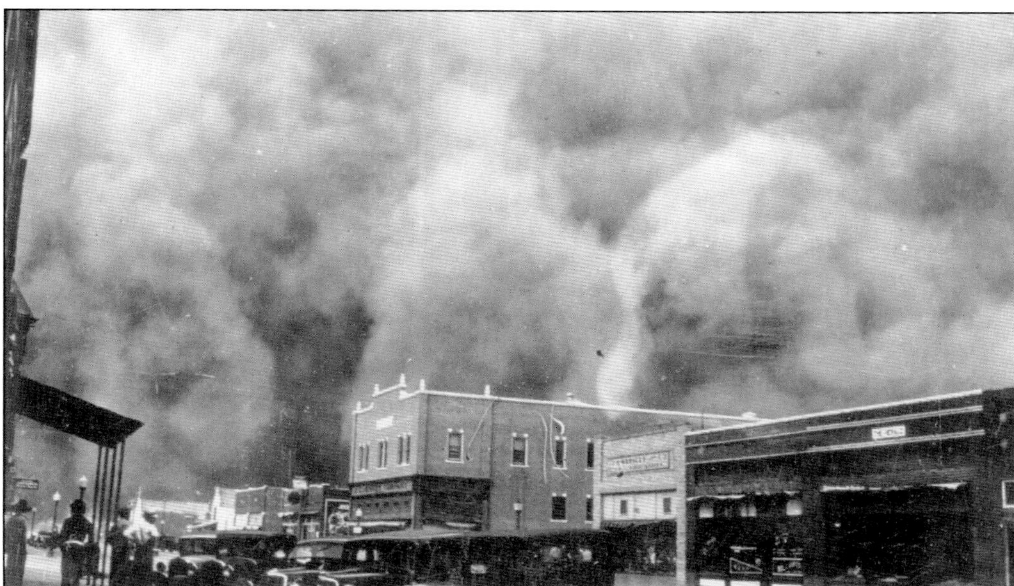

In 2010, area residents remembered Black Sunday with a series of programs sponsored by the Oklahoma Humanities Council, as well as a symposium in Guymon, Oklahoma, during which soil conservationists, climatologists, and historians presented facts about the time. Music composed by Woody Guthrie was performed throughout the day.

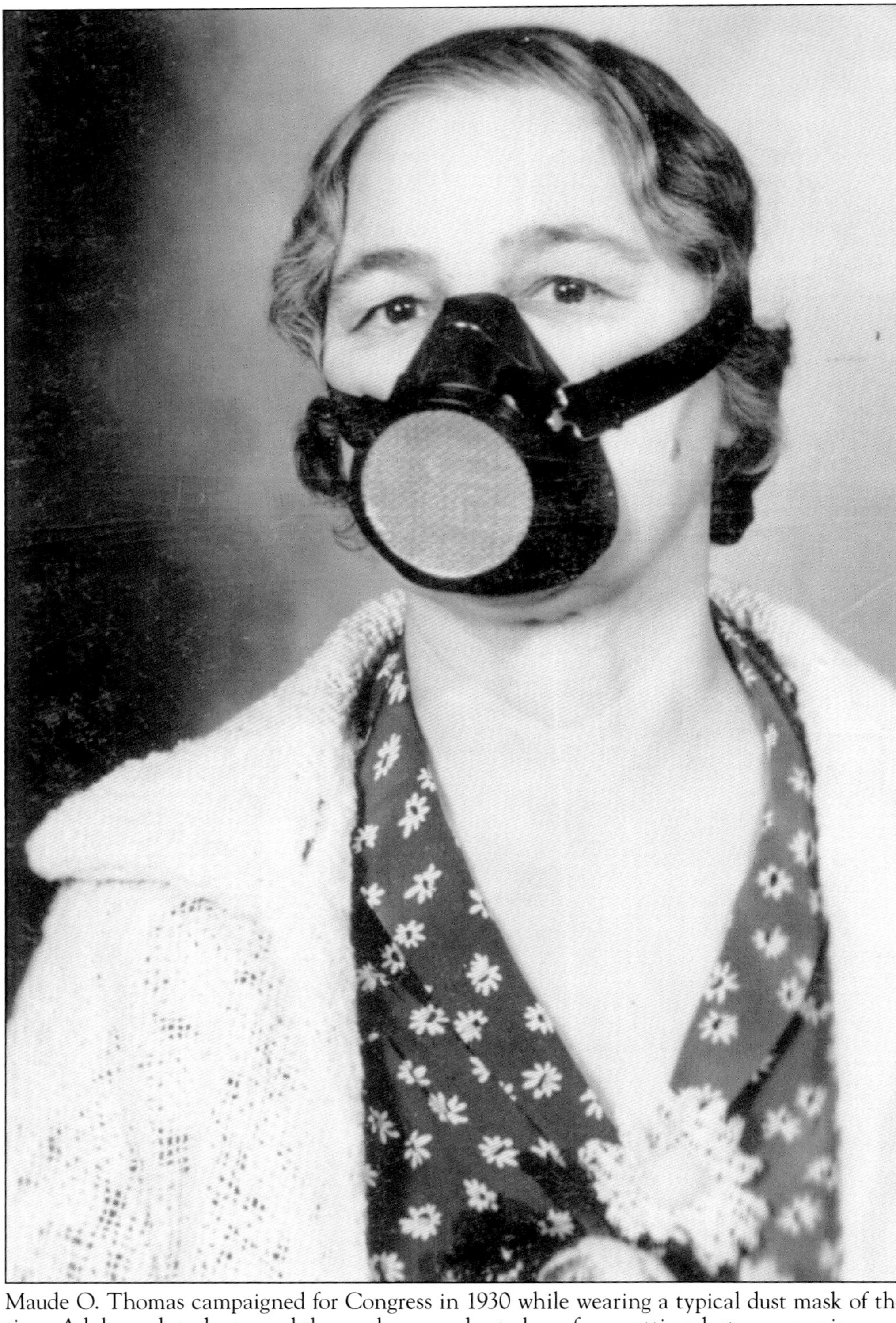

Maude O. Thomas campaigned for Congress in 1930 while wearing a typical dust mask of the time. Adults and students used the masks every day to keep from getting dust pneumonia.

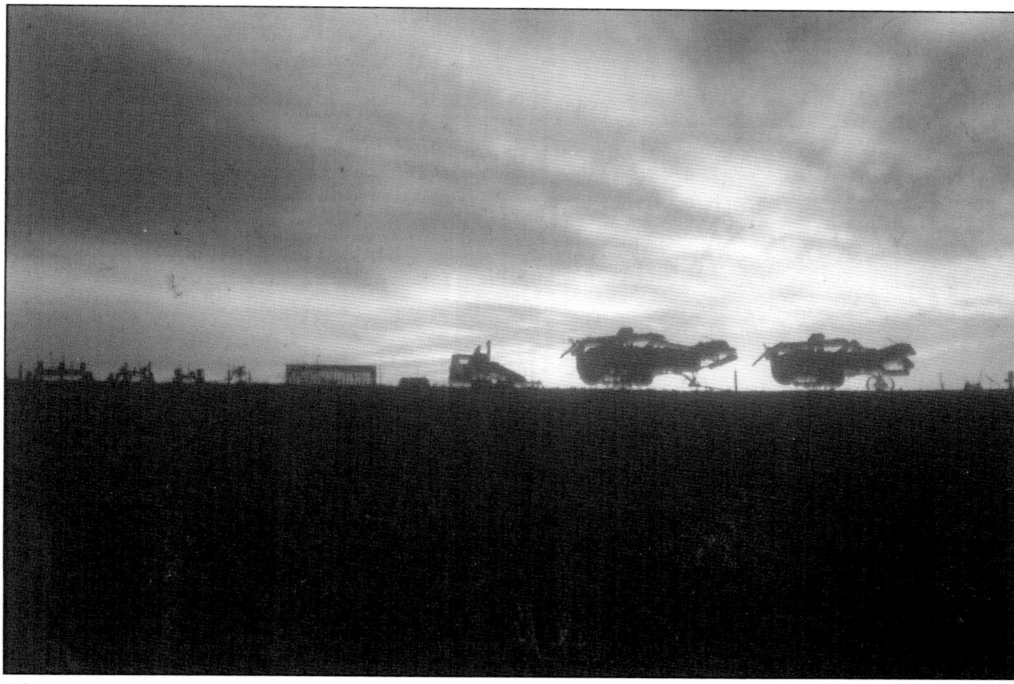

This view is symbolic of the terrible time when farmers lost everything they had worked and hoped for. Many left for California and other states when they lost their farms to bank foreclosure. (HSK.)

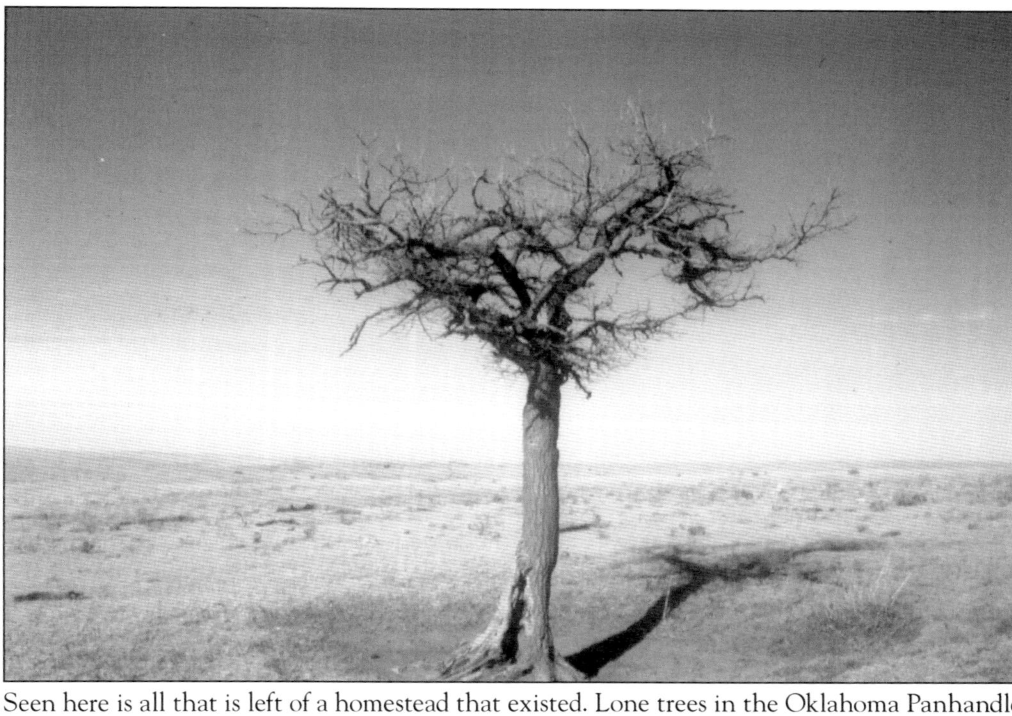

Seen here is all that is left of a homestead that existed. Lone trees in the Oklahoma Panhandle usually mark the site of an abandoned farm or homestead. (HSK.)

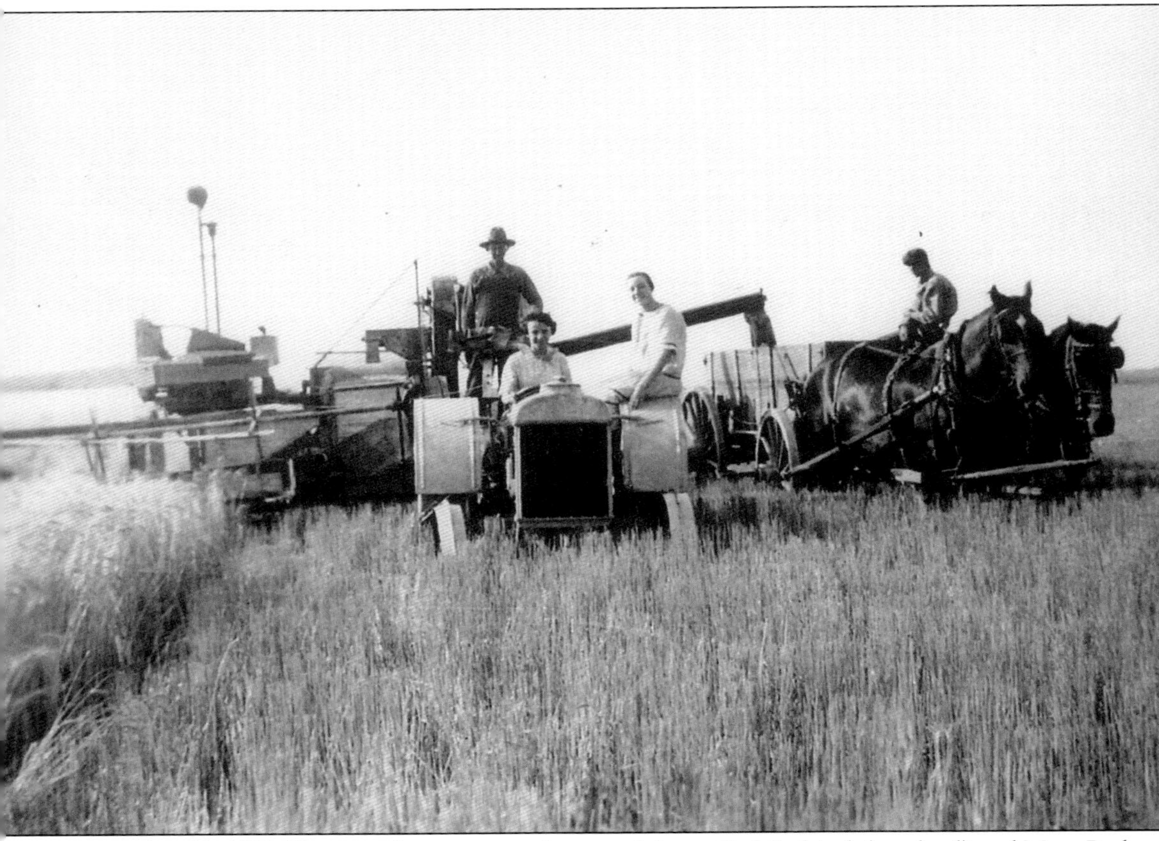

Walter "Jack" Babb is seen here on a combine, and Anna Posl (behind the wheel) and Mary Posl are on the tractor. This photograph was taken in 1939, the first year the rains finally returned and times began to get better.

Eight

Oil and Gas Discovery Changes the Area

Beaver County sits approximately in the middle of the area now known as the Hugoton Natural Gas Basin and has saved many farmers in the area. It was men such as Arthur B. "A. B." Card who were known for their vision and belief that the terrain in Beaver County had the right formations to produce oil and gas. Beaver County had the first well drilled in the Oklahoma Panhandle due to Card's efforts. The well was drilled in September 1935 on land owned by Homer Davis.

With the oil came the automobile and the tractor. These presented many new jobs with motor companies, filling stations, tire repair shops, and mechanics of all kinds who opened up stores and shops in Beaver County.

Colorado Interstate Gas Company (CIG) was organized in 1927 to move gas from the panhandles to Denver, Colorado. CIG engineering developed an automatic pigging system for handling condensation in the pipelines.

The Mocane-Laverne Field in the Oklahoma Panhandle was the site for the development of a solution to the condensation problem. The pigging system is a method of moving liquids by using gas pressure to push a ball or sphere through the pipe, which in turn pushes the liquids ahead of the ball. This system is now in use throughout the natural gas industry.

El Paso Natural Gas Company was another gas business located in Beaver County. Much of its product was licensed to Northern Natural Gas Company. Many of these companies now operate with four divisions: pipeline, petroleum, manufacturing, and chemicals. The Natural Gas Pipeline Company of America also operates in Beaver County. More companies have recently come into the county with the new concept of horizontal drilling for gas and oil.

As one farmer said, "The more gas and oil wells you have on your land, the better farmer you are!"

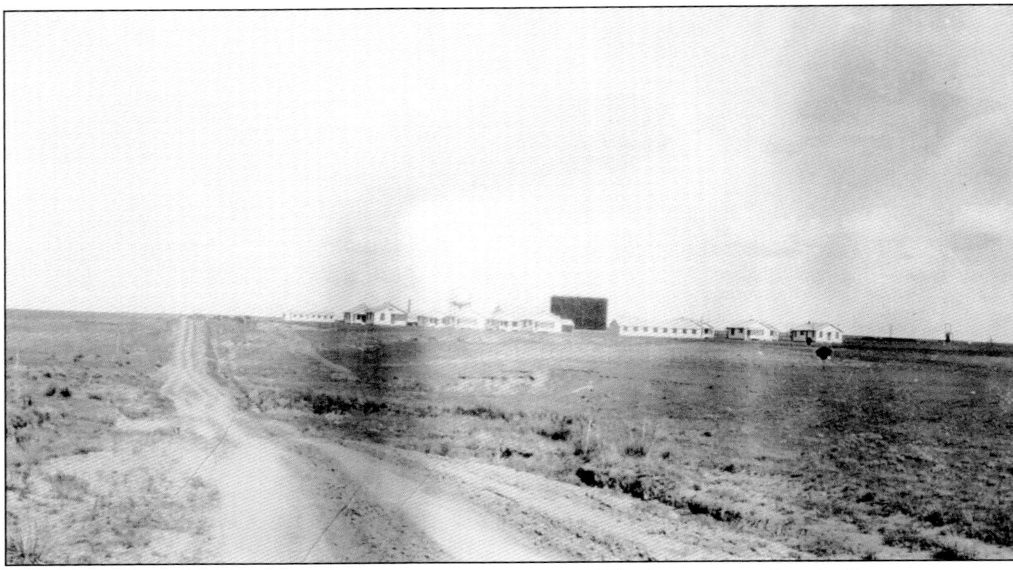

The booster station in Gray, Oklahoma, pictured here on May 23, 1931, was a significant addition to the oil and gas industry in Beaver County. Although ownership of it has changed hands several times, and included Northern Natural Gas Company and Enron, it is still in operation.

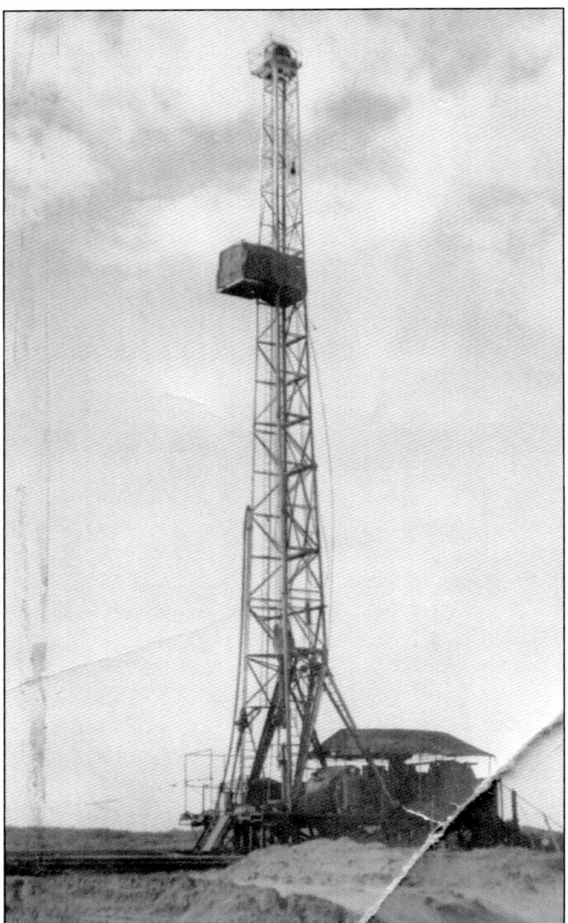

The Flynn Oil Company No. 1 was one of the first drilling rigs in the county.

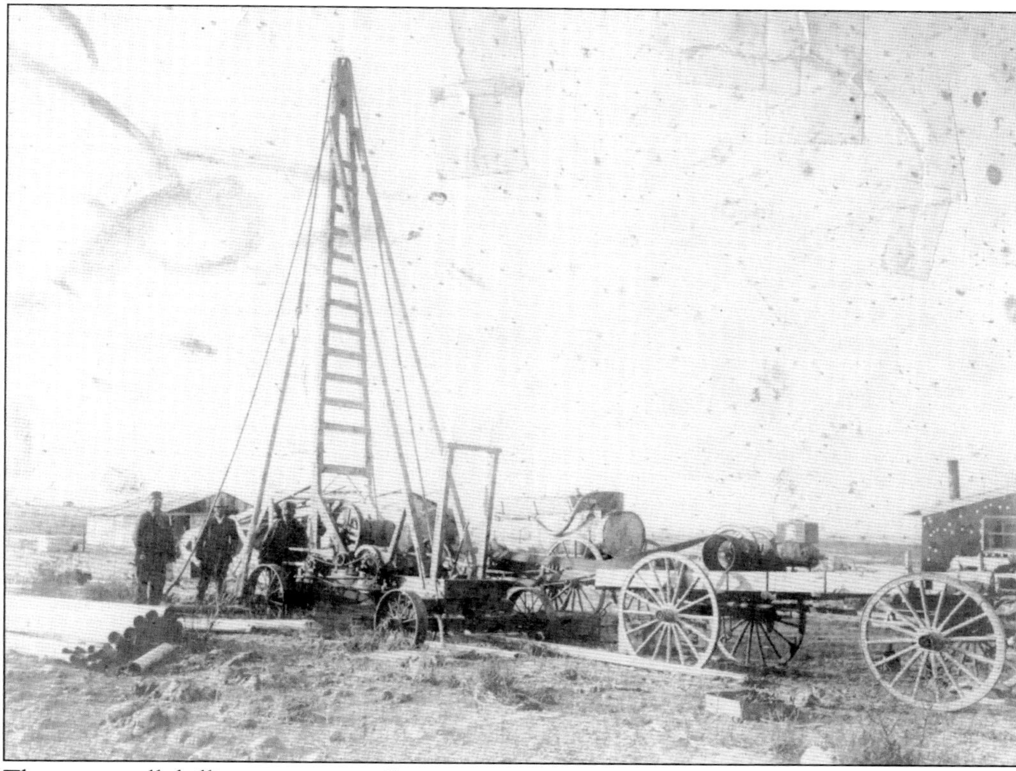

The water well drilling rig was equally as valuable as oil rigs since water was so scarce that people had to depend on deep water wells to survive. This one was owned by the Kile family.

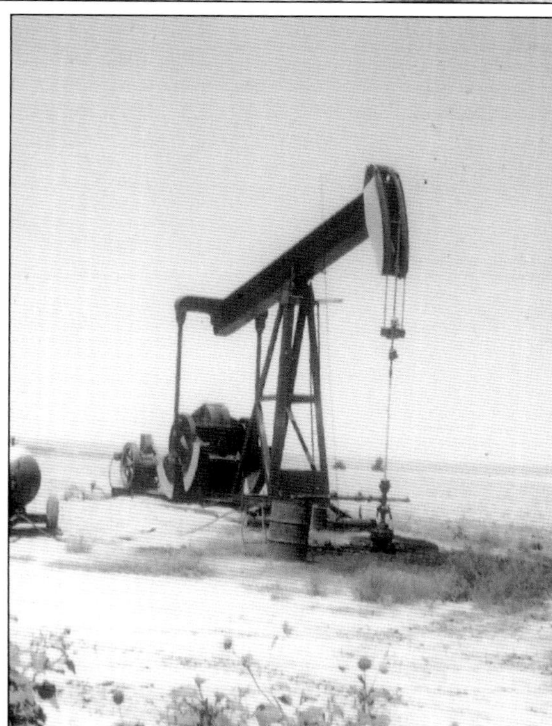

Pumpjacks on oil wells are used to lift the oil to the surface. Oil and natural gas have been lifesavers to Beaver County's economy. (BL.)

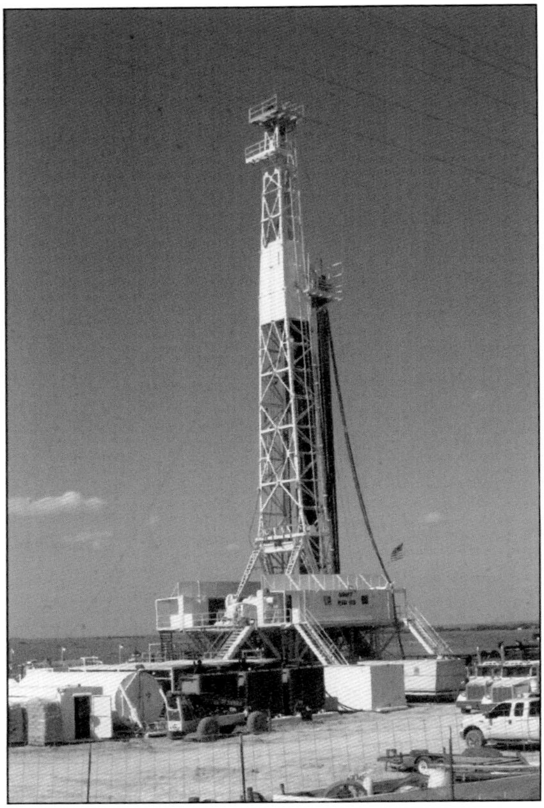

This horizontal drilling rig south of Beaver is an example of a new technique for extracting oil from deep formations or out of wells that are low-producing and have been in existence for several years. (JWL.)

The Taylor filling station, with attendant A. N. Howe Jr., is an example of how customers were treated at gasoline stations prior to the self-service—sometimes called "no service"—gas stations of today. (HSK.)

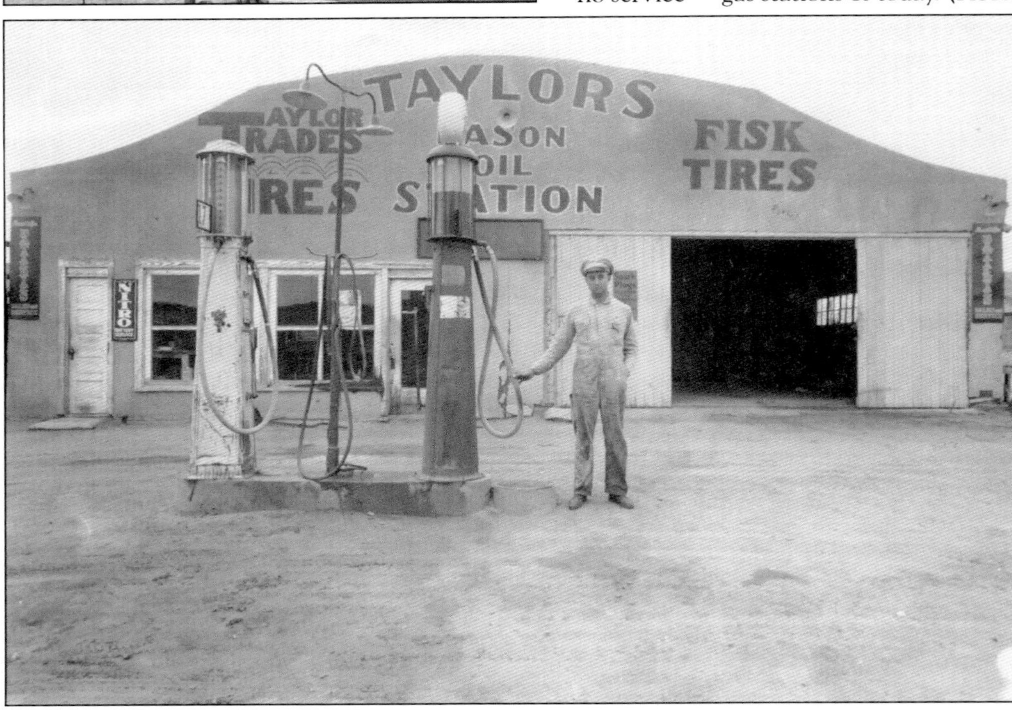

Nine

Present-day Beaver County

Beaver County has moved from early day pioneers living in dugouts, half-dugouts, and "soddies" to residences designed by a prodigy of Frank Lloyd Wright, architect Bruce Goff.

Beaver County has gone from wagon and cattle trails such as the Jones and Plummer Trail to two-plus highways with passing lanes and wide shoulders. The county has gone from no gas or oil wells to almost a gas or oil well on each quarter section of land and from running water found only in small creeks or carried from windmills by hand to solar water systems, large electric wind farms, and electricity in all homes. Technological advances in Beaver County can also be seen in that using mule-powered plows for farming has been replaced with GPS-controlled tractors and combines. Life has gone to computerized everything: cars, trucks, combines, and cell phones. Fuel for the house has become natural gas and electricity instead of cow chips. These days, the only cow chips used are for the famous World Championship Cow Chip Throw contest held each April in Beaver.

Beaver County still has working cowboys who help with the cattle and ride horses. But more often than not, ranchers now load their four-wheelers into pickups and drive to pasture to check on the herds.

The cowboy is portrayed on the television screen, in modern pictures, and in today's writing as a symbol of adventure with natural great courage and living under the law of the six-shooter. However, for those who knew him, the cowboy was an intimate father, uncle, or friend. The real working cowboy was a much more understandable and likeable person than the reflections of him depicted on television, movie screens, and in fictional books.

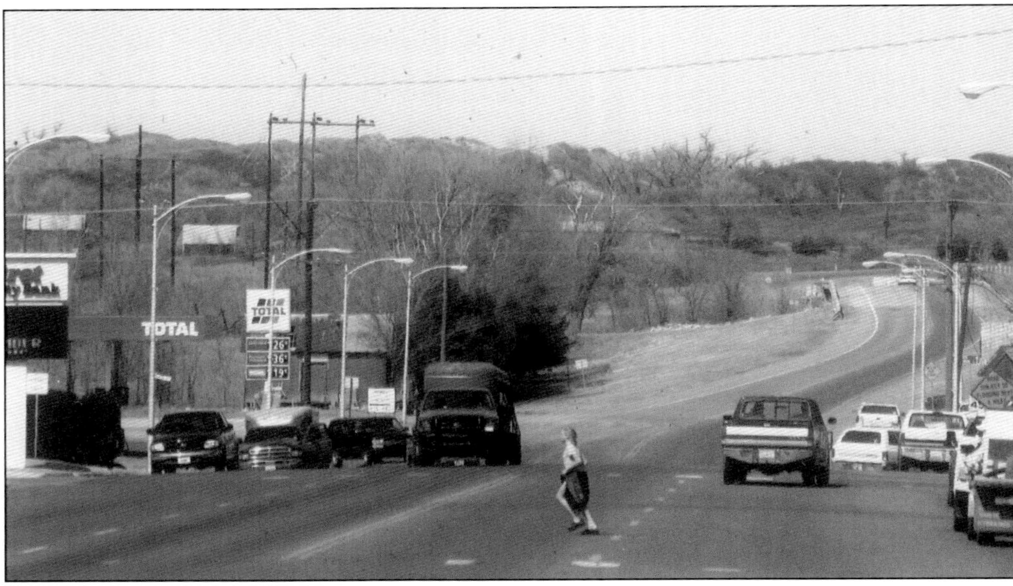

Modern times in Beaver City can be seen in this scene on the north edge of town, which is usually a bustling, busy place until night comes and businesses close and streets are empty. Shoppers do not come to town to visit each other, to sell cream and eggs, or to buy groceries on Saturday anymore. Saturday is often the least busy day in Beaver City except for the World Championship Cow Chip Throw contest in April or the county fair in September. (BL.)

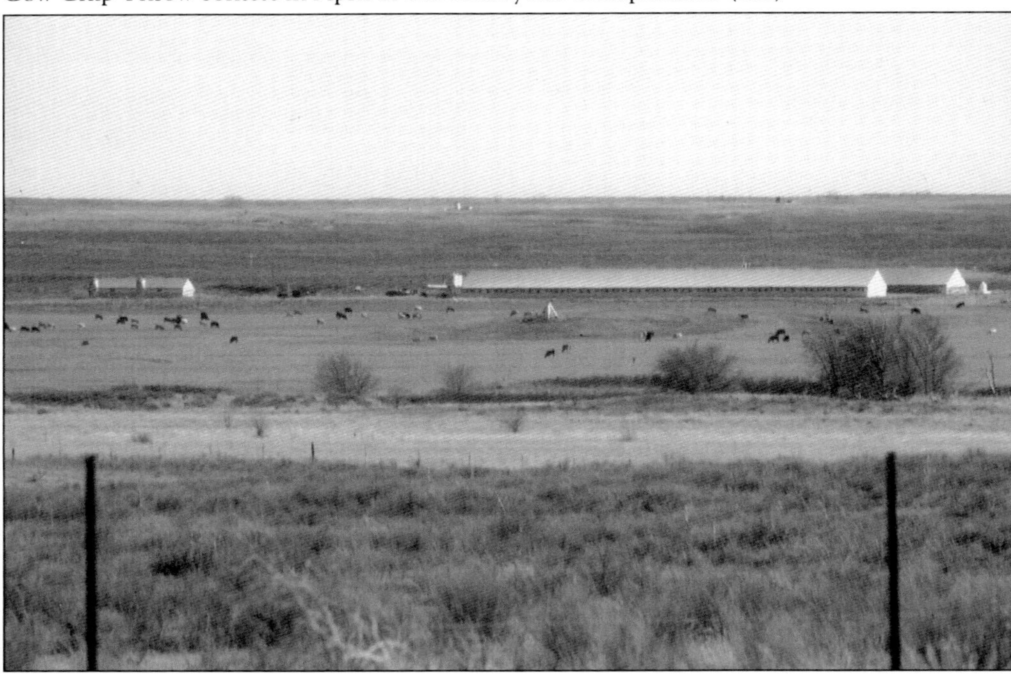

In 1995, Seaboard Farms and other companies proposed erecting hog farms north and west of Forgan, resulting in a near civil war. There was much vocal opposition. However, in the 15 years since the hog farms were built, they have been a boon to the economy and provided many jobs that were not available before. (BL.)

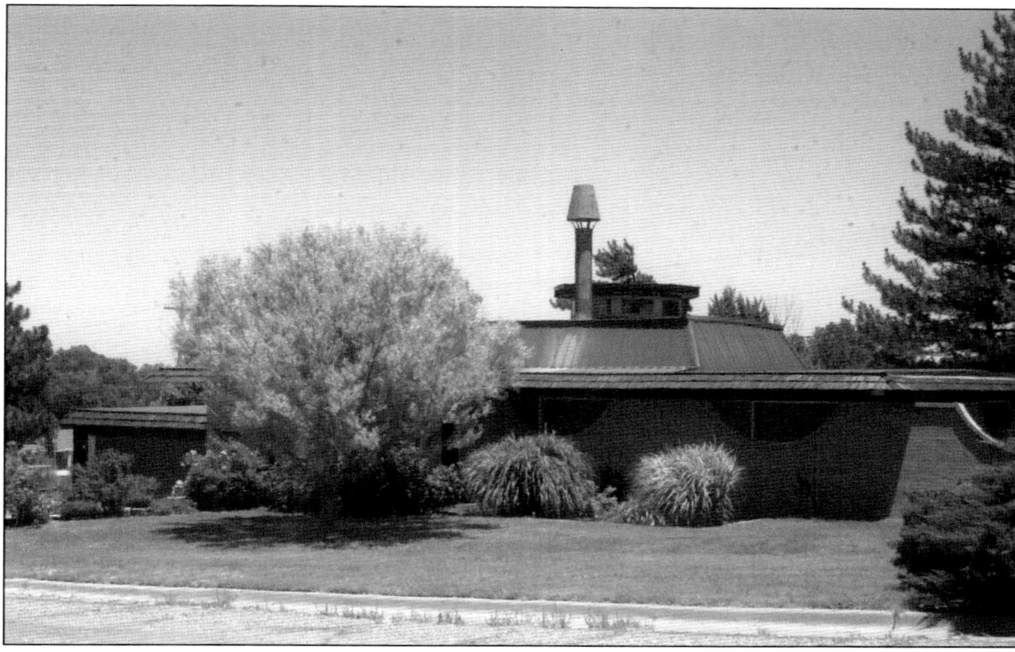

This house, designed by Bruce Goff—who was a pupil of Frank Lloyd Wright in 1963–1964—was originally owned by Celestine Barby and is an example of the popularity of Wright's influence on architecture all over the country. (JWL.)

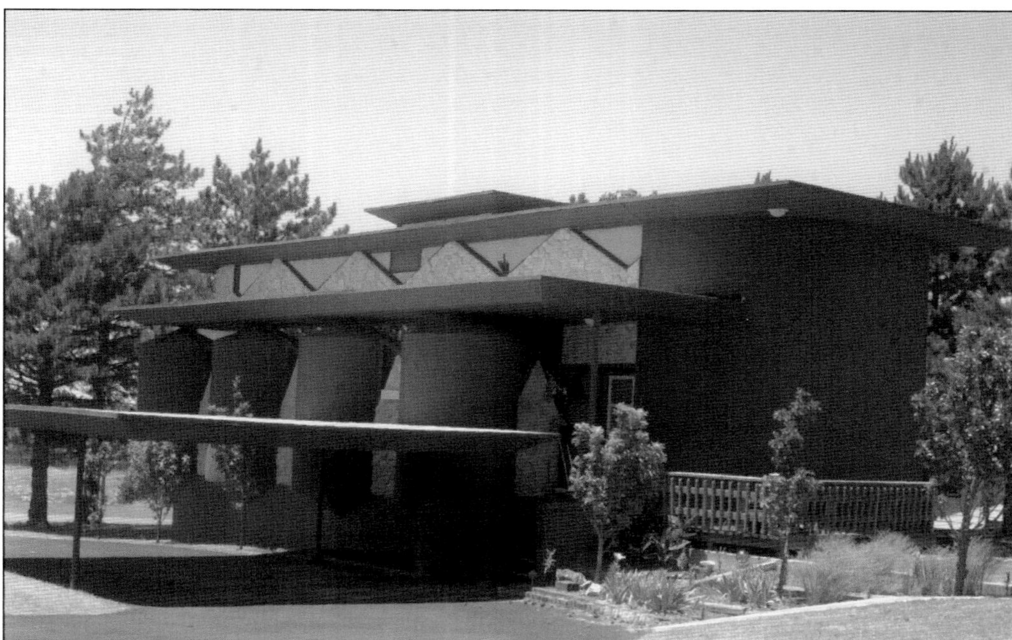

Another house that was designed by Bruce Goff was originally owned by Bill and Dottie Dace. Both this home and the Barby house are located in the northwest part of Beaver. (JWL.)

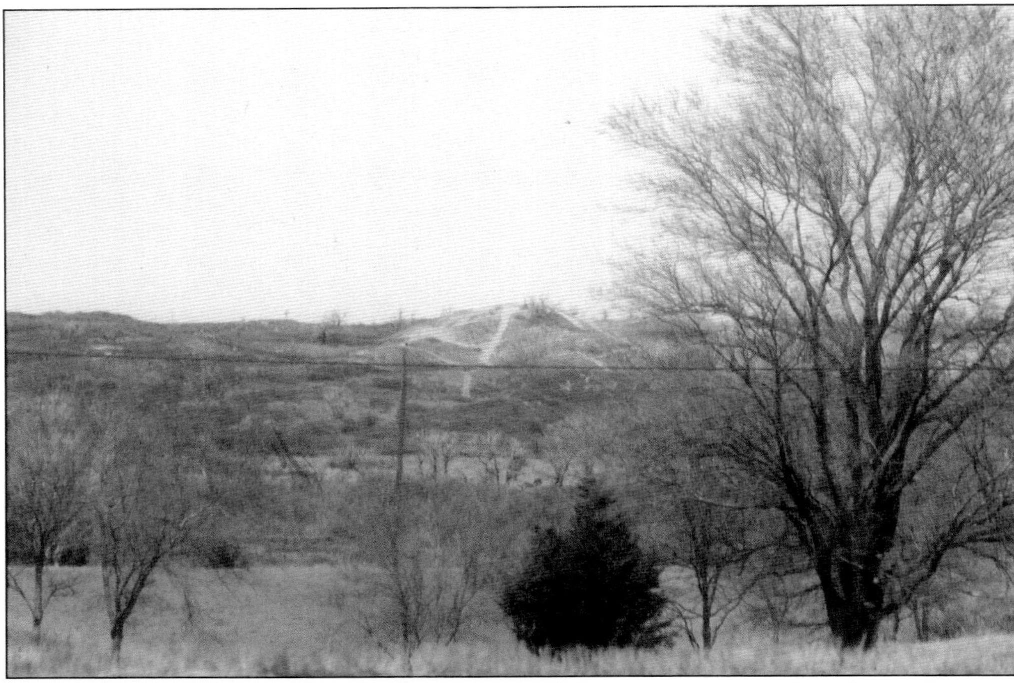

ATV tracks in Sand Dunes State Park denote one of the main attractions for riders and campers on holidays and weekends. (BL.)

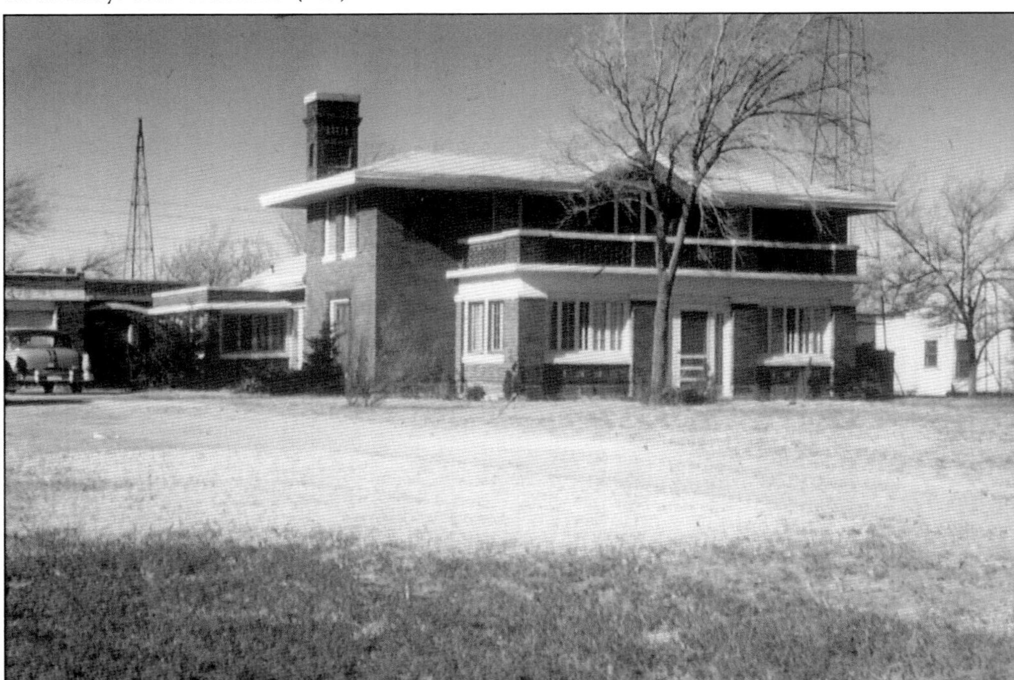

The S. S. Strong house is now owned by Joan and Harold Kachel. Strong was one of the pioneer builders and community leaders. (HSK.)

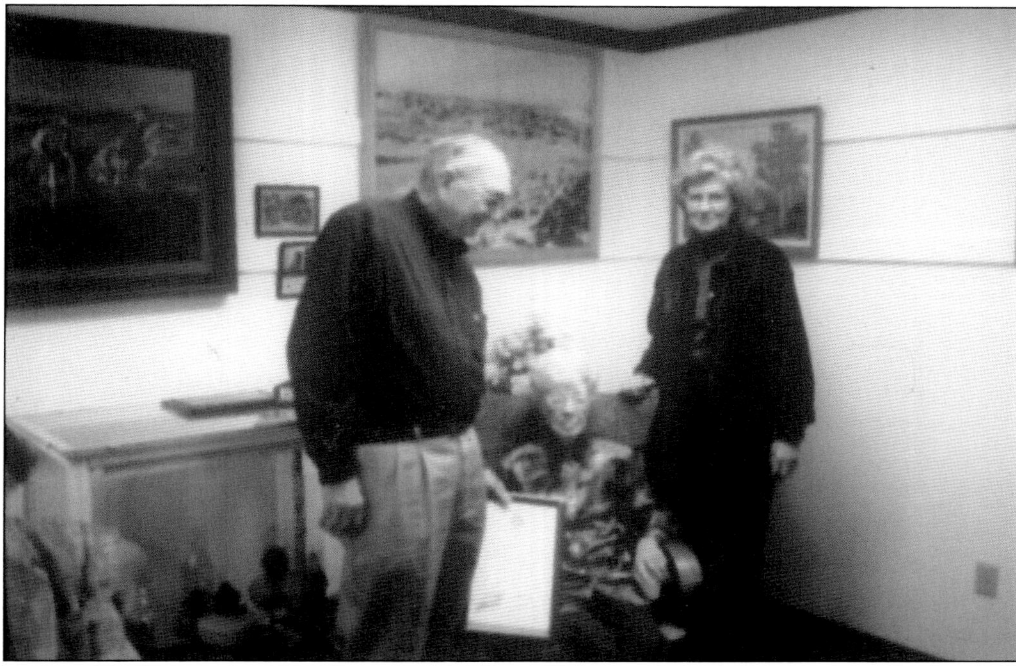

Representative Jack Begley presented Fannie Judy with a Governor's Award for "her pioneer heritage and work to preserve the history of Beaver County." Her work, more than that of any other member, contributed to the preservation of the Jones and Plummer Trail Museum. She worked every day at the Museum until she was nearly 97 and then was an active member until her death. She had grown up on the Cimarron River, married Tom Judy, and ranched on the Cimarron until her later years when she and Tom moved to Beaver. She has been called "one of the last of the dying breed of pioneers." (HSK.)

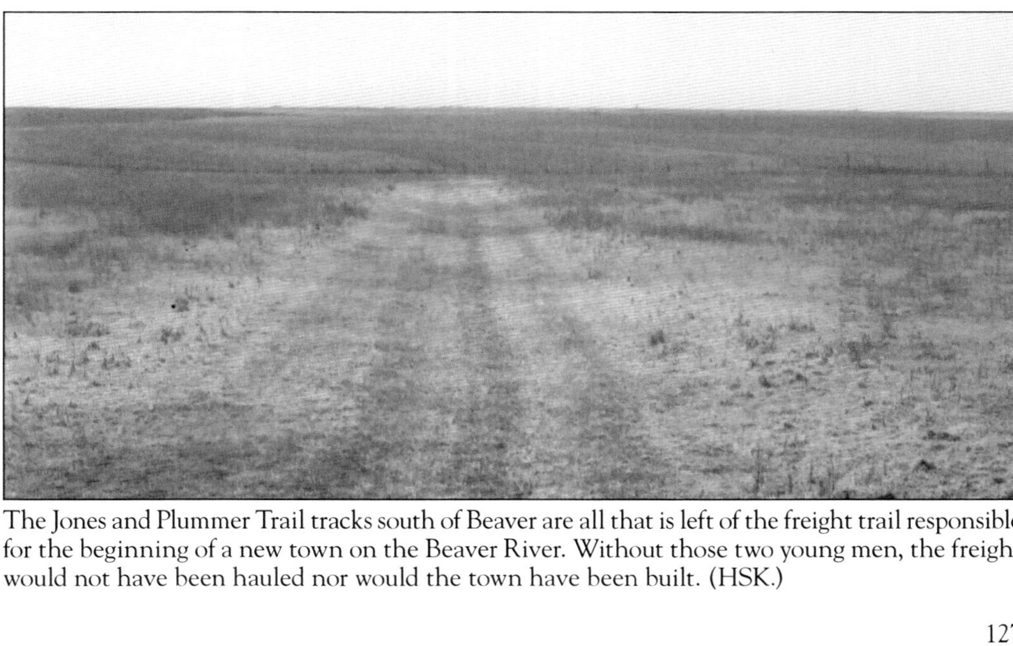

The Jones and Plummer Trail tracks south of Beaver are all that is left of the freight trail responsible for the beginning of a new town on the Beaver River. Without those two young men, the freight would not have been hauled nor would the town have been built. (HSK.)